THE SHAOLIN GRANDMASTERS' TEXT

FOR JEFF,
THE MOST BIG-HEARTED PERSON
I KNOW.

— BEN.

OSC

**The spirit of the dragon dwells deep inside each of us.
This book is for those who would have it come out.**

Whether there is no-seeking in seeking
or seeking in no-seeking,
there is still your seeking.

Tamo

The name, Tathagata, is merely a word.

Shakyamuni Buddha

Desire is like a knife:
if it is continually being sharpened,
it will soon wear away.

Lao Tzu

THE SHAOLIN GRANDMASTERS' TEXT

HISTORY, PHILOSOPHY, AND GUNG FU OF SHAOLIN CH'AN

Revised Edition

by the

Order of Shaolin Ch'an

Published by the Order of Shaolin Ch'an
Beaverton, Oregon

The Shaolin Grandmasters' Text: History, Philosophy, and Gung Fu of Shaolin Ch'an
Copyright © 2004, 2006 by the Order of Shaolin Ch'an

Published by the
Order of Shaolin Ch'an
P.O.Box 566
Beaverton, Oregon 97075

Find us online at: **www.shaolintemple.org**

Notice of Rights:
All rights reserved. No part of this book may be used, reproduced, or transmitted by any means, electronic, mechanical, photocopying, recording, or otherwise, without prior written permission of the publisher.

Notice of Liability:
The authors and publisher of this book are not responsible in any manner whatsoever for any injury which may occur through reading or following the instructions in this book. It is essential that before following any of the activities, physical or otherwise, herein described, all readers should consult with a qualified physician for advice on whether or not to embark on those activities.

Notice of Trademarks:
Throughout this book trademark names are used. Rather than put a trademark symbol in every occurrence of a trademarked name, we state we are using the names only in an editorial fashion and to the benefit of the trademark owner with no intention of infringement on the trademark. All trademarks or service marks are the property of their respective owners.

Library of Congress Catalog Number 2007927062

ISBN 978-0-9755009-2-7

First Printing 2004
Second Printing 2006, revised
Third Printing 2007, revised paperback

Printed and bound in the United States of America.

Cover art graciously donated by Earle Rock. Interior photographs graciously donated by Greg Schutt.

CONTENTS

PART 1: THE HISTORY AND SPIRITUAL PHILOSOPHY OF SHAOLIN

PART 2: THE MARTIAL ARTS OF SHAOLIN

PART 3: INTEGRATING THE PRACTICES OF SHAOLIN

Tamo

Part 1:
The History and Spiritual Philosophy of Shaolin

The Buddha was instructing a young nobleman, who had asked how he could know that the Buddha was teaching truth. The Buddha explained that what he taught was a way to discover truth for yourself. Still, the young man wanted to know if following this path would lead to a happy afterlife.

"If you had been shot in the arm with an arrow," the Buddha said, "would you have it plucked out quickly? Or instead, would you inquire from whence came the arrow? Was it from an enemy archer or an accident from your own men? Would you then inquire if the archer was an untouchable, of military class, or a noble? Would you then require a list of his ancestors and parentage? Would you seek to know the materials that made up the bow and the arrow? Would you only then, after gathering all these facts, pluck the arrow from your arm?"

"No, master," replied the young man. "But I do not understand your meaning."

"My meaning is clear," spoke the Enlightened One. "Life does not give us time to prepare all things before taking action. We must take action as best we can, as we need to, and learn all else we need while we are ourselves in action. Don't put off doing what you can and what you know is important just because you do not know the unknowable."

I have taught a doctrine similar to a raft -
it is for crossing over,
and not for getting hold of.

Shakyamuni Buddha

Chapter One

Welcome to Shaolin Ch'an

*I look upon the judgment of right and wrong as the serpentine dance of a dragon,
and the rise and fall of beliefs as but traces left by the four seasons.*

Shakyamuni Buddha

What is Shaolin?

We begin with a question: "What is *Shaolin*?" This question has many answers... we shall provide the most important one first. Shaolin (known as *"Sil Lum"* in southern China) is a *sect*, or school, of *Ch'an Buddhism*. Ch'an ("*Zen*" in Japanese) is both the most mystical and the most basic of Buddhist *paths*. Ch'an is considered mystical because of the idea that, through meditative discipline, human beings are capable of intuitively seeing reality in such a way that abolishes suffering. Ch'an Buddhism is also seen as mysterious due to its non-logical character,[1] and its incorporation of *Taoist* ideas. (The first appearance of a glossary term will be bolded and italicized.)

Ch'an is perhaps the most fundamental kind of Buddhism in the sense that its "back to basics" attitude encourages a practical interpretation of the *eightfold path* and eschewal of ceremonial religious trappings. Ch'an is also a distilled or crystallized version of Buddhism because it urges each individual to walk the spiritual path, and avoids placing undue responsibility upon religious authorities. In this way, Ch'an is a return to the practices of the historical *Buddha*,[2] emphasizing minimal reliance upon scripture and a life characterized by meditative practice. Ch'an is not merely about meditation and chanting *mantras*, however. Ch'an adherents are first and foremost *Buddhists*, contrary to the "New Age" image many westerners hold of Zen practitioners. Much can be said about Buddhism. For now, we shall keep things simple and say that a Buddhist is one who strives to live according to the eightfold path in order to eliminate suffering.

Shaolin differs from other Chinese Ch'an schools in many ways. Many scholars have long believed that Buddhist sects rooted in the teachings of Ch'an *Patriarch Bodhidharma* share very similar philosophies. It is now coming to light that these schools are actually rather diverse.[3] Shaolin Buddhism, for instance, has been influenced by *Tibetan Buddhism* (sometimes called *"Lamaism"*) more than any other Chinese sect that we are aware of. Compared to other Ch'an schools, Shaolin is perhaps the most pragmatic, and certainly one of the most unusual. Buddhism is often portrayed as pacifistic, yet Shaolin practice martial arts. Our martial practices, often called *"gung fu,"* have even made Shaolin famous.

We see fame (or infamy) due to a martial arts-inspired reputation as a tremendous irony given that physical, martial skill is not the primary goal of Shaolin gung fu. Just as sculptors reveal the form hidden in a block of granite with hammer and chisel, we employ martial arts to unveil and realize our original *buddha-natures*. Shaolin practice forms and engage in combat to chip away at the *ego* until nothing is left of it. You might wonder: well, for instance, why don't the Shaolin practice flower arranging as a means to liberate themselves? We certainly could. Ch'an presupposes a wealth of training modalities. Our specific martial training method stems from our pragmatism—we have found that self-defense and combat training offer an expedient and excellent means of teaching Buddhist lessons. This pragmatic approach—using martial arts as a tool of self development—constitutes a large part of what it is to be a Shaolin *monk*. Shaolin are Buddhists first and martial artists second, or third. This is a different notion of authenticity with regard to our tradition than is often · understood.

Shaolin could be described as Buddhism with Taoist leanings. Taoism provided much of the blueprint for our martial techniques, yet it was Buddhism that provided a mental and spiritual direction for the use of those techniques. This Taoist-body/Buddhist-mind notion is crucial to understanding Shaolin. Shaolin Buddhism values competence and *compassion*, and decries hypocrisy and delusion. The practicality of Shaolin Ch'an surfaces not only in our philosophy, but also in our combat training, as that training gives us practical tools as well as spiritual ones.

We began this section with a discussion of what is distinctinctive about Shaolin. It is not the practice of martial arts which makes Shaolin Buddhism distinct, it is the intense focus upon the role of personal truth and personal responsibility in the elimination of suffering. Shaolin students are not given precepts to take from "the establishment". Rather, Shaolin students are encouraged to explore the Buddha's teaching, and once they have put aspects of that teaching in practice they may take vows affirming their own commitment and realization.

The Purpose of this Book

Shaolin Buddhism and martial arts, as practiced in our temples before 1900, is alive, growing and adapting to new times and new circumstances. It has never been meant to be a fossilized set of rituals, encrusted in an irrelevant past and buried under pointless practices. Shaolin has always been intended as a living contribution to the world's knowledge and individual liberation, using intense training methods to open and strengthen the mind. The martial techniques are first and foremost aimed at combating weakness within one's self by eliminating ego, and thus opening the full mental capacities of the student to enjoy and learn from nature. Our training is designed to encourage a radical spiritual awakening, although there is no guarantee of this.

The Shaolin Order has never produced a book of this sort nor attempted to explain its practices to a public audience. We come forth now, 1500 years from the founding of our Order, for three reasons which work in concert: sharing our philosophy, self-preservation, and conquering ignorance. Of greatest importance, we believe that the Shaolin path has the potential to lessen or mitigate suffering for at least some individuals. While proselytizing is no aspect of Shaolin, we are like many other groups in wanting to share what we believe is a "good thing." Specifically, we wish to share our philosophy in the hopes that people unknown to us will benefit by learning about our Buddhism. Perhaps you, the reader, are one of those people.

In passing this information on, we also hope that by whatever name it shall be called in the future, the essence of what we are as a Buddhist order shall go on into the next generation. Our greatest priority regarding the future flourishing of Shaolin is that the ethical and spiritual roots of our philosophy be preserved, even in priority over the martial components of the Order. By letting people know that our school of Buddhism exists and what its lessons are, this book will hopefully help to strengthen our *sangha* (Buddhist community) enough so that Shaolin will persist into the future, preserving our teachings. Proceeds from the sale of this text support the construction and operation of a permanent place of Shaolin study. If you purchased this book, thank you for your support.

We also feel a responsibility to faithfully represent our beliefs and tradition in the face of an onslaught of misinformation. Ignorance can serve no good purpose here. This text is intended to educate the reader and so provide tools able to help the spiritual seeker distinguish between Shaolin Buddhist teachings and other teachings that often get mixed up with Shaolin. Conquering ignorance, the preservation of the Shaolin Order, and the sharing of Shaolin tradition are interdependent activities. Each relies upon and even includes, to some degree, the others. This text is the spearhead of our efforts. We hope that these efforts are of some benefit to you.

Obstacles to Understanding

When the worldly morons encounter a devilish,
cock-and-bull fellow who babbles a demonic line,
they come up with a demonic interpretation and use it as a compass.
This is beneath contempt.

Tamo

Perhaps the greatest difficulty we face lies in the distortion of our history and philosophy by non-Shaolin commentators. Even the Smithsonian is confused about the purpose of Shaolin.[4] The proliferation of articles, books, and fantastic cinematic representations of "Shaolin" has given the world an extremely distorted and incorrect view of the historical Shaolin Buddhist Order. Many reasons keep those images in place, all of them stemming from either ignorance (often coupled with romanticism) or some form of self-interest. (Although the above quote from Tamo primarily refers to distortion of the **Dharma** and not distortion of history, it is nevertheless particularly fitting here.)

For this book to make sense to the reader who knows little about Shaolin, let us begin by briefly summarizing what most people think of by "Shaolin." The Shaolin resurrection within China appears to be a rebirth firmly rooted in nationalistic propaganda and a desire to improve the tourist trade, and hence the economy. (This is further discussed in the section entitled "A Haunting Question.") Many people envision this "Shaolin" rebirth in China when they think of Shaolin; others think of the television show, *Kung Fu*, from the early 1970s; still others have been indoctrinated by scores of publications prominently featuring the word "Shaolin;" and some recall the wonderful stories of Hong Kong cinema. And so the public is pulled in many directions as to the nature of Shaolin. The true purposes and intent of the Order have been almost completely obscured over the last 30 years by a popular culture that has depicted the Shaolin as an organization concerned only with "fighting" and elaborate stage shows. We maintain that true Shaolin Buddhist practices cannot be found upon a stage, cannot be purchased, and would never be tolerated in today's China. Our **grandmasters** decided in the 1940s to make efforts to ensure that any rebirth of the Order would come from the New World, and warned that claims of monks "discovered" in China, especially those with government endorsement, should be seen with skepticism.

Shaolin has often been a source of controversy. Even prior to 1970, Shaolin misinformation and mythicization abounded.[5] We have heard distinguished professors categorically deny the existence of either Shaolin or its problem-children *tongs*; that only authenticated accounts by the communist Chinese government are to be trusted; and that the temples are fictitious, based solely upon old chivalric novels from the late Ch'ing Dynasty, such as *Emperor Ch'ien Lung Travels South* and others (which are currently not available in English). To the last observation we reply that simply because the Civil War is an event described in the fiction novel *Gone With The Wind* does not mean that the *Civil War* itself is a fictional event!

These statements (as well as this book) may be controversial. Indeed, there are few historical entities that engender as much debate, confusion, and acrimony as the nature and reality of Shaolin. There may be those who will claim that our Order is a fiction, or that the "real" Shaolin monks are in China at the "real" Shaolin Temple. You may believe whatever you wish—that's the wonderful thing about beliefs, isn't it? The point of this book is not to damage the Chinese tourism industry; neither is it to disparage others. Our position is delicate: it is as if we are presenting a spherical map of the Earth to a community who believes that the world is flat. Moreover, some folks are making a lot of money selling flat-Earth maps. Understandably, those people may become upset when someone else comes forth with evidence of a spherical Earth—especially when the round-Earth people distribute highly detailed round–Earth maps in an effort to help navigators travel from place to place. Paradoxically, the truth is sometimes controversial (there was a time when claiming that the Earth was an orb could land the claimant in a bonfire), and this book may spark passionate discussion. Or, to paraphrase a colleague, this text probably has a little something to offend everyone!

By the same tokens of accuracy and rigor, we have tried to avoid denigrating anyone's belief system while simultaneously being faithful to the considerable oral history we have been charged to present. (With respect to our oral history, we only really guarantee a significant degree of accuracy for post-1850 information.) We have attempted to point out our sources, clearly noting when information is coming from our own oral tradition (most of the text), a historical source, or legend. We also indicate corroboration of our information, when we have it, and welcome constructive comments (please see the Additional Resources section at the end of the book). Please also keep in mind that we are not historians! Although we are sharing much of our tradition and oral history, the precise details pale in importance when compared to the Dharma. We do not have all the answers—perhaps we do not have any answers. To wit, the endnotes are not provided to muster support for any thesis. They exist as points of departure for the reader interested in further exploring martial arts and/or Buddhism. In finally publishing *The Shaolin Grandmasters' Text*, our intent is to discharge a responsibility to help the complete context of Shaolin Buddhism survive beyond the 20th century.

> When appearances and names are put away and all discrimination ceases, that which remains is the true and essential nature of things and, as nothing can be predicated as to the nature of essence, it is called the "Suchness" of Reality.
>
> *Shakyamuni Buddha*

Who are the Shaolin?

The authors of this text are members of the Order of Shaolin Ch'an, originally established in 520 C.E. (Current Era). The *masters* who provided the materials for this volume were remnants of a once large and peaceful tile in the grand mosaic of China, a tile that embodied the teachings of *Lao Tzu* and the Buddha in an environment similar to that of some smaller American universities today. Politicians and warlords, however, made these masters' stay in China perilous. Orders were routinely given to destroy temples, murder monks, and torture their families. (Later sections on Shaolin history will explain why this occurred.)

Circa 1970, our *priests* optimistically foresaw a time when China would transform its image of martial arts from the nationalized dancing called *"Wushu"* back towards traditional arts, and attempt to restore credibility to a Buddhist Temple ethic. But they also doubted that China in the twentieth century would truly welcome the return of the monk order called "Shaolin" in the North, and "Sil Lum" in the South. Our Order and all that its monks stand for, as pointers towards self-fulfillment and liberation, are in diametric opposition to the dictates of Stalin, Mao, and other tyrants. We doubt that China in the twenty-first century will truly welcome the return of the Shaolin Order, either. Too much is at stake for the People's Republic of China (PRC), in terms of both money and that ubiquitous *Confucian* practice of saving face.

The three late grandmasters who provided much of the information for this volume were outcasts by the standards of the PRC's ruling class. They were the most senior monks in our temples, and they collectively decided that Shaolin could not survive intact in China during their lifetimes. Once the evacuation of the *disciple* and *student* residents was accomplished, the grandmasters asked the monks to disperse, with the most senior members emigrating to eventually settle in America. It was their belief that only in a land of liberty could the Order regroup and teach a small following the essence of Shaolin *Tao* as monks are taught. The stories of their emigration are not the subject of this narrative; nor do we wish to engage in the unfortunate American (and often Confucian) pastime of exchanging credentials. In Shaolin, diplomas are not issued, for they are transient pieces of paper or parchment (a Buddhist belief in stark contrast to the prevailing Confucian society in which the Order originated; Buddha taught that all things are transitory). Skill is relatively indelible however (to the degree that relativity can apply to something "absolute"), and the reader may listen to or ignore these words as he or she chooses.

The grandmasters took new names upon arriving in America because of concerns about political retribution to their families and friends in China. Grandmaster Li En Huo was the last chief monk at Honan Temple (some use the term "abbot," though that is not quite a proper term: he was a 12th *rank* Shaolin grandmaster—the Chinese term for chief monk is *"fang chang"* [see pages 112-117 for a discussion of ranks]). Grandmaster Hua Ling P'o was the second-ranking monk at Honan. Grandmaster Ben Ch'i Lo was the last chief monk of Fukien Temple. They were accompanied, and aided in their work in America, by Grandmaster Kam Yuen Weng (who had also served as Fukien's chief monk), Master Lin Sze, Master Lo Tang T'ao, and others as well.

To some, the existence of these monks and their legacy in America may seem like a martial arts fairy tale (at best) or a ridiculous fabrication (at worst). There are, scattered around the world today, a handful of senior practitioners in a variety of styles who had ties to the Shaolin Order and its priests at one time or another. Some of these stylists are well-known figures, but most are more obscure ones. Most are also deceased.

This recounting of Shaolin history and substance was left in the care of Grandmaster Li En Huo's designated successor to the position of Shaolin chief monk. Abbot Li's notes included the remark: "To whatever future editor must transcribe and convert our remembrances into a book, our apologies. We humble monks can only wonder at what marvels of publishing will face our meager manuscript in 1992 or 2002!" As editors and contributors to *The Shaolin Grandmasters' Text*, the sense of responsibility tied to representing Shaolin's ancient arts and noble philosophy makes us particularly careful to share the grandmasters' teachings with the greatest precision possible. Presenting this information in the grandmasters' intended context, we often use examples that postdate their materials. References to *Star Wars*, recent historical events (e.g. the Tiananmen Square incidents), and technology (e.g. MRI devices) are liberally sprinkled into the text wherever they help clarify a particular point. Much of the spelling follows the **Wade-Giles** system of transliteration, which is what most English-language martial arts and Buddhism sources used prior to 1995 (and it was used almost exclusively prior to 1979, when the PRC officially adopted the Pinyin system). To many readers, the Wade-Giles spellings (which give us "ch'uan" instead of "quan") will be familiar. Other times, spellings may reflect Cantonese, as opposed to Mandarin, pronunciation. Use of Cantonese and Wade-Giles spellings reflects our own history. Finally, this book is a little disjointed in places. It is the product of many voices.

The Order has decided to present this material to the world, to the best of our ability, because we believe that our message will be genuinely helpful to some, and because the late grandmasters' families and friends are no longer alive to become targets of political retribution. Our hope is that this text will serve as a pointer and a beginning to those interested in and ready to follow the path of Shaolin Ch'an.

There will be some disciples
who upon hearing this teaching
will become bewildered in their minds and will not believe it.

Shakyamuni Buddha, referring to the teachings of the Diamond Sutra

Issues of Identity

Be discreet—I learned too late its value.

Bruce Lee

We have been exceedingly reluctant to publish this material for many years. That reluctance is reflected in our continuing anonymity. The original authors of the core of this book were the grandmasters of their arts and guardians of a long and peaceful tradition (recent movie plots notwithstanding). These arts have only been shared with students if they agreed to preserve the privacy and anonymity of their instructors.

Living members of the Order are the present preservers of a 1500 year old tradition of Ch'an Buddhism. But this book owes its existence to more than just the living authors; this information is also the legacy of our forebears. Many Shaolin have acted to preserve and evolve our philosophies and methods. So we cannot in good conscience affix a few names to this work and call it "ours." Shaolin Buddhism emphasizes cooperation over competition.

Of course there are other reasons why we have chosen to remain anonymous, such as avoidance of the martial arts limelight and other worldly entanglements. The very act of publishing a book like this will erode the privacy of our members; affixing the names of living Shaolin would only make that erosion more severe. We emphasize a focus upon individuals, but to the ends of self-development and liberation. The ultimate authority, for any person, lies within the individual. Look into your own heart for the authority to assess what you read, and ultimately to make all your decisions in life. Names are ephemeral, but they are also powerful as tools of the ego. Shaolin is *about* extinguishing the ego.

Our anonymity is part of what makes Shaolin different from, for example, most Japanese Zen schools. Lineage is very important in many Zen schools because it establishes who has received the transmission of the Dharma, hence who is enlightened and has the authority to teach. But the notion of a "mind to mind" transmission of the Dharma is no part of Shaolin. The buddha-nature is something everyone possesses; the spiritual seeker need only awaken to it. Although authority to teach, for a Shaolin, may come from the Order, the school and its masters are no arbiters of enlightenment.

A public name and its connection to a detailed lineage too easily becomes a satellite revolving around the ego, serving as "proof" of authenticity. But Shaolin Buddhism is not about displaying "proof" of anything; it is about simply doing, and letting the credit—or lack thereof—fall where it may. Historically, Shaolin has been a long continuum of nameless monks. Every once in a while, a particular Shaolin monk becomes famous (or infamous) and this typically marks the end of spiritual development for that individual. Better luck next incarnation. Pass "Go," but do not collect $200. Many civilian traditions in the Chinese martial arts have been born of these Shaolin who have "lost their way." Names, and the notoriety often associated with them, are essentially and literally *no part* of Shaolin philosophy or practice.

If you must affix names to this work, then credit should go to Li En Huo, Hua Ling P'o, and Ben Ch'i Lo. The survival of our tradition to date is largely the responsibility of these three Shaolin priests, all three of whom were ordained in China when our Honan and Fukien temples were still fully operational, all three of whom bore the legendary brands of our order. Too many students of both Buddhism and the martial arts place their teachers upon splendid, high pedestals. At some point, this results in unmet expectations (we all possess faults). The Buddha might even have said that suffering is the product, not of craving, but of unrealistic expectations! As this lesson is well understood by many Buddhists, most do not care about identities—the teaching is what matters. In the martial arts community, many people take issues of identity and lineage very seriously. We hope that by including this discussion of identity, both groups will find something of explanatory value.

Our late grandmasters held that the quality of Shaolin is based on the content of the teaching, and not merely on the identity or public reputation of the teacher. In that tradition we present this book: accept it or reject it as you choose, as its authenticity cannot be "proven" except by first hand experience. Numerous studies have shown that dedicated martial artists tend to have a high degree of overall success in their lives, probably because they learned to forge themselves through discipline, dedication, and a very strong sense of ethics. It is this forging of the self through gung fu which fits so well with Ch'an Buddhism. Certainly, Shaolin philosophy and martial arts have combined to help us achieve our goals. May Shaolin as presented here help you reach your goals and find harmony in your life.

The "Auspicious Design" of Buddhism symbolizes the union of compassion and wisdom.

Martial artists like the metaphor:
"All schools are branches on the same tree."
To understand the growth of the branches,
it is useful to study the roots.

a Shaolin master

Chapter Two

History of Shaolin

All stories have a beginning; over time it becomes difficult
to remember which version is the truth.

The Shaolin/Sil Lum temples were the Chinese amalgamation of an Indian philosophy with Chinese tradition and spiritual beliefs. The Enlightened One, or Buddha, of India presented a world-view that was both liberating and self-fulfilling to humans. The Buddha recognized that the lives of most people are filled with suffering, and conversely that the joy of liberation is the absence of suffering. Meditation ("ch'an" in Chinese, "zen" in Japanese—both are derived from the *Sanskrit* word *"dhyana"*) was an essential vehicle for freeing the self ("ego" of contemporary popular psychology) from its attachment to the worldly concerns that could induce suffering. Because Buddhist teaching avoided extremes of *asceticism* and overindulgence, the route to *enlightenment* via moderation became known as the "middle path." *"Mahayana,"* the Sanskrit word for "Great Vehicle," is the term used to refer to Shaolin and other Chinese middle paths. In time, alternate routes became established, especially in the animistic societies of Tibet, where Buddhism took on highly ritualized and theistic tones. Buddhist sects can be divided into philosophical schools (that place no stock in study or acceptance of deities and the supernatural), and religious schools (that adopt many local, and frequently some Hindu, deities along with teachings about heavens, hells, and the hereafter). Shaolin falls within the category of a philosophical school.

People from many walks of life embraced the Buddha's path, for it required neither riches nor abject poverty to be practiced. Moderation was something anyone could understand. In eschewing a reliance on gods and post-mortem rewards, the now-focus appealed to the masses. For much of the Indian population at the time (or any population), life was already a hell. A path that led away from the infernal reality of poverty and misery was bound to be popular. In addition, Buddhism was, in its earliest incarnation, both non-sexist and class-free. Women could follow the path and teach the message. The lowest Indian *caste*, the untouchables, members of which were seen as filthy and barely human, was elevated to equality with the "higher" castes (such as the kshatriya, and even the brahmin). The higher classes often learned to find reward in using their resources and advantages to help those less fortunate (**Shakyamuni** Buddha's own father, Shuddhodana, was one such kshatriya ruler who helped the Buddhist community—he later became an **arhat** himself). Indeed, many stories are told of arhats and **lohans** who gave their entire fortunes to the less advantaged as they themselves took the vows of monk-hood. Originally, lohans were bandit-like characters in China—but the meaning of the word was reversed due to legends of these rogues who gave up their vile ways for the holy life of Buddhism.[6]

Buddhists use "monk" and "priest" because of their rough equivalence to how those terms are used by other religions. A Shaolin monk is (loosely) any member of the Order (including even students) while a priest is an ordained individual with the authority to teach others to the highest teachable levels. Our relaxed usage of "monk"—a legacy of our more monastic past—differs from most other Buddhist sects where the term *only* applies to those who have been ordained as celibate, renunciate bhikshus.[7] A Shaolin monk *can* be a bhikshu. Bhikshu ordination occurs in the Order of Shaolin Ch'an, although it has not happened in many years. We have great respect for the renunciate Sangha, and do not often use the term "monk" to refer to ourselves today. Yet "monk" is liberally sprinkled throughout this book, as befits our sources and our past. We generally prefer to use the terms "student," "disciple," "master," and "priest" to describe Shaolin of varying levels.

Those who dedicate their lives to teaching the Buddha's message take vows to become priests and adopt the wearing of symbolic saffron robes. Saffron, still among the most prized and expensive of spices, is the color of the rising and the setting sun. The symbolism thus comes from three sources. First, enlightenment is the event of the rising spiritual sun, illuminating reality so it may be seen clearly. All followers of the path seek to become aware of the sunrise in each of us. Second, as the saffron spice is a rare delicacy, so too is the state of walking the eightfold path and, ultimately, becoming enlightened. Third, all things in the universe are transitory; we all live and die. The setting sun symbolizes this impermanence.

An important idea in Buddhism is **reincarnation**. Although reincarnation will be discussed later in the text, the idea of reincarnation is intimately connected to a very important aspect of Shaolin: our nature-focus. Because there is no eternal "soul" in Buddhist thought, reincarnation is not seen as a literal event (as in the Hindu faith). What the idea of rebirth *does* include, however, is this notion that all living things are connected through a network of cause and effect. Taken to its logical conclusion, this idea has tremendous import for our relationship with the plants and other animals with which we share the planet. Buddhists do not consider one species to be higher or lower than another, but equal so long as they have self-awareness or *sentience*. For this reason, a Shaolin Buddhist sees it as morally indefensible to kill any sentient creature except in extreme cases of self-defense. Furthermore, a great deal of our meditation emphasizes direct experience of the natural world.

Among the early dispersers of Buddhist teaching were the patriarchs. These men possessed the odd combination of a sincere desire to teach others the words of the Buddha and a rather non-centrist, almost evangelical urge to carry the teachings far from India. This latter inspiration has enabled Buddhism to flourish down through the centuries to present times, for the teachings were all but destroyed within India by a combination of Muslim invaders, Hindu absorption of Buddhism, and other factors. But by the time the Buddhism had mostly disappeared from India, new sects of Buddhism had been well established by the patriarchs in Ceylon (Sri Lanka), Burma, Laos, Cambodia, Japan, Thailand, Nepal, Tibet and China.

According to legend and historical documents, an Indian monk named Bodhidharma (called "P'u-t'i-ta-mo," or *"Tamo,"* in Chinese) founded our Order in 520. Much information about Bodhidharma is based upon legend, but quite a bit is based upon solid historical documentation, as has been discussed by other authors.[8] (Jeffrey Broughton's *The Bodhidharma Anthology* is a superb scholarly work on the teachings of Bodhidharma and his circle. Much of our verified historical information relies directly or indirectly upon Broughton's work.[9]) Non-Buddhist evidence of his historicity and presence in the Loyang region also exists.[10] Yang Hsüan-Chi wrote *Record of the Buddhist Monasteries of Lo-yang* (*Lo-yang chia-lan chi*) in 547, documenting Bodhidharma's presence in the region. Yang was not a Buddhist monk; he was in Loyang to document the many glorious temples in the area.[11]

The Shaolin Temple at Song Shan in Honan had been built by Emperor Hsiao-wen in 496, but Bodhidharma altered the course of Buddhist practice there so drastically that we consider him the spiritual founder of our Order. He took it upon himself to "edit" the way Buddhism was being conveyed in China, a place where most Buddhist activity centered not on meditation, but on transcribing Buddhist texts from Sanskrit into Chinese calligraphy. It was the Chinese emperor's intention to make Buddhist doctrine widely available to all in the language of the land. This was not a bad thing, of course.

> Self means ego.
> The reason why the sage
> meets suffering without being sad and
> encounters pleasure without being happy
> is that he has lost self.

Tamo

Tamo and Early Shaolin Development

Bodhidharma's story would make a wonderful epic novel. Legend has it that he brought meditative Buddhism to Tibet when he was en route to China. Some scholars think it more likely that he reached southern China by sea,[12] but historical records indicate a moderate likelihood that Bodhidharma (who might have actually been Persian) came to China along the Silk Road from Persia.[13] So there are good reasons to think that he may have traveled through modern-day Tibet. (Bodhidharma's place of origin isn't certain, but we will continue to refer to him as an Indian—ultimately, it makes no difference, as his message is our area of concern.) Bodhidharmatara, as he is known in Tibetan scriptures, was not Tibet's Buddhist patriarch, but one of several teachers who brought Buddhism to the "top of the world." Tibet was a land of many religions and warring clans, and took the efforts of many strong teachers, such as Milarepa and Tilopa, to unify under a distinctly Tibetan brand of Buddhism.

Bodhidharma's role within our present work is to place him, eventually, in the Ch'ien-kang (Nanjing today) court of Liang dynasty Emperor Wu-ti (502-549), successor to the Liu Sung. (When Bodhidharma arrived in China, the land was divided into the Northern Wei Empire and the (southern) Liu Sung Empire. The Liang dynasty endured from 502-557.) This emperor had decided that he wanted to assure himself a place in heaven, so had hired armies of scribes to translate Sanskrit Buddhist texts into Chinese. It is a common belief among those who do not actually read the Buddha's words that deeds such as having works transcribed and preaching will buy one a place in heaven. In fact, the Buddha avoids any contemplation about heaven, deities, or supernatural phenomena, being concerned only with liberation from earthly suffering and unfortunate rebirth. (True, the Buddha considered escape from the *karmic cycle* of death and rebirth, which some argue is a supernatural idea, to be the ultimate liberation, but it was to be achieved by very pragmatic means.) When the emperor learned of Bodhidharma's arrival in the Chinese capitol, he arranged an immediate audience.[14]

The Indian monk, however, was not what the emperor had expected. He was neither subordinate nor meek. He looked nothing like the Buddhist monks in China. Bodhidharma was swarthy, bearded, and blue-eyed. His crown was naturally bald, but his remaining hair hung long and unkempt. Instead of traditional saffron and maroon robes, the patriarch wore blue and gray. The emperor was confronted with a self-assured, rugged man who had trekked over the Himalayas and walked to the Chinese capitol, a trip that took several years. Bodhidharma explained that noble deeds cannot be bought, and that enlightenment was not to be had from the labors—however noble—of others. In fact, enlightenment does not function as the effect of good (or bad) works at all. The emperor would have to reach enlightenment on his own merit, and the journey would not be hastened by building monasteries. Not surprisingly, the Indian was shown the door and he left the capital city, traveling north across the Yangtze River to the Lo-yang region and eventually to a temple that had been built for the purpose of housing scribe monks.

The temple was built on a mild slope of a hill, around which had been planted thousands of saplings. From this sylvan setting came the temple's name: "Young Forest," or, in the Mandarin dialect, "Shao Lin." Bodhidharma was given access, but his critical evaluation of the monks and their task earned him the ill-will of the chief monk, who subsequently banished him from the premises. It is not surprising that the first abbot of Shaolin (known as "Bhadra" or "Batuo") would have denied Bodhidharma entrance. Bhadra was a Theravadin missionary whose ideas about Buddhist practice must have been rather different than Bodhidharma's. Bodhidharma's early training was with an Indian teacher, Prajnatara, who was a master of the Sarvastivada sect, which is considered a proto-Mahayana school.[15]

Still undaunted, Bodhidharma set himself to demonstrating the liberating powers of meditation. He retired to a cave that still overlooks the grounds of the Temple, and engaged in a detailed program of meditation. Legends tell amazing stories of Bodhidharma boring holes in cave walls by the laser-like intensity of his gaze. Whatever the truth was, after eight years he eventually impressed the monks such that they recognized his true worthiness as a patriarch of Buddhism, admitting him to the Temple and giving him his Chinese name, "Tamo." As Tamo, he taught the monks the simple but demanding basics of the way of life that would henceforth be known as "Shaolin." Tamo's true claim to fame rests on being the founder and first patriarch of the Buddhist practice known in China as "Ch'an," and in Japan and much of the rest of the world as "Zen."

Despite legendary accounts, Tamo did not invent the martial arts styles we refer to as gung fu. There is no reason to doubt that he was trained in Indian self-defense arts from his native India, for such training would have been a normal part of the education of a young man from his princely social class.[16] His skills were almost certainly enhanced while he traveled north into Tibet and China, and local people may very well have exchanged combat secrets with the monk. But once he entered the Temple and became the acting abbot, his curriculum did not initially contain a special martial arts practice. In fact, Shaolin's signature gung fu didn't enter the mainstream curriculum for about another 700 years. Tamo's initial interest was to include a physical component to the daily routine of the monks at the Temple. The men assigned to the new order by the emperor had been given the formidable task of transcribing Buddhist books and commentaries from the Sanskrit language into Chinese characters. There was little else in their routine other than writing and performing necessary household functions—cleaning, laundry, cooking and so on. When Tamo attempted to introduce these scribes to the meditative practices he felt were the core of Buddhism, he quickly learned that none had the stamina to undergo a session without falling asleep.

The Indian undertook a drastic change in curriculum by instructing the monks in the *eighteen movements of lohan*, a series of postures with their emphasis on proper breathing based on *yoga*. His choice of yoga would fulfill two needs. First, it would give the monks physical training to improve their stamina. Second, traditional yogas included the exercises that stimulate and help develop the inner power called *prana* in India and *ch'i* in China. (Ch'i is absolutely central to Shaolin Buddhism, meditation, and gung fu. It will be discussed later in this volume.) Many exercises were developed just for the monks, including the bone-hardening exercises and the marrow washing sequence (both have been lost to posterity though a totally new exercise has been dubbed "marrow washing"). Eventually, the realities of life in a remote temple surrounded by dangerous animals and roving bandits prompted Tamo to introduce a martial aspect into the Temple's physical curriculum. These additions, though, were not permanent nor the foundation of Shaolin's later gung fu. The skills Tamo taught probably disappeared from the Temple shortly after he died though other monks no doubt brought in different styles as they left worldly life to become monks.

Seng-ch'ou, a famous dhyana master and contemporary of Tamo who visited the first abbot of the Shaolin monastery shortly after the Temple's founding, may have influenced early martial training there. Seng-ch'ou was well known for emphasizing mindfulness. He resided at the nearby Sung-yueh monastery and later became famous for using his tin staff to separate fighting tigers.[17] Then again, he may have had nothing to do with martial training at Shaolin, but the historical record is useful for two reasons. First, it establishes as a fact that monks traveled (and perhaps resided) in dangerous areas where martial training would prove advantageous. And second, it shows that many Buddhist monks carried staves and already knew how to use them in combat. It is also possible that Bhadra had a strong impact on martial training at the Temple. Some sources claim that Seng-ch'ou and Hui Guang were two of Bhadra's disciples, and that these two monks developed much of the early martial training.[18] The time was ripe for the founding of the Shaolin Order.

An artistic depiction of the Honan Shaolin Temple's front gate.

Development of Shaolin After the Time of Tamo

The Shaolin Temple had been established by a Chinese emperor, and close links would bind the Temple to imperial governments—despite Tamo's unfavorable audience with Liu Sung Emperor Wu-ti. The martial prowess of the monks was first utilized for a specific combat purpose when the small order supported the ascent of the young T'ai-tsung (629-649) as a T'ang dynasty emperor. Shaolin Master Hsiao-shan and twelve other masters supervised portions of the imperial army and soundly defeated opposition to Emperor T'ai-tsung. The court appreciated the support of the "warrior monks," but the senior priests were less than enthused about this new title. The reputation would come back to haunt the Order during the next emperor's reign.

After Tamo departed Honan (by some legendary reports to bring Ch'an to Japan; more reliable sources have him passing away in Northern China in 534[19]), there was a period of some years with little innovation in the training of monks. Our oral tradition maintains that around 610 the third abbot of the Temple began instituting additional martial training, in large part as a response to the increased banditry and passing gangs of private soldiers.

Shaolin were always encouraged to develop new skills that would give them an advantage over attackers. As monks practiced their new skills, they found tremendous inspiration from observing the local wildlife. Shaolin believed that nature had many lessons to teach those who would pay attention. Meditating upon the actions of animals had already become central to the Order, so familiarity with the defensive habits of the creatures was a natural outcome of such observations. The early styles followed the Indian tradition of creating single-man shadow boxing routines, known as *"kuen"* or forms. The monks also named individual techniques after specific moves of animals (*tiger's claw, white crane skewers frog in the pond, white ape attacks snake,* and *snake creeping down* are examples) as well as from important Buddhist symbols. The *lotus fist*, for instance, gets its name from the lotus, a traditional Buddhist symbol of purity. One popular observation is that while lotus flowers may bloom beneath, at, or above the water level, they are still all lotus flowers. A similar parallel is drawn for people who, though rising to different levels in life, are all still humans.

Along with the novel introduction of martial arts training into Shaolin, the third abbot also added an extensive program of learning the use of weapons to the training regime. To other Buddhists, bound by doctrinal prohibitions against the use of weapons, this action was unfathomable. After all, given the fact of human weakness, how could someone learn to use weapons and then be expected not to use them? But the Shaolin abbot stood firm: how, he posed, can a person learn to defend against a weapon if he does not understand that weapon? Weapons training stayed. With very few exceptions, a monk was not allowed to take any weapon out of the Temple. The general exclusion from this rule was the long staff, a walking staff that also makes a formidable weapon. If a monk were attacked, though, he might disarm an opponent and use the enemy's weapon in his own defense. This helps explain why we spend so much time training in weapon disarmament techniques.

By the Order's centennial, martial arts were firmly united to Tamo's brand of Ch'an, and a legend was established. The novelty and, to many minds, unorthodoxy of the Shaolin Order kept it from becoming a widely dispersed sect. Monks were not always cut from pure cloth; many were criminals who took Buddhist vows with the intent of making repentance and starting new lives. So long as they kept their vows, they could stay in the Temple (though rarely did any of these become priest-level). Additionally, Shaolin training requirements discouraged all but a very few from wanting to join the Order. Because the number of priests available to supervise students was always limited, the Temple policy restricted entry of new students to once every three years. Rapid, widespread proliferation was never a Shaolin goal, but offering high quality instruction always was.

Staying clear of kings and ministers, make your home in deep mountains and remote valleys, transmitting the essence of Ch'an Buddhism forever, if even only to a single true Boddhiseeker.

Ch'an Master Ju-ching

28

It was about 130 years after the founding of Honan Temple that a second large temple was constructed in Fukien Province. The martial skills of the Honan monks engendered so much fear in the emperor of the time that he ordered the Temple destroyed and the inhabitants executed. This was the first of many purges of the Order that would occur over its lifetime. Our oral tradition maintains that, in 680, three thousand imperial soldiers surrounded the Honan Temple at night and set fire to the grounds, surrounding fields, and a nearby village. The Temple was, at that time, relatively small, and seven of the thirteen priests and some forty disciples managed to escape the siege. They made their way to friendly Buddhist and Taoist temples in Fukien far to the southeast, and set about establishing a new temple there.

The very existence of a Shaolin temple in Fukien Province is heavily debated by those outside the Order of Shaolin Ch'an. One early source claimed that the Fukien Temple was located in the Chiu Lien Mountains.[20] Draeger and Smith contend that the Chiu Lien Mountains are in Kwangtung and Kiangsi Provinces and not in Fukien. They furthermore repeat the supposition that claims of a Fukien Temple stem from the book *Emperor Ch'ien Lung Travels South*.[21] Meng and Loewenhagen, based on their recent research, maintain that the Chiu Lien Mountains do indeed extend into Fukien Province, and that the Southern Shaolin Temple was established there in the 7th century.[22] It may seem curious to some, but the exact location of temples in China is not a pressing concern of the Shaolin Order today. We shall simply state that there was indeed a Fukien Temple; many of our masters trained there and certainly had no reason to be untruthful.

Over time, Fukien Temple would become the second major force in the Shaolin Order (where the prevailing dialect pronounced it "Sil Lum"), even rivaling the more famous northern temple. It was at Fukien that White *Crane* permanently became part of Shaolin's martial repertoire, and where many of the styles began to take on the manifestations still seen today. Unlike the Honan Temple, Fukien's was built from an existing temple in a lush forest, on a series of low hills near a wide river. It was less accessible than the parent temple, which also made it difficult for a large armed body to approach. This Fukien Temple would face attacks over its lifetime, but none by massive siege forces such as those Honan faced so often. (This description refers to the *last* location of Shaolin's Fukien Temple. During the approximately 1100 years of that temple's existence, its precise location within Fukien Province changed numerous times due to exigent circumstances.) By the time Fukien Temple was transformed into a fully Shaolin temple in 683, it had begun to sever ties to imperial and other patronage of all kinds. The ultimate schism was effected by a formal *Decree of the Guardian* in 915. The Decree's core doctrine, which has been a central tenet of Shaolin ever since is as follows:

Enlightenment is the uppermost reason for walking the path of the Buddha. This path leads us away from birth, death, rebirth, and worldliness, and must include renouncing the ties and fealty to the secular world. From this date forward the Shaolin Order shall live and act separate from imperial law, shall not partake in government or civil administration, and shall abstain from any act of war.

With the initial transformation of Fukien Temple into Shaolin (it had been part of another Buddhist sect before that time) in 660, the Order had begun to establish a new position within its organization. The second temple was taken as symbolic that several temples might be built over time, spreading Shaolin across the huge breadth of China. Consequently a *guardian successor* would be appointed as the abbot over the whole Order. Chosen for this position was the priest or priestess with the greatest breadth of Shaolin education, who could conceivably resurrect the Order from minimal resources should later emperors or warlords destroy the temples. Because the guardianship was initiated in Fukien, where Taoist influences were particularly strong, it was decreed that this monk be given "heavenly protection" by Shaolin's and Taoism's most potent guardian creature, the gold dragon. A special throne was constructed for the guardian successor's use during ceremonial occasions, with a large green-eyed gold dragon surmounting the backrest. The office of *Seat of the Gold Dragon* had been established as a unique aspect of Shaolin Ch'an Buddhism.

The Dark Side of Shaolin

The southern lands were also more influenced by Taoism than the north during this period (ca. 650-900), to the extent that Taoist and Buddhist philosophies became firmly united in many local temples. For Shaolin, it was a wedding of ideas that never divorced. The eightfold path and the *yin/yang* blended well in a harmonious school of nature study. Shaolin selected from Taoism the theories of ch'i, gung fu yoga, moving meditation, and many other practical aspects. Yoga as practiced by the Taoists consisted of a series of postures that were designed to exercise all portions of the body systematically, internal organs as well as muscles. These exercises are very similar to Hindu yoga and accomplish much the same ends. They are meant to unify the body as a functioning, whole entity and improve its state of being through relief of tension and improvement of balance, poise, and circulation. *Pa Kua* (Baguazhang) is such a Taoist art.

Like Buddhism, Taoism also can be divided broadly into "philosophical" and "religious" branches. The philosophical Taoists interpreted Lao Tzu's *Tao Te Ching* as a guide to *metaphysics* and ethical behavior that would, ultimately, lead one to a higher plane of existence. It is this branch—again, without any reference to, or belief in, the supernatural—which Shaolin eventually embraced. But Taoism also has a very animistic, supernatural religious aspect whose senior practitioners were China's famous and respected alchemists. Somehow, these adherents of Lao Tzu believed that through becoming "harmonized" internally they could use their ch'i magic to alter matter and energy against its natural flow. Two camps of these religious Taoists proliferated. In the North, the more orthodox alchemists gained a great deal of influence, blending martial arts, alchemy, philosophy, and ch'i enhancement. But many would completely succumb to a dark side of this quest for harmonic balance and, like *Star Wars'* Darth Vader, fall far from the source of their spiritual training by using their skills to obtain power and influence over others. (The *Star Wars* movies offer many good examples of ideas in Buddhism and Taoism—many of those examples having been originally inspired by eastern philosophies.) Especially during the T'ang dynasty, heretical Taoist sects like the Lung Hu ("Dragon and Tiger") Style and Mou Shan Style enjoyed prominence in southern China.[23] The most famous of the dark priests with respect to Shaolin was *Pak Mei* ("White Eyebrow" in English) of the 17th century.

Shaolin embraced this "dark side" of Taoism into its curriculum several times, probably because many masters realized the value of the more legitimate advances made by the "Amulet Sect" (as the heretical Taoists were called). Indeed, it is believed that their innovations in subterfuge went on to form the nucleus of Japanese Ninjutsu.[24] Unfortunately, many of these arts were taught within a shroud of secrecy that forced a practitioner to forfeit more and more of his integrity in order to learn the secret arts. Many of the Shaolin who would take up arms against one oppressive emperor or another were led to the decision based on the influences of "dark" Taoism. ("Dark" Taoism is also discussed in the Shaolin's Taoism section in Chapter Four.)

Pak Mei's style is considered "closed door" within the Shaolin Order, and is primarily studied by high ranking Tiger and Leopard masters.

Temples and Early Styles

Shaolin has certainly adapted and evolved through the centuries. Around 683 the Fukien Temple became fully Shaolin, in part because of the need for martial arts training in a bandit-rich region, and in part because the Order's nature-based practices of observation and learning were well complemented by the diverse local wildlife. Because the Fukien Temple was not far from a main trade route linking China with its Indo-Chinese neighbors, the Temple became a center that promoted and modified its Buddhism, martial arts, and other activities over time.

The monks' need for protection against bandits and wild animals is difficult to fathom from our civilized perspective. But southern trade routes were notoriously dangerous; southern China is quite vast and was mostly untamed till quite recently. Marco Polo reported in the 13th century that traveling alone in the South was quite dangerous due to the large tiger population! Also prior to modern times, three varieties of leopard were prevalent in northern China: Manchurian Leopard (*Felis villosa*), North China Leopard (*Felis fontanieri*), and Snow Leopard (*Felis uncial*).[25] And monkeys have always been numerous in China. During the 1990's, two members of our Order traveled to Omei Shan and were confronted by monkeys in the forest. They reported that the monkeys displayed no fear. Monkeys are no longer numerous in more settled regions of China, but in earlier times the simian population was considerably larger and widespread. As late as the mid-19th century, penal authorities in northern China used apes as "watchdogs,"[26] likely due to the apes' intelligence and strength. Banditry has also been an historic problem (Yang also remarks upon the ubiquity of robbing and killing by hordes of bandits in Chinese history[27]). Even as late as the early 20th century, Chinese trade caravans required heavy security as protection against thieves and marauders. Because wild animals and dangerous people abounded, combat skills allowed Shaolin monks to travel with much greater freedom than the average Chinese citizen.

Near the end of the first millennium, the spread of Buddhism in China was almost complete. Shaolin had temples in the populous North and at a strategic place in the South, but was poorly represented merely by lone monks in the West. Around 945, a small mountaintop monastery at Omei Shan in Szechwan Province allowed a contingent of monks from Honan to take charge of much of the grounds and direct instruction. Being along major routes spanning western and eastern China, and the linking roads between Tibet, India, and Mongolia, Omei Shan quickly became a center of information exchange for a broad cross-section of Buddhist and Taoist practitioners. Of particular interest to the five resident Shaolin monks was information about foreign and exotic healing arts. Colleagues soon brought texts from as far west as Asia Minor to their curious Chinese comrades, and within its first century Omei Shan was recognized as a leading center of Chinese medical knowledge. According to our oral tradition, Omei Shan's medical library would come to hold almost every known medical text, spanning Babylonian to Chinese sources. Apparently, many of Omei Shan's western medical texts had been bartered or captured from European crusaders as they invaded the Middle East.

Over the next several hundred years, the monks at Omei Shan would establish particularly close ties with the lamas of Tibet. Shortly after the monk *Ordator* founded the White Crane style, it found its way to Omei Shan, the temple with which the style is most often associated. Because Omei Shan's doctor-monks were also expert in White Crane, a link was forged that remains firmly in place today: few crane practitioners are not well versed in some aspect of the healing arts. (Omei Shan is sometimes listed as a northern school, but is geographically in western China's Szechwan Province.)

Our tradition is unclear about why monks from Fukien set out to found another temple in the South, this time in Kwangtung. Whatever else can be said about this temple, it certainly had the most peaceful existence within the Order.

A few years after Omei Shan was established with a Shaolin contingent, another group of monks from both Fukien and Honan joined with Taoist companions to establish a temple at Wutang in Hupei Province. Shortly after choosing a lofty mountain site in 980, two other Buddhist sects joined in the construction, and the Wutang Shan Temple was born. Although Wutang has always been a Taoist temple, for many long stretches of time, there were Shaolin monks in residence.

At the Honan Temple, a priest named Chueh-yüan ("Kwok-yuen" in Cantonese) was put in charge of physical training (or merely studied at the Temple for a time), and he decided to broadly expand the range of the martial arts of the Temple. He increased the number of empty-hand movements from Tamo's eighteen to seventy-two. This priest and his refinements are a matter of some contention. Our oral tradition maintains that he developed seventy-two techniques during the 7th or 8th century. Another source lists his given name as "Hung Yun-szu" and places him in the 13th century[28] (while the *Shao-lin Ch'uan-shu mi-chueh* [*Secrets of the Shaolin Fist Arts*] published in 1915 held that Chueh-yüan studied under a Shaolin monk by the name of "Hung Yun"[29]). Yet another source, along with *Secrets of the Shaolin Fist Arts*, places Chueh-yüan in the 16th century.[30] Other sources have him developing techniques in the 11th or 12th century.[31] It is extremely unlikely that Chueh-yüan was alive during the 16th century, as some Shaolin styles had already been codified and extensively developed. It is furthermore something of a stretch to think that he had a reputation of any sort during the Mongol Yuan dynasty of the 13th century, since the Mongols outlawed all martial arts practice. Indeed, anyone caught practicing a martial art was sentenced with seventy-seven strokes from a heavy wooden paddle.[32] Regardless of the specifics, we're content to say that he lived "a long time ago."

Later, Chueh-yüan collaborated with two famous local *boxers* named Li Sou and Pak Yook-fong—or these two expanded on his developments at a later point. Li had been a martial arts instructor to imperial guards and Pak was supposed to have been a great master from T'ai-yuan in Shansi Province; and so both brought a considerable body of practical combat experience to the collaboration with Shaolin. The (two, or) three men developed one hundred-seventy maneuvers that were the basis for the classical *five-formed fist* of northern Shaolin gung fu. *Secrets of the Shaolin Fist Arts* maintains that this collaboration occurred at Loyang's T'ung-fu Monastery.[33] Yang cites the book *Shaolin Temple Record* as claiming that Pak developed these maneuvers based on earlier work with the others, and subsequently wrote the book, *The Essence of the Five Fist*.[34] *Secrets of the Shaolin Fist Arts* provides circumstantial evidence of Pak's authorship of such a book, describing how Pak became a Buddhist monk at Shaolin in his 50s, taking the name "Ch'iu-yueh," or "Autumn Moon." The movements were divided into five *systems* based on the behavior of animals. Each system comprised the maneuvers of one specific animal and no other. Techniques based on these animals had been practiced in the Shaolin Temple for quite awhile before this codification,[35] but the work by these men is the first known case of a text being written during this early period. According to our oral history, this all took place in the distant past, certainly before the development of styles we see beginning in the mid-16th century. The first emperor of the Sung dynasty, T'ai Tsu, supposedly developed Long Fist style during the late 10th century.[36] It seems most likely that this early synthesis of the five-formed fist took place before Long Fist came about, before 975 or so.

There is also a fair probability that the five-formed fist had been in existence for a very long time when Pak Yook-fong wrote *The Essence of the Five Fist* around 1050-1200. Chronicling the internal practices of the Temple for a wider audience has never been a high Shaolin priority, so it is likely that Pak received credit for a martial science that he merely recorded, and did not create. Also of note: as William C.C. Hu has pointed out, the 1915 *Secrets of the Shaolin Fist Arts* is filled with all sorts of inaccuracies. Given that this book is the root source for most of the stories circulating about Chueh-yüan and Pak, most of what is commonly considered "fact" about the development of the five-formed fist may be fabrication instead.

In the early 1550s, Emperor Jiajing harnessed Shaolin martial prowess for a variety of purposes. At the time, the southern coast of China provided a tempting target for pirates, and many Shaolin volunteered their assistance in repelling the bandits. This political-military activity may appear at odds with the 915 *Decree of the Guardian*, yet there are a few other factors to consider. First, the pirate threat was not part of any internal, Chinese political machination—it was the equivalent of today's much-hyped terrorist threat. So the Shaolin who volunteered to fight pirates were fulfilling a sense of duty to country. Second, and most important, those who fought were *volunteers*. The Shaolin Order did not repel pirates, a group of individual monks did. The distinction here is critical. The Shaolin creed places tremendous emphasis upon individual choice and responsibility. Third, monks at the Honan Temple, due to proximity to the Imperial Court and its unique pressures, found it very difficult to adopt an isolationist policy with respect to the government. (It was partly for this reason that Honan Shaolin were much "stingier" instructors than their Fukien counterparts. Because of political involvement by many who stayed at the Song Shan Temple, the senior masters established a teaching policy which reserved the most advanced aspects of training for monks who had proven their intentions as *Buddhists* over a period of many years.)

Around 1565, one of the style masters made the intuitive leap of logic that gung fu forms and combat practice should be taught as moving meditation. Seated meditation was already a well established Buddhist practice, but after studying local animals the Shaolin felt that motions requiring intricate and practiced movements were also meditation. This same master was also trained in Taoist traditions and therefore saw a need to balance static meditation (yin) with moving meditation (yang) to achieve a harmony of mind, body, and spirit. Her name was *Ng Mui* (a different Shaolin Ng Mui would invent *Wing Chun* in the 1770s) and she modified existing martial training into a new style that would use the movements to cultivate and perfect ch'i. Because her style would transcend physical and mental practices while blending Buddhist and Taoist philosophies, she modeled her style after a composite creature that had great significance to a wide range of students. She named her style *"Dragon,"* and many variations of that style exist today. Dragon would become a pinnacle style within the Order, taught to only a select few of the most promising and worthy disciples. Admission to the Dragon style was also an unofficial prerequisite for later advancement to the most senior positions within both a temple and the Order at large. (One civilian Dragon lineage holds that Ng Mui developed Dragon before a burning of the Honan Temple in 1570[37].)

Similar philosophical reasoning led to the development of the *Snake* style, though the history of its roots has been lost to us. We mention Snake now only to highlight the fact that Snake and Dragon are the oldest genuine Shaolin styles still in existence. Although Dragon was codified during this period, dragon-like techniques go back another 1000 years to the late 7th century.

Shaolin During the Early Ch'ing Dynasty

The history of the Shaolin Order during the Ch'ing dynasty is a complete mess. There are two primary reasons for this. One, keeping historical records has never been seen as very significant or important within the Order. Two, as Shaolin gained some notoriety, a plethora of secret societies and martial stylists began tracing their lineage to monks of the Order. And of course, their "historical" accounts all differ. Looking at extant records of various Chinese martial traditions, we discover that the Honan Temple burned in 1570, 1647, 1735, and 1774. Those same sources report that the Fukien Temple burned in 1637, 1647, 1673, 1720, 1723, 1735, 1768, and 1774. We can state with complete confidence that some, all, more than, or none of these dates are accurate. It is especially likely that the Fukien Temple was a frequent target of imperial arrows between 1644 and 1735. There was tremendous resistance to the new Ch'ing dynasty in Fukien Province, especially in Putian County, where many Buddhist monasteries were concentrated.[38] It also seems very likely that the Honan Temple was attacked and burned shortly after the Ch'ing came into power, in part because many northern rebels had sought shelter there. This would make 1647 a very likely date for the destruction of the Honan Temple, and is corroborated by **Praying Mantis** lineal information.[39]

To understand what really occurred during this period, we must look at historical information. The Manchu Ch'ing came to power in 1644. Emperor K'ang Hsi didn't assume the mantle of control until 1662, and he ruled until 1723. Emperor Yung Cheng ruled from 1724 to 1735. And Emperor Ch'ien Lung ruled from 1736 up until 1799. Assorted details about these men are relevant. Supposedly, 128 Shaolin helped K'ang Hsi put down bands of marauders (Ming insurgents by some accounts[40]); because he didn't allow people to carry weapons, he supplied the monks with weapons.[41] K'ang Hsi visited the Honan Temple in 1704, bequeathing upon the Order his imperial seal and a sign which read "Shaolin Ssu," or "Shaolin Temple." Yung Cheng was a generally despised emperor who outlawed all martial practice in 1727,[42] and who reportedly burned down both the Honan and the Fukien Temples.[43] Ch'ien Lung visited the Honan Temple in 1750 and even composed a poem about the experience. K'ang Hsi and Ch'ien Lung clearly held no animosity towards Shaolin, at least during certain periods of their collective rule. But one or both of them may have been poorly disposed towards the Order at one or more points, and given the orders for destruction.

We do know that both temples served as shelters for rebels during this period. How could rebels resist coming to the Shaolin? The Shaolin temples not only offered protection from the Ch'ing, who greatly respected Buddhism (perhaps even more than the Ming dynasty had), but our temples were also excellent places to learn martial techniques. For the most part, genuine Shaolin monks and high level priests were *not* involved in plots to overthrow the Ch'ing dynasty. Since 915, it has been an official part of Shaolin philosophy to avoid war and secular, political activity. Our focus is upon self-improvement and the cultivation of wisdom and compassion. It is critical for the reader to understand that the Order never condoned political activity, yet as a Buddhist organization, neither did the Order turn away those who came in *apparent* sincere need.

During the Ch'ing transformation, the new Manchu conquerors wanted to assert authority over the avowedly non-secular monks; either because they felt the Shaolin Order was a threat, they wanted to harness

Shaolin military power, or both. The *guardians* ("guardians" here refers to both the guardian successor *and* style masters/abbots, who are also appropriately called "guardians") refused to become imperial "warrior monks" for the Manchu. Aided by one senior Shaolin master named "White Eyebrow" (the same Pak Mei mentioned earlier as a priest of dark Taoism), imperial troops surprised and overtook Honan Temple, likely in 1644 or 1647. A few masters and a handful of disciples escaped the invasion, and headed to safety in the South. White Eyebrow was given "command" of the Temple and an imperial garrison of elite troops, whom the monk was to train in advanced gung fu. Pak Mei later traveled to Shaolin temples at Wutang and Omei mountains, accompanied by Fung To-tuk.

White Eyebrow's style became forbidden in the sense that a Shaolin could speak neither his name nor his history. His style would be discussed under other names, depriving the renegade monk of the honor his art should have brought to his name. We mention this here to clarify this situation and put White Eyebrow into his historical context vis-à-vis the Shaolin Order.

Legend of the Five Elders

Sometime during the early 18th century, the Fukien Temple burned. According to some legends, the Temple was betrayed by a senior monk, Ma Yee Yuk (or Ma Ning Yee), who was known as "Pak Mei" (or "White Eyebrow"). As the legend has it, Ng Mui, Gee Sin, Mew Hing, Hung Si-kwan, and Fung To-tuk escaped from the Temple. (Other versions include Pak Mei at the expense of Mew or Hung.) Gee Sin traveled around and eventually took shelter on the Red Boats (early Chinese opera boats that provided entertainment up and down the rivers [especially the Pearl River] of southern China). He is known for teaching many laymen, including: Luk Ah-choy, Leung Yee-tai, and others; as well as those with Shaolin affiliation, such as: Hung Si-kwan, Fong Wing-chun, Mew Hing, Fong Sai-yuk, and others. Ng Mui invented Wing Chun, Fung To-tuk invented White *Tiger*, and Hung Si-kwan invented *Hung Gar*. And the betrayer, Ma (Pak Mei), invented the White Eyebrow style. Or so the story goes. (There are many variations, especially in Hong Kong cinema.)

Most of these characters, though they appear in works of fiction from the 1880s onwards, really did live. We have internal evidence for the historical existence of some of these personages. For instance, Ng Mui was a relation of Sitaigung Hua Ling P'o (mentioned in the first chapter of this book). Most of the stories told about them are patently fictitious, however. The Pak Mei for whom the style is named, for instance, lived around 100 years prior to the Five Elders Legend. Surely, the same Pak Mei didn't persist for two hundred years!

We believe there are many reasons why Pak Mei continues to "pop up" in Chinese folklore. We shall discuss two. First of all, he was the "Darth Vader" of his day, a fallen Shaolin monk, and he was understandably immensely popular as a villain. And so any time a really nasty scoundrel was needed, "Pak Mei" was invoked. Second, recall that the original Pak Mei was a practitioner of the darker aspects of Taoism. What did he receive for aiding the imperials in their conquest of the Honan Temple in the mid-17th century? According to our histories, Pak Mei was deeply interested in the Taoist quest for immortality, and was rewarded by the Manchu with access to knowledge and worldly control over other Taoists. The Taoist societies, much like the anti-Ch'ing secret societies, had a practice whereby the leader would assume a symbolic name. It is both probable and logically consistent that one or more of these societies always had a "Pak Mei" at the helm. So when the Fukien Temple was betrayed in the 18th century by "Pak Mei," it was one of these later Pak Meis. It is even possible that the original White Eyebrow spawned a secret cult of his own which perpetuated a grudge against Shaolin—a grudge eventually resulting in bloodshed.

The Legend of the Five Elders maintains that Pak Mei slew many Shaolin, including Gee Sin, Fong Sai-yuk, Hung Si-kwan, and others. Some versions even claim that Pak Mei slew Fong Wing-chun's father. Fong later married Hung Si-kwan; and, as the legend goes, Hung slew Fong's father's killer as part of his courtship.[44] But this is no part of the official Hung Gar lineage. As the story goes, Hung developed Hung Gar by blending the White Crane style of his wife with the Southern Tiger style he had learned from Gee Sin. Hung was, by all accounts, amazingly strong, and this stylistic synthesis suited him well. On the pretext of lingering to look for other comrades, some Shaolin disciples prepared to take revenge on White Eyebrow and recapture the Temple. For several years, these disciples, led by Hung Si-kwan, planned their strategy and honed their gung fu skills while "hiding" as riverboat acrobats. When Hung confronted White Eyebrow, Hung was killed. His son, Hung Wen-ting, supposedly slew Pak Mei with Hung Gar techniques a few years later. According to the legend, the death of Pak Mei symbolized the "righteousness" of Shaolin being reasserted over the imperial-mandated destruction of the Temple.

From the Shaolin perspective, there are serious problems with this legend. First, as already mentioned, is our own oral tradition, which maintains that White Eyebrow lived in the mid-17th century. We recognize the fallibility inherent in the transmission of oral history (that is, we might be wrong about all this!). Yet while our monks who trained in China during the late 19th century verify the existence of Gee Sin, Hung Si-kwan, Luk Ah-choy, Ng Mui, and others who lived during the 18th century, they maintained that Pak Mei lived much earlier (as did Fung To-tuk).

Then there is the case of Hung Si-kwan. Seen as a historical hero by many, he was an outcast by Shaolin standards. Hung was known to have developed skills with the express intent of killing someone, perhaps in the case of Fong Wing-chun's father; and perhaps others, as Hung was involved in fighting the Ch'ing. He may even have honed his fighting skills to battle a latter-day "Pak Mei." Hung was engaged in both political machinations and taking revenge—for these activities he was disowned by the Shaolin Order. This partly explains why Hung Gar, certainly an excellent martial style, has never enjoyed the prominence within the Order as it has in civilian circles.

Finally, affiliated with the Five Elders Legend, is the common assumption that *only* five Shaolin survived this assault on the Fukien Temple. This assumption is part of the "story," the folklore aspect of history. During this period, other Shaolin temples were active, and numerous masters resided in these other locations. Monks frequently traveled between temples, and it was fairly common, for example, that a Fukien abbot would have trained at Honan, a Honan abbot at Fukien, and a Kwangtung abbot at Omei Shan. Many monks also spent prolonged periods among the general populace, and still others lived in a solitary fashion, close to nature. It is also a Shaolin custom to *run away* in the case of attack. So, while the Fukien Temple was razed during this time period, it isn't true that the upper echelons of the Order were decimated (or worse).

Shaolin During the Late Ch'ing Dynasty

By the late 1700s, Shaolin ties with other Buddhist temples, notably those from Tibet, were greatly expanded, and monks were often sent for five or ten year exchanges to learn from the other schools. Tibetan Buddhism could hardly be more different from Shaolin if it tried. When Indian monks brought Buddhism to Tibet, they encountered fierce local peoples who were strongly bound to their local deities and **Bon** religion. Rather than convert people and suppress their native beliefs, Buddhism acted like a growing snowball, incorporating Bon ideals into a new synthesis. By the time of the Tibetan unification of Buddhism, the number of deities, hells, and spiritual beliefs it incorporated was staggering. In stark contrast, Shaolin's Buddhism has no link with any deity, hell, or supernatural entity. Tibetan Buddhism has a strong tradition of ceremonies and ritual magic, all of which must be practiced at particular times and according to rigid guidelines. The ceremonies of Shaolin are less restrictive, and more celebratory and secular in nature, as are our contemporary birthday parties and graduation exercises. Still, both traditions possessed two strong elements in common: both incorporated Tamo's concept of Ch'an, and both had developed martial skills. These links would overcome the differences and, in fact, serve as the conduit through which a close relationship would develop.

Shortly after the implementation of martial arts practice as a required part of Shaolin training, around 1760-1770, some of the masters gave names to the new styles. (Prior to this point in time, much of the martial training offered within the Shaolin Order was elective—some monks did not choose to enroll in this elective martial study.) Many styles have been lost to history, and others modified or incorporated into the styles that have existed over the centuries. Sometimes a particular name would be used for very different styles. Most popular among names must be "Tiger", for there are, or have been, Tiger, Tiger's Claw, Black Tiger, White Tiger, Mountain Tiger, Tiger and Crane, Angry Tiger, Tibetan White Tiger, Southern Tiger, Shantung Black Tiger, and others.

By the 1760s, the Temple's arts would be known almost exclusively by the names of various animals, though a few other styles—notably *Buddha Hand*, Wing Chun, and *Lohan*—would also come from the Order. By tradition, gung fu from Shaolin is generically referred to as the five-formed fist. The more ancient aspects of the five-formed fist are the Crane, Tiger, *Leopard*, *Cobra* (in the North), and Dragon styles; whereas the modern aspects of the five-formed fist are the Crane, Tiger, Snake, Praying Mantis, and Dragon styles.

Today, when many people talk about Shaolin gung fu, they are often referring to various subsystems and evolutionary descendants of Long Fist (Chang Ch'uan). We attribute this, in part, to the popularity of using the "Shaolin" name, which has become a widespread practice. This trend is also largely due to the fact that the new hybridized martial arts practiced by the "Shaolin warrior monks" at Honan Temple are based upon Long Fist.[45] But the primary cause is simply that the complete animal styles were normally only taught to those who remained in the Temple. Hence the these Shaolin styles tended not to get disseminated, and the styles that *did* get widely disseminated (such as Ch'ang Chuan, Choy Li Fut, and Hung Gar) have become strongly connected to "Shaolin" in the minds of many people. The "Shaolin" name is used quite legitimately with respect to these styles, as their pedigree is indeed Shaolin, but they were not the core martial teachings of the Order. As an aside, many of the more "closed-door" styles have civilian traditions as well. Southern Dragon, White Eyebrow, and other styles were taught to lay students at various points, and these styles have been passed on outside the Order. If all the *pai* traditions were to be collected together, much of Shaolin's martial teachings would be represented.

There were popular uprisings against the Ch'ing in 1774 and 1775 (during which one or more of the temples may have come under imperial attack), but Shaolin continued along rather peacefully from 1800-1870, with only a few odd bumps here and there. In 1878, the guardian successor learned that monks from Wutang (including Shaolin living at Wutang) had been routinely joining bands aimed at overthrowing the imperial government. Shaolin had no fondness for the decrepit imperial system or its involvement with the spread of opium among the people and the resulting Opium War with the British (1839-1842). Nevertheless, political interference was strictly taboo in the Order, and the military activities of the Wutang monks went far over the line of prohibitions. By order of the guardian at Honan, Wutang lost its affiliation with Shaolin in 1878, but its monks were free to rejoin one of the other temples if they would recant or had not taken part in the political intrigues. Many failed to "come home."

One of the Wutang Shan monks, who *did* recant and later rejoined the Order at Fukien Temple, recorded his thoughts about the experience as follows (a paraphrase):

> We are all of us like ants in a great nest. Some of us are moving grain after grain of sand out of the nest, but we are focused on keeping the tunnels clear so that the entire nest may remain sound. Others of us pick up a grain of sand and become obsessed with the fate of that single grain.

The guardian at Honan had asked each Wutang monk to find his center. Those who succeeded returned to the Order. Those who failed had mistakenly inflated the importance of events *at that time* to an epic magnitude. They focused on individual grains of sand in lieu of understanding why the grains were moved (i.e. to keep the tunnels clear). These monks failed to realize that any particular act is a transitory piece of history. As is true of many historical sequences, this is a cautionary tale and offers valuable lessons to the attentive.

Shaolin and China in the 20th Century

By the end of the 19th century, western nations and the Japanese had parlayed military superiority into economic infiltration of China. The British had turned the imperial family into an impotent puppet regime primarily through the import and sale of opium, and the consequent drug-devastation inflicted upon the poor population. This lead to the incursion of other European powers, including Russia, Germany, France and Holland, and later the Japanese and Americans. By the late 1800s, China was effectively divided into national zones of influence, each controlled by one of the outside powers (military losses to foreign powers forced China to pay indemnities to those powers, as well as provide trade opportunities and some degree of regional political control). The long-standing animosities between China and Japan worsened, and many Chinese extended their anger to include all other "foreign devils" (especially Christian missionaries) as well.

The Boxer Uprising began in rural districts in late 1898 as the group calling itself the Spirit Boxers began to actively threaten Christian converts in northern Shantung Province. The Boxers consisted of mostly disaffected youth who had suffered poor environmental and economic conditions, yet among their numbers martial artists—some, alas, from Shaolin and

Wutang—could be found. These were not monks, necessarily, but people who had studied at the temples, or from temple masters. The Boxers began by threatening and killing foreigners, especially missionaries, and in 1900 brought their rebellion to Peking (Beijing). The Ch'ing Empress saw what was happening and sided with the Boxers, declaring war on all foreigners. The combined western legation forces held out for some two months until a joint western army relieved them. The Boxers were summarily put to rout. Though the Boxers' initial assaults on the military powers of the occupation governments were not entirely successful (many believed in Taoist magical spells that would make them impervious to gunfire), their temporary defeat would lead to a more modern reformation that included adopting modern military weapons and tactics.

The restlessness uncorked by the Boxer Uprising failed to die out. Coupled with growing disdain by the Chinese for their powerless and self-indulgent empress, the Boxer Uprising (though failed) inspired a nationalist movement with extensive grass roots support. For a decade, various factions eroded the remaining power and prestige of an imperial court that, most Chinese believed, was both powerless and had sold the country to the West. By 1911 the people finally ended the imperial system under the leadership of Sun Yat-sen and instituted a weak but hopeful republic in its place. Meanwhile, the gung fu stylists and monks associated with Wutang became very dissatisfied with the Shaolin. Wutang Temple, where the Taoist "internal" styles of *Hsing-I* (Hsing-I Ch'uan), Pa Kua Chang, and *T'ai Chi Ch'uan* were developed and practiced, promoted largely Taoist principles. In contrast with the predominantly Buddhist leanings of mainstream Shaolin, the Taoists saw no problem in staging rebellion, but hated the Buddhists for their non-involvement. To this day a schism exists, to the extent that many Wutang practitioners actually deny the existence—at any time—of Shaolin or its martial arts. This is sad, given that the events of a century ago cloud the links between very different yet well-known schools. It is as if two siblings who were close as children had a fight as young adults and never could arrive at a truce afterwards.

There are other ramifications of this discord between Wutang and Shaolin. Wutang stylists often claim that there are no Shaolin styles, and that Shaolin (if it *did* exist) is only gross, hard technique, while Wutang styles are soft, flowing, and have true power. We have read, and heard, T'ai Chi Ch'uan instructors tell people that there was only one Shaolin temple (when they admit we existed at all) at Honan, but no others because no one they spoke to from other towns ever admitted they knew of the existence of such temples. It is a poorly structured argument by any analysis: Shaolin didn't exist, but if it did it was only a hard style that was done at only one temple. On a personal note, we have great respect for the "internal" styles of Wutang, particularly Pa Kua, and believe that any student able to find a competent teacher of such styles would benefit from the study of them.

The withdrawal of western forces from China was prolonged over many years, and by the end of World War I China was in an almost feudal state of civil war. Not only were national troops fighting loyalists, but both sides had to fight the Japanese (who still held much of the northern Manchurian region of China) as well as many powerful regional warlords. Many parts of China were virtually anarchies, but by 1931 almost all non-Asian occupants had been successfully driven out. Interestingly, retaining their welcome in the late 1930s were the volunteer American airmen known as The Flying Tigers, who helped repel Japanese forces prior to World War II. At this point, the major combatants within China were the nationalists and the communists. Both sides displayed the typical jingoistic attitude of forces in mindless warfare: "if you aren't with us, you are against us." (This slogan, sadly, continues to appear in the world to this day.) Neutrality, for both nationalists and communists, meant nothing except the possibility of a later enemy.

Consequently, soldiers from both sides routinely murdered Shaolin and other monks. Regime change is often marked by the massacre of religious leaders and priests, in addition to educated individuals who "might" question the new powers or who represent traditional ways. Witness Pol Pot's policy of sending hit squads to university campuses with orders to execute all those wearing eyeglasses. Although not in China, Pol Pot's actions are representative of the kinds of tremendous atrocities occurring in China during 1900-1949. Our senior monks were seen as a threat by the various regimes vying for power during this period, and to spare those connected with them in China they simply "disappeared," fleeing the country and assuming new names. Records of events within China during the early 20th century are not very complete, but we are told (by our monks) of incidences where entire villages were "eliminated" because residents had offered aid to those of our, and other, religious orders. This program of murder during the early 20th century led to the exodus of many monks into the hills, or abroad, with the hope that Shaolin knowledge might survive even if the temples themselves did not. Throughout the history of China, there have been many Buddhist purges, or programs of extermination. The third patriarch of Ch'an, Seng-ts'an, hid out in the mountains for ten years in order to avoid execution. But these purges never lasted long in a society that placed so much value on the spiritual life. (According to the observations of Herbert Giles in the late 19th century, the upper crust of Chinese society often had great contempt for Buddhists, and adhered to a blend of Materialistic and Confucian philosophies.[46] But Buddhism was more respected among the "lower" classes, perhaps because it is an egalitarian philosophy.) The end of a dynastic China marked the end of, if not complete religious freedom, at least a degree of reverence for religion and religious values.

The exodus of our senior monks occurred prior to the miserable fates of a multitude of scholars, officials, and monks in China shortly before and after Mao Tse-tung came to power. In 1949, the communists in China clamped down on Taoism and Buddhism, expropriating religious buildings and either executing clergy or sending them to labor camps, which amounted to the same end.

Even in very recent times, the Chinese government has persecuted

Buddhists. The BBC reported in 1998 on China's crackdown on Tibetan Buddhists, when abbots and abbesses in Tibetan monasteries were all replaced with party officials, references to the Dalai Lama were cut out of all religious texts, and Buddhists in Tibet were "reeducated." Monks who repeated or wrote the phrase "Free Tibet" were given a seven year prison sentence. The Chinese government furthermore required monks to criticize the Dalai Lama, arresting those that refused. The government arrested more than 800 monks and nuns as a result. By the best current estimates, the Chinese government has killed between one and one-and-a-half *million* Tibetans between 1949 and 2003. This example harbors no malicious purpose; it is merely an attempt to inform readers about the religious atmosphere within China during the 20th century. The recent persecution of Tibetan Buddhists is one (very recent) aspect of a larger movement that has included the destruction of many Buddhist temples and the "reeducation" of many Buddhists throughout China. (It is worthwhile to consider how the American people would respond to such religious persecution if it were to occur within the United States.)

> We must guard ourselves against the barbaric Red Communists, who carry terror and destruction with them wherever they go. They are the worst of the worst…They have robbed and destroyed the monasteries, forcing the monks to join their armies or else killing them outright. They have destroyed religion wherever they've encountered it, and not even the name of Buddhadharma is allowed to remain in their wake…we must be ready to defend ourselves. Otherwise our spiritual and cultural traditions will be completely eradicated. Even the names of the Dalai and Panchen Lamas will be erased, as will those of their lamas, lineage holders and holy beings.
> The monasteries will be looted and destroyed, and the monks and nuns killed or chased away. The great works of the noble Dharma kings of old will be undone, and all of our cultural and spiritual institutions persecuted, destroyed and forgotten. The birthrights and property of the people will be stolen. We will become like slaves to our conquerors, and will be made to wander helplessly like beggars. Everyone will be forced to live in misery, and the days and nights will pass slowly, and with great suffering and terror.

Thupten Gyatso, the thirteenth Dalai Lama, 1933

Buddhist temples were unfortunate victims of war in a land that had abandoned its historical practice of respecting posterity and ancestors. All the Shaolin temples were ransacked and looted by various armed groups. Omei Shan Temple, in Szechwan Province, was situated on a mountaintop and deemed by Chinese officers to be a fitting target for artillery practice. It was shelled in turn by nationalist and communist armies. In a fitting twist of fate, the communists rebuilt this one-time site of medical and natural history knowledge in the mid-1970s, and used it for some time as the National Park and Research Headquarters for the panda reserve. (This was told to us by two Chinese zoological researchers who had worked at that facility—we have no corroboration.)

There are various stories coming out of China today referring to the history of Shaolin, particularly over the past 300 years. However, many of these stories are suspect, with the more commonly "authenticated" versions coming from government records. (Compare Chinese accounts of the events at Tiananmen Square with BBC or any other news coverage. There is very little agreement between the accounts.) The fact that Chinese authorities persecuted Buddhists, Shaolin, and martial artists makes any story about Shaolin history from the PRC suspect. The currently prevalent sport of martial arts-like choreography called "Wushu" originated as a result of a compromise between the post-World War II government's desire to suppress genuine martial arts and the national need for, and history of, a martial arts tradition. Modern Wushu, however, was not designed as a martial art (strictly illegal until quite recently) by the Chinese government, but as a national and largely acrobatic art. Claims to the contrary date back only to the early 1970s, following on the popularity of the *Kung Fu* television show. The Shaolin Temple in Honan Province is now one of the top three tourist attractions in China. According to the Chinese government, the Temple and its martial and Buddhist practices have all been fully and authentically restored. The Chinese government is now seeking World Heritage Site status for the Honan Temple.

Shaolin in America

Beginning in 1902, senior Shaolin priests began arriving in the United States. They spent time in such cities as San Francisco, Chicago, Vancouver (Canada), and Toronto (Canada) before convening in New York. They generally kept very low profiles, and not only because they were Buddhist monks with little desire to "make names for themselves." This was also the time of the Chinese Exclusion Act (1882-1943) and a host of other oppressive immigration laws. These laws ensured that most Chinese coming into the United States would keep a low profile.

The Chinese Exclusion Act and its legal offspring are horrible contradictions of the spirit of the U.S. Constitution. This congressional act forbade the naturalization of Chinese already living in America and prevented immigration of any Chinese not given a special work permit. In addition, any Chinese wishing to enter America had to pay a special tax. Later laws prohibited Chinese from owning real property; and the Oriental Exclusion Act of 1924 barred the immigration of foreign-born wives and children of Chinese living in America. It was also possible to buy and sell Chinese slaves long after black Americans had been emancipated from such degradations. This situation was not surprising given the reception early Chinese immigrants to the United States were offered. The phrase "not a Chinaman's chance" came about to describe the general prediction of Chinese fates in Californian mining camps during the California Gold Rush. A Chinese who injured a Caucasian miner even in self-defense could fully expect that a mining court would find *him* to be the guilty party in the altercation, exonerating the true offender! Seen in this light, the "Gold Mountain" loses some of its luster.

Public sentiment towards the Chinese (and many other Asian groups) was surreal in its severity, and did not diminish. The Expatriation Act of 1907 mandated that an American woman who married a foreign national would lose her U.S. citizenship. But while the Cable Act of 1922 partially repealed the Expatriation Act, an American woman would *still* lose her citizenship if she married a *Chinese* man. From a contemporary perspective, it can be difficult to understand why these draconian laws were enacted. Part of the stimulus for the Chinese Exclusion Act was a growing anti-Chinese sentiment in America due to the perception that Chinese did not assimilate "properly" to American culture. Combine this issue of image with the fact that Chinese immigrants worked for much lower wages than more entrenched "Americans," and the recipe for extreme prejudice was complete.

These oppressive laws and the sentiment driving them certainly influenced the evolution of the Shaolin Order in its new home. Public displays of our Buddhist heritage were eliminated in an effort to "blend in." Monastic robes, shaven heads, and other public signs of our religious practice were discarded. Shaolin has never been dogmatically faithful to appearances anyway, so this was no great sacrifice. The environment created by these laws also contributed to our secrecy. If Chinese living in America were not liked, a "strange" eastern religion wherein practitioners were also masters of unarmed combat might not be tolerated at all. To avoid unwanted attention, which might result in persecution or even deportation, Shaolin were secretive and prudent.

And so accidents of politics, by their fickle and transitory nature, infused the Order with a greater sense of caution. Chinese politics forced our priests to flee China, and American politics changed some aspects of our practice. We don't see these changes as necessarily "good" or "bad," however. Worldly change is inevitable. Appearances may have changed, but the core of our practice remains much the same as it has for hundreds of years. The Buddha's message is constant. Shaolin Ch'an is, today, a very small yet very sincere school of Buddhism.

The reality of the survival of Shaolin without a formal structure highlights an important part of Shaolin philosophy: that which is learned by many people cannot be burned down, misappropriated, or otherwise destroyed. The Shaolin Order has rebuilt many times from a small foundation of masters. Perhaps the future will mirror the past.

A Shaolin Time Line

ca. 800 BCE	Beginnings of Chinese boxing can be reliably traced at least this far back, to the Chou Dynasty.
563 BCE	Siddhartha Gautama of the Shakya clan born.
527 BCE	Siddhartha Gautama of the Shakya clan becomes enlightened and is henceforth known as "Shakyamuni Buddha."
483 BCE	Shakyamuni Buddha dies at age 80.
520 CE	Tamo founds Ch'an/Zen school of Buddhism and is first Ch'an patriarch near Shaolin Temple of Honan Province.
528 CE	Tamo officially recognized as Shaolin Ch'an Patriarch at Honan Temple.
610 CE	Martial arts become a minor part of Shaolin training.
ca. 650 CE	Dragon-like techniques known to exist.
ca. 660 CE	The Order establishes senior abbot position of guardian successor. The Order establishes a sister temple with other monastic orders in Fukien Province.
ca. 680 CE	The first destruction of Honan Temple, by imperial troops.
ca. 683 CE	Establishment of Fukien Temple as an exclusively Shaolin.
915 CE	Guardian successor decrees that Shaolin will refrain from involvement in worldly matters such as government, war, and non-Buddhist paths.
ca. 945 CE	Omei Shan Temple in Szechwan accepts Shaolin presence.
ca. 970 CE	Kwangtung Temple established, China.
ca. 980 CE	Wutang Temple established jointly with Taoists and non-Shaolin Buddhist sects.
1100-1300 CE	"Heroic Period" in Shaolin history that saw the rise of a pragmatic attitude towards the martial arts. Some temples are burned during this period.
ca. 1399 CE	Fukien Temple rebuilt and expanded, with a curriculum of distinctly southern gung fu and strong revision of Buddhist doctrines as having priority over Taoist ones.
ca. 1470 CE	White Crane founded by Tibetan Lama Ordator.
ca. 1500 CE	Omei Shan Temple becomes fully Shaolin.
ca. 1565 CE	Southern Dragon is known to exist, but origins cloudy. Most likely initially developed by Shaolin Master Ng Mui.
ca. 1627 CE	*Wang Lang* founds Northern Praying Mantis style.
ca. 1644 CE	Honan Temple destroyed by imperial troops, aided by Master Pak Mei. White Eyebrow and White Tiger styles develop.
ca. 1670 CE	Black Crane taken to Japan by Chen Yuan-peng.
ca. 1680 CE	Northern Dragon emerges as a distinct system.
ca. 1700 CE	Individual animal styles become the norm in Shaolin. Temples' teaching splits the Order into Northern

and Southern schools.

1735 CE	The famous main gate at Honan Temple is constructed.
ca. 1765 CE	Shaolin develops its own "brand" of gung fu, modifying outside sources and creating new ones. Gung Fu becomes a universal and signature part of Shaolin training. Formal awarding of ranks begun, equivalent to academic degrees in western schools.
ca. 1770 CE	Leopard merges with Tiger.
ca. 1776 CE	Wing Chun developed by Shaolin Master Ng Mui. Hung Gar developed.
ca. 1830 CE	Southern Praying Mantis originates. Choy Li Fut develops.
1872 CE	The main gate and front walls of Honan Temple are renovated and enlarged, taking their now familiar forms.
1878 CE	Wutang Temple disciples and masters are involved in plots to overthrow Chinese government; the Wutang Temple is severed from Shaolin affiliation.
1899 CE	Many members of Wutang Temple incite mobs to take up violent overthrow of imperial government and expel foreigners.
1900 CE	The Boxer Uprising leads to the end of imperial China. Fukien Temple totally destroyed at about this time. Honan Temple severely damaged.
1902 CE	Shaolin chief abbot leaves China for the United States. 1902 to 1930: Shaolin's senior echelon flees China.
1911 CE	Chinese factions terminate the imperial system. China becomes fragile republic. All foreigners ordered to leave.
ca. 1927 CE	Senior Shaolin priests begin convening in New York City to establish a temple.
1928 CE	Warlord Shi You-san burns down Honan Temple.
1931 CE	Ascending warlords and fractionalization in China; "foreign devils" generally expelled. Temples looted, and damaged or destroyed by this point.
1949 CE	Mao Tze Tung establishes China as a communist state; all religions, temples, and monks are to be destroyed. Martial arts outlawed and Buddhist practices "discouraged."
1964 CE	Bruce Lee introduces gung fu to American public.
1972 CE	*Kung Fu* movie and television series present fictionalized account of Shaolin to America and popularize the Order and gung fu.
1974 CE	Honan Temple main gate restored as historical monument.
1985 CE	The Order of Shaolin Ch'an sends a disciple to the Honan Temple to determine if any genuine remnants of Shaolin practice persist there. This representative found no Buddhist or traditional gung fu practice, only Modern Wushu and the seeds of a tourist attraction.
1989 CE	Communist China rebuilds Honan Temple as a "restored cultural facility." See page 125 for more information.

Chapter Three

Shaolin Ch'an Buddhism

Truth can not be cut up into pieces and arranged into a system.
The words can only be used as a figure of speech.

Shakyamuni Buddha

Buddhism is a philosophy that originated in northern India in the 5th century B.C.E. Most students of philosophy, world history, or comparative religions know the story of the wealthy young Indian prince, Siddhartha Gautama, whose father kept the unpleasant realities of the world hidden from his son. One day, however, these efforts failed, and the young prince was able to witness disease, poverty, and death. Naturally enough, these realities frightened him, especially after he learned that he, too, was mortal and subject to these influences. One night he stole away from the palace and he began a pilgrimage to seek the spiritual path that would release him from suffering. After trying many approaches (including asceticism) he finally rested under a tree and went into a deep meditation. During this meditation he became enlightened ("buddha" means awakened one or enlightened one, roughly translating further into "one who sees truth"), meaning he understood the truths of the world and saw the path to alleviate suffering.

From that day onwards Shakyamuni (Sage of the Shakya Clan) Buddha taught anyone who would listen, regardless of age, sex, or caste (a very big concern in India even today). When many people think of Buddhism today, they bring to mind the view that life is eternal, resurrected generation after generation through rebirth or reincarnation. In this view we are all linked by a spiritual lineage and the acts of one affect the lives of the others. The notion of reincarnation, though, is controversial within Buddhism, with various sects having greater or lesser belief. Depending upon which *sutra* you read, the Buddha himself seemed equivocal on this subject. Sometimes he taught about how we must learn to escape the cycle of rebirths and on other occasions he expounded a doctrine of non-self. If there is no self, then what can be reborn? Several sects hold to the idea that the very familiar image of reincarnation was used metaphorically to help practitioners better visualize their interdependence and relatedness to all other living things. Other sects push a more literal interpretation to achieve the same ends: if we see our neighbor as the possible reincarnation of a former best friend or beloved pet, will we not treat him better? Buddhist teaching does not include an unchanging, permanent self or "soul" of any kind however—hence a more literal understanding of rebirth becomes problematic. Part of the difficulty surely lies in the context of the Buddha's ministry. To communicate with the people of that time, who were Hindu, Shakyamuni employed familiar metaphors. Shaolin has no dogmatic take on this issue: the precise nature of reincarnation, whether actual or metaphorical, is left up to the individual.

We might think of reincarnation as follows: In each life we must learn certain lessons. If the whole of our earthly life and reincarnations is depicted as a wheel, then in each incarnation we add spokes to brace the outer rim. Sometimes we make more spokes, and other lifetimes we make fewer, but eventually we fashion a full wheel. It is at that point that we escape the cycle of rebirth. Though the rim and spokes remain intact in each lifetime, the individual consciousness is unaware of its existence or state of development. Thus, in each incarnation we begin life with some advance over the previous, but without a collective knowledge of that wholeness. A fuller awareness would impede the learning to be done in the present lifetime. This metaphor is helpful for understanding an incremental approach to awakening. Within Shaolin, some make active use of such allegory. Others find the whole subject of reincarnation to be not particularaly crucial. The truth or falsity of reincarnation, and the nature of that reincarnation, should not really be central to a Buddhist's practice.

Compassion *does* occupy a central place in Shaolin thought, underlining the fact that the relationship between a Shaolin adept and the natural world involves more than just emulating a few creatures for their combat prowess. Passing pain to another creature only adds **karmic debt** to ourselves. To harm another is to harm one's self. Yet we are willing to accept this price, if necessary, to prevent *others* from reaping such a karmic harvest. We are all part of the same interrelated network of life. Compassion in action is an affirmation of that bond and helps us overcome the ego, which is always trying to separate suffering into "mine" and "other."

The place we accord compassion in our practice is reflected by the places we inhabit. Temples often contained beautiful and elaborate gardens (actually, most of the gardens were outside the temple walls, but still on temple grounds) that were places for meditation, contemplation, and teaching. Many included pools where fish, turtles, and birds would be kept. Though Shaolin did not keep pets as thought of in most countries, we did allow many creatures to share our space, and it was a rare temple that did not serve as home to several dogs, birds, and goldfishes. It was through this proximity with domesticated and semi-domesticated creatures that we sought to forge our first deep links with other sentient species. Close association with these creatures reinforced our belief that we shared more features in common than not, and allowed us to develop compassion for all sentient life forms.

There are a few interesting symbols associated with the Buddha's enlightenment which deserve explanation. The first is the *swastika*. While Shakyamuni was meditating under that tree, he was also recovering from a fast (his most recent failed path to enlightenment). When he awoke, he was met by a young shepherd who offered him water and bread. The young boy was named "Svasti" (hence "Svastika") and blessed by the new Buddha. (According to some sources, Svasti is the grass-cutter who provides bundles of grass for the *bodhisattva* to sit upon in his final awakening.[47]) A symbol of crossed jagged lines would represent the boy and his act of generosity and compassion. It is precisely because this symbol carries so much power for so many people that the Nazis adopted it as their own (but printed it tilted and reversed from the most common representation—though the swastika is printed *both ways* in some cultures). As with so many other actions by that party, the very use of the swastika was a major desecration of a sacred symbol. Today, the swastika is still used widely in India and East Asia as a symbol of compassion (it is incorporated, for example, in the logos of many Karate schools). In some Ch'an and Zen schools, the swastika symbolizes the limitlessness of the Dharma.[48]

The second symbol is the cobra. After the Buddha began teaching, he would rarely be alone. However, on one of these rare occasions he sat meditating in an open field on a hot day. A cobra came by and observed the spiritual teacher. He moved behind the Buddha, raised up and opened his hood widely. In return for this gesture of shading the man, Buddha touched the hood of the snake and blessed it for its help. To this day, the "eyeglass"-like marks on Asian cobra hoods are seen as the symbol of the Buddha's fingers in blessing the snake and its descendants. (A more popular but related story tells of how the great *naga* king Mucilinda spread the hoods of his seven heads to protect the Buddha during a rainstorm, then transformed into a young man who paid homage to the Buddha.)

Based on historical information, the Buddha has the distinction of having lived to teach his philosophy longer than any other founder of a spiritual path. He lived on for several decades after his awakening, finally dying at the ripe old age of eighty. It is generally conceded that food poisoning was at least partially responsible for the Buddha's death. After Buddha's passing came his Dharma-successors, referred to as the patriarchs. As they dispersed across Asia, they modified aspects of Buddhism to accommodate local peoples and their beliefs. Perhaps the greatest amalgamation of systems is to be found in Tibet, where the official Buddhism includes many features that are quite foreign to Shakyamuni's initial teachings. Nevertheless, one who accepts the *four noble truths* and follows the eightfold path is considered a Buddhist, a follower of the

Dharma (the universal teaching, the Buddha's formulation of which is presently available to us) and member of the Sangha.

The Buddha also differs from other holy leaders in that **he never claimed to be anything more than a man who discovered the path to enlightenment—without supernatural help.** In his lessons were the essential messages that humans are the source of their own salvation, that salvation does not require supernatural intervention, and that enlightenment is a state that any sentient being can attain. These are aspects of the practice of Buddhism that distinguish it from those religions requiring deistic worship or belief in the supernatural.

For the reader unfamiliar with Buddhism, a key distinction between Buddhism and middle eastern religions (Judaism, Islam, and Christianity) is that Buddhism encourages questioning and testing of all its precepts, while western monotheisms typically require blind faith and obedience of their followers. This ideal was in stark contrast, for example, to the Catholic Church during much of its first 1500 years. The popes forbade anyone but certain clergy and nobles to learn to read (preventing anyone asking embarrassing questions about the Bible or papal decrees), a law that if broken was punishable by death. Finally, while the great middle eastern religions have historically limited the involvement of women, Buddhism generally makes no distinction among its devotees by sex and is unique among world religions in this respect (there is always an exception to the rule, however: you can find misogynistic sects if you look for them).

Many Paths: a Buddhist Sects Education

All the sects are like beads on one rosary.

T'ai Hsü

The reality of a diversified Buddhism must be taken into account by followers of the path. The various sects have thrived, moved, been replaced, or changed over the 2500 years since the Buddha's last lesson. India, the birthplace of the Buddha, is still largely a Hindu nation. Buddhism survives in the island of Sri Lanka off India's southeast coast, and in places like Thailand, Burma, and Japan. It once thrived in China, and is presently returning to that huge country. In each of these places it has taken on a different nature, sometimes resulting in two or more distinct sects. The introduction of Buddhism into China, long before Tamo, was close to the Tibetan model of that time. By the time of Tamo, though, the new masters were intent on returning Buddhist practices to the individual and deemphasizing the role of the community. Only an individual, they claimed, could attain enlightenment. If people only focused on community efforts, none would become liberated. Universal suffering would persist.

The Buddha observed that people follow one of three basic philosophical approaches to the spiritual life. He referred to these approaches as: low path, middle path (madhyama-pratipad), and high path. The low path is the path of the common man, the life of one unaware or unprepared to develop his spiritual self. The worker who struggles merely to survive is not seen as low or lowly in a pejorative sense, but as one not yet aware enough, or without the time/resources to see beyond the immediate needs of food, clothing, and shelter. By "low" a Buddhist means that the individual's focus is self- and earth-centered, totally governed by the mundane needs of (generally) subsistence level survival. Working hard at a menial occupation is *not* synonymous with traveling the low path; in fact, menial tasks can often be vehicles of enlightenment. Regardless of physical occupation, one is on the low path if he is "unaware or unprepared to develop his spiritual self."

The high path is the practice of denial, fasting, and other asceticisms that, though aimed at spiritual development, often lead to abusing the practitioner's mind and body. The Buddha considered excessive deprivation and pain as counterproductive, dangerous to spiritual growth. Many mystical spiritual traditions around the world follow a high path.

The middle path is the way of the Buddha: the eightfold path. Balance is of tremendous importance: balance between aspects of the path, and balance between the social, emotional, intellectual, physical, and spiritual dimensions of life. Yet even among sects following this middle way, there are surprising differences.

> Consider dietary laws. Generally speaking, the priests of Sri Lanka, an island, may eat seafood. Japanese priests may eat seafood and filet mignon, too, providing somebody donates it to them. Chinese Buddhists are vegetarians no matter where they live or what they are given. What about sexual conduct? Japanese priests may marry. Chinese priests are celibate. Thai priests may not so much as touch the flesh of a female human being or even sit at a dining table with a female priest or…any male who is not a priest. At the other extreme, priests of any "left-hand" yoga or tantric order receive instruction in ritual sexual intercourse. What about reincarnation? Most Chinese and Japanese Buddhists virtually ignore the subject while the lives of Tibetan Buddhists are so shot through with transmigrations that there is no room left to house the creation of a single, unique, wholly-new individual. Everybody is, or was, somebody else.[49]

This is somewhat "tongue in cheek," but also accurate. As you might surmise, Shaolin Ch'an shares more of its practices with some Japanese and Tibetan Buddhist schools than it does with other Chinese Ch'an sects.

Most religions or spiritual traditions offer "lower" and "higher" paths or approaches depending on individual circumstances. Among

Buddhist schools there is a sort of "high path," best characterized by the *Theravada* school (Sanskrit for "Doctrine of the Elders," some scholars describe Theravada as the only extant *Hinayana* Buddhist tradition). In some places it is a strongly religious school that combines the Indian pantheon of gods and goddesses with the existing local pantheon. Its most successful sects are in Sri Lanka, Thailand, and other countries located in Southeast Asia. This school emphasizes self-purification, to awaken the spiritual or divine from within the practitioner. Central to Theravada practices are strict obedience to moral precepts, rigorous study of the Pali Buddhist Canon (especially the *Abhidharma*), meditation, chanting, and ceremonial activities intended to remind the subtle soul-self of its earlier incarnations. Such awareness then advances the monk towards enlightenment.

In a way, the Theravada school is founded on the idea that humans are base, but capable of approaching an awakening if they *act* divine. Monks and nuns must be celibate, shave their heads, perform assigned tasks, attend rituals, and memorize volumes of sacred texts. Theravadin models for divinity, in some areas, are often drawn from Hindu texts but strangely ignore many of the very human activities of the gods.

If Theravada constitutes the "high" aspect of the broader middle path, then our Shaolin Ch'an (all Ch'an and Zen, really) probably corresponds to the "low" part of the middle path—especially in the sense that our Buddhism is practice-based as opposed to sutra-based, ritual-based, or rule-based. Sometimes debate arises as to which sect is most faithful to the Buddha's earliest teachings. We don't know! Yet in assessing this, consider that the Buddha's message was transmitted in a mostly oral fashion for a few hundred years before monks in Sri Lanka put the Pali Canon together from memory. Much time had passed since the Buddha died. The Shaolin perspective, along with that of some others,[50] has been that although the Pali Canon focused on many of the Buddha's formal teachings, the conservative Theravadins missed or downplayed many aspects of the Buddha's teaching—aspects essential to Ch'an practice. Much of the *Vinaya* basket (collection of rules) of the Pali Canon seems ad hoc when compared to the Buddha's core message. To cite just one example, the *Vinaya* prohibits Buddhist monks from entering the homes of "low-caste" individuals. Shaolin, like some Tibetan sects, sees some of the *Vinaya* rules as less than vital to the path. In most Tibetan orders, monks are supposed to follow all the rules, but simply end up breaking the "minor" ones. In Shaolin, one *can* be a bhikshu, taking and following all the *Vinaya* rules—yet one can also be ordained as a priest without following those rules. There is a wide latitude in practice. Although Theravadin sects, and many Mahayana sects, are very different from Shaolin Ch'an, we do acknowledge that they are all paths to the same destination—just suited to very different kinds of people. We are thankful for this diversity.

In China, Mahayana teachings gave rise to the Ch'an, Hua-yen, T'ien T'ai, and Pure Land schools. In India, Mahayana gave rise to the Madhyamaka and Yogachara schools, and in Tibet arose the Vajrayana (or

Tantrayana) school. The Madhyamaka school, founded by Nagarjuna, is, literally translated, the "school of the middle way." The term "middle way" often expressly refers to Madhyamaka, but we are using the term here in its more general sense of indicating the teachings of Shakyamuni Buddha. (In the *Dhammacakkappavattana Sutta*, also called the "*Setting in Motion the Wheel of the Law Sutra*," Buddha says that the middle path simply is the eightfold path.) Ch'an Mahayanins believe we live in the here and now, and should act and think accordingly. The overwhelming focus is on accepting our humanity and kinship with nature, awakening to the four noble truths, following the eightfold path, and aspiring to the bodhisattva ideal. This school is unconcerned with the supernatural or deities because the Buddha taught that, by definition, the supernatural could be neither confirmed nor explained by resources available to humans. The most important things a person can do in a lifetime, then, are to acknowledge kinship with all sentient life and to eliminate ego and the causes of attachment.

Shaolin Ch'an is included in the middle path, primarily because it walks a line between hedonism on one side and asceticism on the other. Individuals are *supposed* to be individuals. This is a path that avoids extremes, staying on the middle of the road. Like orchids, we believe that human beings need to be stressed in particular ways to thrive—hence our rigorous martial and meditative training. But stress an orchid too much and it dies. Humans are no different than orchids in this regard. Fasting, abject poverty, excessive praying, and devout practice of daily rituals do not necessarily lead to enlightenment. In fact, Shakyamuni Buddha's own cousin, Devadatta, urged the Buddha to make certain ascetic practices obligatory within the Sangha, such as: life in the open, wearing only rags taken from cremation grounds, strict vegetarianism, and avoiding meals at laypeople's homes. The Buddha refused on the grounds that such ascetic practices should be voluntary and were no essential part of the middle path.[51]

Lotus Position

Inquiring about a difference
is like asking to borrow string when you've got a good strong rope.

Ch'an Master Hsu Yun

To attain Zen enlightenment, it is not necessary to give up family life, quit your job, become a vegetarian, practice asceticism, and flee to a quiet place, then go into a ghost cave of dead Zen to entertain subjective imaginings.[52]

Zen Master Dahui

Shaolin Ch'an also holds that systems of intellectual inquiry will never lead to Ultimate Truth. Discursive reasoning and logic are useful in dealing with our everyday world, but intuitive understanding is necessary for grasping ultimate reality. In this way, Ch'an Buddhists can correctly be called "gnostics." "Gnosis" is a Greek word for knowledge, but specifically refers to intuitive knowledge—the kind of "knowledge" one can acquire through meditation and adherence to the eightfold path. Gnosis might even be seen as mystical knowledge (although Shaolin espouses a practical approach to Ch'an, Ch'an *is* considered the mystical school of Buddhism), as it constitutes an understanding that comes from awakening, through meditation, to our own buddha-natures and grasping our fundamental unity with the universe. The opposite of gnosis, for a Buddhist, is ignorance.

The theme of gnosis conquering ignorance is not unique to Shaolin; it is seen in all Mahayana sects, if to varying degrees, and elsewhere as well. When Shakyamuni Buddha was in his 60s, he began spreading a revised teaching, a teaching that pierced through and transcended his original teaching.[53] This evolutionary teaching—which included the messages that *shunyata* itself is empty, and that Buddhists should put this "emptiness of emptiness" to work in liberating sentient beings—the Buddha called "perfection of wisdom" (prajnaparamita). Not many grasped this teaching of the Buddha, and although both the early Theravadins and pre-cursor Mahayanins had written copies of perfection of wisdom sutras in the second century BCE,[54] this literature was marginalized by the Theravadins and not included in the Pali Canon. There are two reasons for this. First, much of the perfection of wisdom literature was esoteric in nature, and so not readily accessible to most disciples.[55] Second, the precursor to the *Diamond Sutra*, which gently rebuked asceticism and monastic discipline, could not have been popular with the Theravadins, who valued those ideals.[56] The perfection of wisdom literature forms much of the body of the Mahayana school; and the *Diamond Sutra*, with its gnostic message of awakening to no-mind and hence the highest compassion, is the heart of Mahayana. No-mind (wu-hsin) is a very Ch'an concept, whereas compassion is truly the core of Mahayana thought. Shakyamuni's esoteric prajnaparamita teaching partly consisted in the message that these two elements are inextricably linked. The notion of gnosis as awakening or *seeing* Ultimate Truth also appears in early Christian writings such as the *Gnostic Gospels* and in Tibetan Buddhist writings; one tantric Mahayoga thesis states that "the infinity of gnosis [is] nondual."[57]

The Four Noble Truths and the Eightfold Path

Following this way you shall make an end to suffering.

Shakyamuni Buddha

"Awakening," as the Chinese usually refer to becoming enlightened, may be usefully understood as *seeing* Ultimate Reality. But how does one wake up? This is where the Buddha's core teaching becomes important. It is said that Shakyamuni's actual enlightenment under the bodhi tree consisted in his deep intuitive grasp of the four noble truths.[58] These truths, originally expounded in the *Dhammacakkappavattana Sutta*, are simple and excepting perhaps the fourth truth, self-evident:

1.   **There is suffering in the world;**
2.   **Suffering is caused by desire, including desire for love, wealth, fame, and even life itself;**
3.   **Suffering can be eliminated in the individual through the elimination of desire;** and
4.   **The way to eliminate desire is through destruction of the ego, via the eightfold path and eventual enlightenment.**

Many westerners criticize Buddhism for being a very negative, pessimistic religion. To wit, the first noble truth says that life is filled with suffering. But the Sanskrit word for suffering, "duhkha," is a much more inclusive term. The meaning of "duhkha" includes the concepts of suffering, imperfection, unsatisfactoriness, frustration, and impermanence. So it isn't that the Buddha was pessimistic, but neither was he optimistic. The Buddha was a realist.[59] Shakyamuni simplifies the four noble truths by saying: if you learn to free yourself from desire you free yourself completely. To a Buddhist, fear of death equates to desire not to lose life. Overcome that desire and fear of death dissipates like smoke in the wind.

Thich Nhat Hanh, in his excellent *The Heart of the Buddha's Teaching*, writes that, according to the Buddha, desire is one of many afflictions that can cause suffering, along with anger and ignorance. This point is important, lest we oversimplify the Buddha's teachings. Suffering means more than just pain, and desire is a placeholder for more than just lust. Shaolin tries to acknowledge the breadth of the Dharma by encouraging education and curiosity to combat ignorance, understanding and compassion to combat anger, equanimity and renunciation to combat craving.

High spiritual attainment is no easy thing, but the path is well-defined. Buddha defined the route as an eight-part practice. The steps are not strictly sequential, but must be followed together and in harmony. Here is a very brief, Shaolin interpretation of the eightfold path:

1. **Right views.** When you ask yourself "Why do I do what I do?", what answers do you have? By right views the Buddha meant your motives and your goals. Do you seek to become a politician for the fame and power, or for a genuine desire to help others? No action in your life should be mindless; a spiritual person knows why she acts. A right action leads to a well-defined goal that moves you towards your spiritual enlightenment. This does not mean that each move must be grand; in fact, most journeys are made up of myriad tiny steps. Right views will help you determine if you are on the right path. Right views also ask you to study and understand the four noble truths and the eightfold path. Eventually, right views lead to meditation and acceptance that all things are interconnected as part of a whole. Much of this explanation also fits into the section on right action. You will note that most of these concepts are overlapping and not at all exclusive.

2. **Right resolve**. Are you prepared for the task at hand? What are your preparations of thought, speech, and motivation? Is the task at hand worthy of your time and effort? Rightness in resolve means two things. First, is the activity worthy of your effort? Does it contribute to bettering life for any fellow creatures (harmlessness and good will), or help even *one* other being move towards enlightenment? If the answer is yes, then next ask if *you* are the person to make a contribution towards achieving that goal. Your motivation must be unselfish, with no thought of fame or reward (renunciation). You must have the knowledge or special skills needed to make your contribution. Only when you can merge these two factors harmoniously do you have right resolve. (The three classical elements of right resolve—renunciation, good will, and harmlessness—are highlighted by parenthetical remarks.)

3. **Right speech**. Words are powerful, which is why the sages and shamans of so many cultures believe they have magical power. We all know how careless words may hurt others and open you to attack. Nobody likes a gossip or a liar. The U.S. Navy was quite serious when, in World War II, it placed posters on ships and on bases warning sailors that "loose lips sink ships." Buddhists are aware of the power of words and the thought-entities they can evoke.

Buddhists also acknowledge that words cannot be recalled, and once uttered will stay with a person depending on their tone and content. Something said in fury may stay with a person for a lifetime—even though the words were said in the heat of the moment and later recanted. (Recent neuroscience research even indicates that social snubs register just like visceral pain to the brain.) The mere fact that such words can be uttered means that a person is capable of thinking such vitriol, and that acts as a corrosive between relationships. Buddhists believe very strongly in the power of words: words can move us to tears or anger, tenderness or contemplation, passion or boredom. A Buddhist tries always to "say what you mean and mean what you say."

4. **Right action**. Once you decide on a task, is your procedure well thought out, or is it haphazard? If you wish to become an M.D., you must gain admittance to a medical school. Each step leading to that end must be precise. One does not normally enter medical school directly from a driver's position at a pizza parlor (but a pizza delivery driver *may* become an M.D. if he takes the appropriate actions).

Right action is not simply about doing the "right" thing, but about taking the right (read "necessary") steps for you to get from point A to point B. If preparation is a cornerstone of Buddhism, then it is an entire foundation to Shaolin. Our training is not about being perfect, but about being competent. We may not perform the "best" action in a crisis, but we shall perform an acceptable action, and without being inhibited by fear or other distractions. Meditation prepares our nerves for crisis, and our other preparations come from our overall training and career preparedness.

Most Buddhists adhere to a limited number of guidelines regarding right action. These include avoiding the harming of other living beings, being sincere, abstaining from illicit sex, and avoiding drugs and any substance that may deprive the mind from maintaining control. Right action also dictates the use of Shaolin martial skills. Actions that gratify the ego—such as winning in tournaments—are seen as highly contradictory to this goal. You will not see genuine Shaolin masters engaged in any gratuitous competitions.

5. **Right livelihood**. Buddhists believe that work is a manifestation of spiritual development. Enlightenment is difficult to achieve if you are in the wrong occupation for you; e.g., a vegetarian may find extreme moral difficulty working as a butcher. The choice of career is important, and Buddhists believe that the choice must come from within, not from "following in the family footsteps"—that is, unless you truly find fulfillment in that business. To a Buddhist, profession is an expression of intention. In American society it is common to hear people say of themselves: "I am my job." If you ask someone to tell you about herself, she will typically start by saying something such as "I am a writer" or "I design books." So linked with our sense of identity is the way we make our living that a poor match almost always causes grief and suffering. Finding right livelihood is especially important in walking the spiritual path.

It is easy to read this definition into a statement supporting a strengthening of the ego, e.g., "I am only a writer." Such a view is indeed going to reinforce ego. But a person who is writing *is* a writer *when engaged in writing*. Later, the same person will become a cook preparing the family dinner, and a dishwasher later. Any livelihood is honorable so long as it is legal and avoids cruelty.

From the Shaolin perspective, right livelihood is both a very economic and a very ecological notion. You get everything that you need to survive from "the world." What do you return to your community in exchange? A great part of right livelihood is finding and truly understanding your niche in the world.

6. **Right effort**. Having embarked on a path, are you giving the journey the logistical and emotional support it needs to be accomplished? Buddhism frowns on half-hearted efforts. "Do or do *not*" is a Buddhist doctrine borrowed by *Star Wars'* Master Yoda. (*Star Wars* creator George Lucas found considerable inspiration for his space fantasy from Asian philosophies that were popularized by his friend, the notable scholar Joseph Campbell. Buddhism and Taoism permeate Campbell's work and the *Star Wars* saga.) The most important things we do in life cannot be achieved without the full strength of our hearts and minds—the concentration of our ch'i.

According to the sutras, right effort also importantly means ceasing to possess intentions that result in the accumulation of **karma**. One way of thinking about this is that a person successfully exercising right effort possesses a well-calibrated "internal compass." For instance, such an individual does not merely abstain from stealing; stealing does not even enter his mind as an intention. The Shaolin interpretation of right effort is supremely practical when compared to this more classical notion of right effort, yet they are inextricable. You cannot give your full effort, in a practical sense, if your intentions are sabotaged by the ego.

7. **Right attention**. Are you giving enough conscious attention to yourself, to gauge your moods and relationships to be sure you are still on the right path for you? If you cannot hear yourself, how well can you hear others? Do you focus on the important or the trivial matters in your life? In short, are you able to make decisions about what does and does not seem to fit into, or integrate well with, your life? Right attention requires enough self-awareness to be knowledgeable about whom you are in the deepest sense those words represent. This self-awareness includes both deep self-reflection and daily mindfulness. Be mindful of your thoughts and experiences in following the path.

8. **Right meditation**. Have you the discipline to fully focus on the task at hand? (Yoda's comment in *The Empire Strikes Back* about Luke Skywalker: "Never his mind on where he is!" is appropriate.) You need not be single-minded; life is, after all, made of many experiences and relationships. But the task at hand deserves your full mindfulness, or it is unimportant. Can you tell which? Right meditation is about simply being where you are, doing what you are doing. Since we are strong advocates of moving meditations (not simply gung fu—one patriarch famously achieved enlightenment while washing dishes), we do not interpret right meditation to refer solely to specialized, seated meditations such as *zazen*.

As a student of the eightfold path, be mindful that the elements of the path are organic and interrelated. But there is a sort of rough order of practice: one begins with the practice of ethics (right speech, right action, right livelihood), moves on to mastering the mind and its abilities (right effort, right attention, right meditation), and finally achieves wisdom (right views, right resolve). Right views include understanding the four noble truths at the deepest intuitive level, and this was said to have constituted Shakyamuni Buddha's enlightenment, as has been mentioned. Please note two things before moving on: 1) the Shaolin interpretation of the eightfold path is a very pragmatic one, and 2) much more can usefully be said about the different aspects of the path. For greater elaboration, a student can find many good sources on the eightfold path.[60]

Beyond the eightfold path, however, the Buddha provides a lesson that underscores the proper approach to spirituality for those confronted with a confusing plethora of religions, philosophies, and ideologies (as we are in today's culture). When some town-folk asked the Buddha what to believe, given the wealth of circulating belief systems, he replied:

> Do not accept authority merely because it comes from a tradition, appearances, a great man, or is written in a sacred book. Believe only that which you can test for yourself to be wholesome and good.

This lesson (from the *Kalama Sutra*), so often omitted in modern teachings, is considered by Shaolin to be an important lesson of the Buddha. It anticipated the scientific method by well over two millennia, and served to help Buddhism largely remain free of the kind of autocratic control that perverted or inhibited many other religions and philosophies. In short, Ch'an Buddhism rejects the blind obedience of the "faithful," and prefers its practitioners to know life from experiencing it in all its glory and despair. It absolutely requires the individual to experience something before accepting it as real. In Shaolin, therefore, all teachers have first-hand experience of what they teach. Few other disciplines are taught in such a manner.

What Does the Buddha Mean by "Right?"

What sort of thing is the path, that you want to cultivate it?

Hui-k'o

The eightfold path places strong emphasis on the concept of "right," and a student *should* wonder what the Buddha meant by that term. After all, "right" can mean good, correct, or appropriate. In Buddhist terms, all three definitions are applicable to a student of the way, probably in the reverse order given with respect to complexity. The original term as used in the time of the Buddha meant "perfect," but our translation means something somewhat different than the original term. There *is* a single criterion for what the Buddha meant by "right," but it may not be as easy to understand. Right activities are, ultimately, activities that lead to the cessation of duhkha (suffering); but grasping the Buddha's intent in this would be tantamount to having already made significant progress on the path. It will be easier, then, to say that a right action is one that moves us towards the "light" and "good," to use additional subjective terms.

An appropriate action is one that fits with the ideals and life ethics of the practitioner. If a student wants to be a healer, then anatomy, physiology, behavior, genetics, medicine, and surgery are all appropriate interests, and their study constitutes right action. Would an interest in baseball be appropriate to the healer-student? If the goal was to practice sports medicine or a branch concerned with kinesiology, by all means it would. Otherwise, it might be a diversion and thus inappropriate. (Of course, some physical activity is beneficial to any person, but in this simplified example, rightness is only being invoked relative to those activities *directly* related to healer training.)

We will define a correct activity as one that matches the student's levels of comprehension and expertise. To continue the medical student analogy, it might be correct for a first year student to observe a surgery, but it would not be correct to let her *conduct* the procedure. First must come proper groundwork training, more observation, practice by assisting and then, finally, performing an operation first-hand. We do not walk before crawling, nor fly a plane solo before completing ground school. Correct activity, then, may be seen as a fundamental and required learning block in the context of the entire learning process.

In one of the most important scriptures to the Shaolin Order, the *Diamond Sutra* (or *Vajracchedika Prajnaparamita Sutra*), the Buddha lists the qualities needed to become a buddha. In these characteristics are the guidelines for what Buddha meant by "right." These traits are 1) charity, 2) selfless kindness, 3) humility and patience, 4) perseverance, 5) tranquility, and 6) wisdom. An action cannot be "right" in the sense of being a good activity if it violates one of these traits. These traits are often referred to as the six paramitas, and are essential qualities to cultivate on the path to bodhisattva-hood. Calling something a "good activity" will always involve a bit of an ethical context, and the six paramitas provide us with an excellent tool for reflecting on goodness. Also relevant to the Shaolin interpretation of "rightness" are the words of Aristotle, who nicely captured the relationship between "the good" and what we now call "gung fu:"

> The good of man is the active exercise of his soul's faculties in conformity with excellence or virtue [good = exercise of gung fu!]—this activity must occupy a complete lifetime; for one swallow does not make spring, nor does one fine day; and similarly one day or a brief period of happiness does not make a man supremely blessed and happy.

But often, in Shaolin, normative ethics are confined to the supremely practical. Is it good (right) for a person chronically upset by the sight of injury to become an emergency room physician? Is it good for a colorblind person to become an interior decorator? Is it good to allow small children to play with household cleaning agents? The answer, generally, is "no." Much of right action, for instance, relies upon common sense (which is downright uncommon and should probably be given a new label). The first step to cultivating common sense, and the ability to do the "right" thing, is to develop an understanding of the law of karma, also known as the law of cause and effect. Without a firm grip on cause and effect, i.e. wisdom, actions motivated by the highest of virtues and the best of intentions are liable to result in tremendous heartache and suffering. Although not a Shaolin aphorism, "the road to hell is paved with good intentions" is apt here. The Buddhist notion of "right" entails much more than just whatever is morally good—appropriateness and correctness are also essential.

Nirvana

During a dream there is no awakening;
at the time of awakening there is no dream.

Buddhist nun Yuan-chi

What is *nirvana* and why is it important to a Buddhist? Is it a place, like the Judeo-Christian heaven, or something quite different? To start, it was thought by many early sects of Buddhism that nirvana was not achieved at the moment of enlightenment, but only after death. Remember that Buddhism has a central belief in reincarnation, and that souls/spirits keep returning to earth in new forms until they learn how to be free of illusion and attachment. For early Buddhists, only then was the spirit free to move to the condition called "nirvana" and be free of rebirth. Enlightenment provided the knowledge of how to attain freedom, or liberation.

Some Shaolin, heavily influenced by Lamaism, believe in *bardo*. Following the eightfold path, an enlightened one dies and enters a state of post-life contemplation known as the bardo state. In bardo, we encounter a review of our lives, and we make the self-determination of what to do next. If we still suffer, we return to earth in a new life and work to eliminate desire. This is the fate of most spirits. Alternately, the spirit may be free, truly a buddha, and ready to be free of rebirth. According to the Buddhists who believe this concept of bardo, our post-life state is ego-free and thus capable of examining itself objectively. We monitor our own learning between lives and thus insure our continued education on earth if it is still needed.

According to some Buddhist sects (including some Shaolin practitioners), there is yet another choice for buddhas. A buddha may elect to postpone the reward of nirvana and instead return yet again as a living being, with the goal of helping other beings attain enlightenment. Such a soul is called a bodhisattva, literally an "enlightenment being" who is a buddha-teacher. The other choice is to proceed to the state of nirvana.

The Buddha never made promises about nirvana or "ultimate reality" that were beyond the ability of people to know. He neither accepted nor denounced gods or a happy afterlife. Like *Star Wars'* Yoda, he believed that true enlightenment was about what you do and where you are *now*. Other concerns are beyond us and, therefore, of little practical importance. He did not offer us a lush image of a heaven; he offered us a way to be free of pain and suffering. His view of a living nirvana state was one where we saw without illusion, and saw the potential for goodness in spite of the reality of suffering.

Shaolin Ch'an is more a philosophy than a religion; you might call our way a perfection of human cognition or a "philosophy of human education," as some others have denoted Ch'an.[61] But many sects have accepted deities, demons, and Buddha as a god. Buddha was adamant about his being a man, a mere mortal like anyone else who had achieved something that could be achieved by anyone else. Nevertheless, he was posthumously deified by many followers, leading to the religious sects of Buddhism. In contrast, a some sects—including Shaolin—accepted the teachings literally, believing that any person can attain enlightenment and that we all contain a buddha-awareness that simply needs to be recognized or realized. In other words, we are all enlightened already, but we generally don't recognize it as such. That is why the realization of buddha-nature is called "awakening."

This group of philosophical sects does not accept concepts of the supernatural, deities or demons, but is appropriately agnostic (*not* atheistic) in its views about the supernatural. An agnostic, according to the coiner of the term, Thomas Henry Huxley, is one who acknowledges that whatever his *belief* a person cannot prove or disprove the existence of God. To him, all honest people must be agnostic. Under Huxley's interpretation, a theist is one who believes but does not *know* that God exists (even though he may *think* that he knows). Likewise, an atheist believes but does not *know* that God does not exist (even though he may *think* he knows that God does not exist). In the word "agnostic" is the honest claim "I do not know," for humanity has been given no objective test or method that can either prove or disprove the existence of deities. "I believe" is, to a Buddhist, not equivalent to "I know." Thus, Buddhism regards anyone who claims to be an *objective* theist or atheist as deluded, peering through the veil of illusion. A Ch'an Buddhist, then, may believe in a god but still refer to himself as an agnostic. Thus the Buddhist can maintain intellectual honesty while also recognizing the reality of the veils of illusion.

The Shaolin Buddhist doctrine centers on the concept of learning truth for your self. We encourage doubt, questioning, and self-discovery. Although there is recognition that doubt can be a hindrance to spiritual progress,[62] there is also an understanding that doubt (at certain points) is a useful goad for progress. In our focus on self-discovery, Shaolin adheres to the Buddha's teaching that enlightenment can *only* come from within and not from a "secret teaching" or mysterious "passed power" from teacher to student. (Bruce Lee aptly describes "secret teachings" in the martial arts as a kind of "psychological constipation" that cannot compare to clarity of understanding.[63]) A Shaolin teacher is, therefore, more properly described as a guide than a teacher. Like all Ch'an sects, however, Shaolin holds to the "teaching outside of doctrine," meaning that enlightenment does not come primarily from analytical study of the sutras (which becomes philosophizing, two consequences of which are tremendous barriers to spiritual peace: doubt and clinging to opinions).

As a penultimate note on the worldly conception of nirvana, do not be misled into thinking that there is a permanent spirit, or soul, that somehow *enjoys* nirvana. We may use the words "spirit" and "soul," but we certainly don't mean them in quite the same way as the Greco-Judeo-Christian tradition. "Soul" is simply a moniker for the non-physical, but transient, elements that make up the individual. "You" and "I" are always in a state of flux on every level; the Buddha combined the findings of contemporary metaphysicians and quantum physicists long before those groups separately discovered that A) a human being today is not identical with the person that he was yesterday, and B) components of our physical universe are not fixed and immutable. The Buddha saw that every component of a human being, whether physical or mental, is always undergiong change. But the non-physical elements of the flux that "I" call "me" keep on changing, just as the physical elements do. Our bodies decompose, providing nutrients to other plants and animals. Ch'i, as well, must go somewhere! In this sense, the karmic cycle of rebirth is not a supernatural idea at all. It is a sensible prediction based on worldly truths we already know, such as the law of conservation of mass-energy. Buddhists have a reasoned faith that some corollary of this law applies to our non-physical components. Yet keep in mind that this is not the only acceptable Buddhist perspective. Consider Vimalakirti, as he quotes the Buddha in the *Vimalakirtinirdesha Sutra*, "Bhikshus, in a single moment you are born, you age, you die, you transmigrate, and you are reborn."[65] Notions of karma and nirvana need not imply a literal physical rebirth.[66]

From a practical perspective, nirvana might be better conceived as a state or condition rather than a place. It is attained when the ego is subsumed and the buddha-self is allowed to emerge. Whether the buddha-self somehow "goes" to a nirvana after the body dies…we cannot know for certain prior to death, even if we choose to believe it.

Conceiving nirvana as a mere state, however, seems incomplete. It isn't precisely an attained state, but rather a seeing of the true nature of phenomena, as Nagarjuna pointed out.[67] Nirvana is **samsara** (both words describe the world we live in), but we use the word "nirvana" to describe what life is like upon transcending samsara. Awakening, which is simply the event of "reaching" nirvana, isn't something that is somehow achieved or attained—it is more a *seeing* of Ultimate Truth (and a dissolution of the aggregates that constitute what we commonly think of as "self"). Nirvana defies complete description. Like much in Buddhist practice, nirvana must be experienced to be understood. Given Shaolin's non-dogmatic attitude, the precise concept of nirvana is left to the individual to fathom.

Spiritual Enemy Number One: the Ego

Just as a man shudders with horror when he steps upon a serpent, but laughs when he looks down and sees that it is only a rope, so I discovered one day that what I was calling "I" cannot be found, and all fear and anxiety vanished with my mistake..

Shakyamuni Buddha

To one extent or another, the ego has been a target of most spiritual practices. Focusing on the individual is seen as selfish (which, literally, it is) and detrimental to "the good of the whole." Sacrifice and hard work are the common prescriptions for subduing ego, at least in many religious traditions. Buddhism and its close relative, Taoism, also advocate a tempering of the ego—the former seeks nothing less than its extinction—though in somewhat different ways and for somewhat different ends. What, we may ask, is ego and why is it to be so thoroughly controlled?

Western psychologists have used a variety of terms to describe different levels or functions of the rational mind. While the Freudian model of mind may be outdated, it is still useful from a Buddhist perspective. The superego is something of an overlord, governing all our conscious activity based on conscious and subconscious knowledge. The id (from the Latin pronoun meaning "it") is more depersonalized; it is our basest self. From the id come our abilities to kill and love, hate and nurture. To some people, the id is equivalent to our animal nature or instinctive self. Superego imposes ethics and morals on the id lest we behave in a manner not acceptable in civilized society.

The ego (from the Latin for "I") is our most superficial—and most distinctly human—level of consciousness. It is the part of us which is personality and person, behavior and likes—the "self" of "selfish" and "self-centered." To a Buddhist, the ego represents that part of the individual that clings to the mundane plane of earthly existence. Perhaps more importantly, the ego is also what generates hate, delusion, and craving. So keep in mind that although we employ a Freudian metaphor here, the Buddhist notion of ego *does* differ in some ways from Freud's.

Suppose a group of scientists wishes to study deep-sea life, but no manned submarine can do the work required. Teaming with engineers, they jointly design a remote robot (unmanned) submarine. It is small, operated by a team on a large surface ship, and will relay data and take orders through a long cable between the surface ship and itself. The human minds working on the ship are similar to the superego, a vast intellect able to communicate and coordinate with other intellects to provide overall supervision and purpose to the submarine. The tether is akin to the id. It is a mindless relay of multitudes of data, with no ability to understand, interpret, or govern those data. The submarine, all but alone deep beneath the sea, is the ego. It is the whole point of the ship and data tether, yet it cannot exist without them. From them it has a link to more resources, control and safety than it could possibly have alone. It is the eyes and ears to the abyssal world, yet it can only see as well as its equipment will allow. True colors are almost impossible to detect at depth. Sediments in the water can distort or completely block the sub from viewing even nearby objects. Pressure, darkness, and incredible cold are around the sub always, yet it survives and even excels at its task because it is functioning harmoniously with the men above and the linking tether.

Our egos are like that submarine. To extend the metaphor, extinguishing the ego would correspond to eliminating the remote submarine. But then how would we navigate the depths? The Buddhist notion is that with the extinction of the ego, the buddha-self awakens. So, at the same time we destroy (or loose) the submarine, a superb sonar imaging device (the buddha-self) kicks in, allowing us to discern every aspect of the deep sea. In truth, we are better off for destroying the sub (ego), but this is a monumentally difficult task because the sonar device (buddha-self)— although a superior tool—is something we are superficially unfamiliar with. The buddha-self operates in a way completely unlike the ego, with its self-centered, comforting reminders that "*I* am important" and "*I* want/like/dislike/am X."

We see only through a veil that is sometimes thick and sometimes thin. Reality is often disguised or distorted to us. Our superego and id, if working in concert, provide guidance and knowledge. If we are astute, however, they also always remind us that what we are seeing is samsara, or the world of illusion. Illusion can be "real" (like those pink elephants you saw last New Years' Eve) or "imaginary" (what you *think* someone meant, but didn't). We also see our "selves" as reality, as if our bodies (and minds) and their short earthly time are all there is to us. We often fail to see the reality of our interconnectedness, though we occasionally give lip service to having, perhaps, "breathed the same air as Cleopatra." In fact, we all breathed some of that air, but we are also so much more. The chemicals that make up "your" body once made up another, and before that maybe a thousand others, and so on to the beginning of life. Before that, the chemicals that made the first cell came from our primordial planet, the same materials that make up our sun. We are, in absolute fact, the stuff of stars! How, then, can we learn this fact and not recognize our kinship with all things? The sun, the galaxy Andromeda, the silt at the bottom of the sea, your coffee table, and your faithful dog—all are kin. The first opening in the veil of illusion for most Buddhists is to recognize this simple fact

Impediments to seeing through the veil are legion, and the greatest adversary is ego. We see and believe what we wish, often in the face of overwhelming evidence to the contrary. People cling to fear and ignorance like Charles Schultz's character, Linus, clings to his security blanket. Consider a contemporary example:

Scientists invented a wonderful machine that scans inside the human body, providing far more detail than a simple x-ray. The machines were originally called "NMR" machines, standing for "Nuclear Magnetic Resonance." So many people were frightened by the word "nuclear" that the devices were renamed "MRIs" — "Magnetic Resonance Imagers." The new name, eliminating the fearsome term "nuclear," entered the lexicon to appease the fears of the ignorant. How much easier is it to appease than to educate! Are our educational systems so lacking that the majority of people don't even know that every one of the trillions of atoms that make up their bodies contains a nucleus? We have become afraid of something so basic and fundamental to all matter because of the fantastic power released in a nuclear explosion. So blinded are we by this tiny sliver of reality that we deny the many other realities of the atomic nucleus, such as its universal presence at the core of absolutely everything we call "matter."

There are many examples of how we typically face the veils of illusion. You need only look at how you view your world, the people around you, and the values you hold. People create mythologies, religions, and icons to accommodate the fear of facing the unanswerable or unknowable. We fear that which we cannot see, measure, or name. We typically embrace the veil as a pair of psychic sunglasses, altering the way we *can* perceive the world in order to avoid the harsh realities that do not agree with how we assume things to be. The veil is there to be clearly seen (and removed). So long as our sight is clouded by this veil, our ego is alive; when we see clearly, it is because the ego has been extinguished.

The Freudian metaphor is merely a tool, however, which we hope will be helpful in illustrating some key ideas in Buddhism. Another way to approach the issue of self, being, and ego, is to examine the nature of self-identity in Buddhist thought. The Buddha's basic idea is that the "self" comprises a collection of things (thoughts, perceptions, feelings, and so on) which change from moment to moment. There is no continual and unchanging "self," just as one's physical body is not immutable (good scientific estimates hold that it takes somewhere between seven and thirteen years for all the cells to be replaced, or cycle, in a human body). Understanding this transience at a deep level permits liberation, because one is no longer acting to appease the cravings of the "self." Indeed, there is no self to be found. "I" am not the same person "I" was yesterday, but neither am "I" someone else.

Sometimes the Buddha's teaching is described as the world's first systematic psychology. There is some truth to this perception. The Buddha discovered and taught a way to restructure the mind which eliminated suffering. For all of Shaolin's idiosyncracies, this way, this path, is what we are dedicated to. All of our practices are assessed as to how useful they are towards eliminating suffering. This is the way of Buddhism everywhere. And one truly marvelous feature of the Buddhist path is that every branch of the Buddha's teaching employs slightly (sometimes greatly) different methods of conquering ignorance, and hence suffering. This has helped Buddhism endure as a religion with the capacity to speak to many different kinds of people all around the world.

Shaolin Ch'an and Other Religions

I believe that at every level of society
—familial, tribal, national and international—
the key to a happier and more successful world is the growth of compassion.
We do not need to become religious, nor do we need to believe in an ideology.
All that is necessary is for each of us to develop our good human qualities.

Tenzin Gyatso, the fourteenth Dalai Lama

An extremely common question heard by many Shaolin instructors comes from students with a religious affiliation: "Can a [particular religious faith] be a [particular religious faith] and a Shaolin Buddhist, too?"

We came to America because its guarantee of religious freedom made it a likely place for our sect to survive and be resurrected. There is no *legal* prohibition against becoming, say, a Presbyterian Buddhist. It may be against the original religion's rules to belong to—or believe in—anything except the original faith. But Shaolin is not a faith as most religions are normally conceived. Many in the Order share the sentiment of author Robert Heinlein: "One man's religion is another man's belly laugh."

Buddhism's ability to peacefully coexist (often within the same individual) with another religion is not well understood in the West. Westerners often wonder how the Catholic Church has been so successful in converting so many Southeast Asians. In fact, part of the success of missionaries is that many of the converts are simply adding Christianity to their store of beliefs. Many, but not all, of the "converted" remain just as Buddhist as before. Shaolin, like many Buddhist sects, is especially tolerant of, and compatible with, other religious paths. A Shaolin's philosophical commitments reside in the four noble truths and the eightfold path. A Shaolin's practical commitments reside in much the same place. This helps extinguish hypocrisy and promote harmonious coexistence with others.

If you wish to add Shaolin Ch'an to your belief system, do not look to us for permission. The choice is entirely yours. But don't fool yourself about what it means to be Shaolin: put aside the notions you have gotten from movies, television, and most magazine articles. Shaolin monks are not "warrior monks" or knights on a grand mission. We neither seek nor encourage adventurism or proselytism. We do not promote missionary works or any action aimed at converting people to our way of thinking. Shaolin monks avoid fights at almost any cost. Our way is about peace, our tool is meditation, and our goal is self-perfection. In merging Shaolin spiritual practices with a religious faith, the question usually comes down to: will the faith allow Shaolin beliefs? Be clear, however, that Shaolin is not a "feel good," anything-goes, psuedo-spiritual martial arts school. Shaolin is a school of Ch'an Buddhism.

Chapter Four

Lessons in Shaolin Philosophy

Shaolin's Taoism

The Tao that can be named is not the true Tao.

Lao Tzu

Shaolin originated in a China under the strong influence of three major religious and philosophical schools. The Buddhist influence predominated, as we have already seen, and would itself be remolded into a new and definitely non-deistic form. The influence of Tamo and his followers would produce a very distinct version of Buddhism.

At the same time, the philosophy of Confucius had become the dominating force for social order throughout China. It was an understandable attraction for the imperial family, for Confucius had prescribed a social order based on strict obedience to elders and those in power. There was little room for recognition of merit and all social advancement meant passing rigorous—if typically pointless—examinations. Some scholars have remarked that China's Buddhist establishments were ardently Confucian as evidenced by the formal social structure (featuring students, disciples, and masters) in each monastery. In fact, Shaolin Buddhism avoids "squeamish rituals upholding Confucian virtues"[68] as most other schools of Ch'an do, and is strongly founded on promotion and recognition based on merit. With each step taken being firmly based on skills and earned honor, Shaolin tenets have always been quite distinct from the premises of Confucius.

One telling illustration of this is the notion of the gung fu family.[69] In most civilian traditions, a student would address someone in his teacher's generation who had been studying longer than his teacher as "Sibok" (roughly: elder uncle). The same student would always address his teacher as "*Sifu*," even if that teacher became quite advanced in skill. In Shaolin, time-in-rank is of lesser importance. Individuals are not recognized due to Confucian hierarchical position so much as they are recognized based on merit. In the Shaolin Order, titles are based upon degreed rank only. A student addresses a disciple of (sometimes 2nd and) 3rd rank as "Sifu" and a disciple of 4th (and sometimes 5th) rank as "Sibok." This is so even if that sifu or sibok began studying *after* the student in question. K'ung Fu-tzu's (Confucius's) ideas *did* impact Shaolin culture in some ways, but not nearly to the degree that Taoism did.

Aside from Buddhism, Taoism had the most influence upon Shaolin thought and art. Conceived in China within a few years of the Buddha's teaching in India, Taoism was supposedly the brainchild of a court accountant and philosopher, Lao Tzu. At the end of his distinguished career, Lao Tzu was persuaded to write down the principles of his life and the way he saw the world. The resulting work became the *Tao Te Ching*, which is perhaps the single most widely read book ever published. Like Buddhism, Taoism began as an agnostic philosophy that taught the manner in which to live a proper life. The Tao itself represented an ethereal concept of a universe in balance or harmony, in which the constituents were polar opposites. In other words, Tao includes all that there is, in all possible or parallel universes, in terms of Realism, Existentialism, Idealism, or a host of other "isms." The opposites were obvious everywhere Lao Tzu looked: hot and cold, male and female, light and dark, good and evil, hard and soft. To one aspect of the duality he assigned the name "yin," and to the other "yang." Only when there was one, he claimed, *could* there be the other. In fact, he claimed, the creation of one *required* the existence of its opposite. For Lao Tzu, we know light only by comparison with dark. Herein lies the source of one of the great misconceptions about Taoism: dark (or any yin aspect) absolutely cannot exist without at least some light (yang aspect). By "Tao," Lao Tzu meant a continuum in dynamic flux (not unlike the views of the pre-Socratic philosopher Heraclitus), with even the major aspect of one containing a small portion of the other. In the famous yin/yang or double fish symbol we still see the tiny "fish eyes" of yang/yin.

By the time the Shaolin Order was well underway, the teachings of Lao Tzu were widely known and adopted by the monks. Taoist principles of balancing harmony and the guidelines for leading a life of intellect and humble aspect meshed well with Tamo's brand of Buddhism. Shaolin taught a modified version, in which three, not two, aspects had to be kept in balance: body, mind, and spirit. The Taoist teachings on quiet leadership, instead of by coercion or blind obedience, were also heavily promoted within the Shaolin Order. Additionally, Taoist emphasis on nature, as opposed to the Confucian emphasis on a humanist philosophy, played a strong role in the Shaolin Temple. The long-term influence of Taoism would become particularly pronounced in the development of the Order's martial arts, especially with regard to breathing and the psychology of combat.

One of Shaolin's favorite Taoist teachings is a chapter of the *Tao Te Ching* about leadership. According to Lao Tzu, when a task is to be undertaken, a good leader motivates and guides people who, when finished, say "*we* did it." The true spiritual leader need not take or receive credit for a job well done, but leave "glory" for the workers. The leader's reward is in the success of leading, and the freedom that detachment from the work or its glory could engender.

Tamo himself introduced a Taoist approach to the monastic life by insisting that meditation be balanced by vigorous physical activity. The balancing of yin/yang also merged into specific martial practice. For example, a technique is to be executed with considerable subtle energy yet delivered via a very physical punch or kick. It was never appropriate to "merely" use brute strength to achieve a goal, but required the proper application of ch'i energy. Shaolin practitioners were expected to become like the Tao—looked for, it cannot be seen; listened for, it cannot be heard; felt for, it cannot be touched.

Though Lao Tzu rarely used the term "compassion" in the *Tao Te Ching*, he did write about combat in a very emotional way. In chapter 31 he refers to weapons as cursed things, and teaches "even when victorious, a good soldier does not rejoice, because rejoicing over a victorious battle is the same as rejoicing over the killing of men." To a Taoist, then, even a victory is "as a funeral ceremony," and combat is to be avoided whenever possible. This can best be done, we are told, by learning how to live well and properly. In a person who is at one with the Tao (in a state of emptiness and bliss similar, if not identical, to enlightenment), "a tiger has no place for its claws to attack, and a weapon no place to place its point. Why is this so? Because in such a person, there is no room for death to dwell."

Lao Tzu was not writing about a magical formula for immortality or invincibility, though later students would read such meanings into the *Tao Te Ching*. Instead, the sage was trying to shift the focus from how a person lived to how a person should engage living. The difference is not subtle: when Lao Tzu considers how a person lives, he refers to the following of rules, conduct, and etiquette—the mental "software"—that we are taught to obey and emulate. To this person, "rightness" is about following the software, doing what is expected, and becoming a conformist (and certainly within the parameters taught by the Confucian school). To a Taoist, this life would be pointless if not actually destructive, because it limits the person's ability to recognize herself in relation to the wider world. We would become less human and capable of "human-ness" and instead become little more than large social "insects," disconnected from the rest of nature. To be aware of life, though, and to actively engage in living by making frequent value judgments puts us firmly in charge of our greater destinies. Lao Tzu tells us that responsibility is indeed a heavy load, but one which no "greater" person—the thinking human trying to achieve peace and harmony—can possibly avoid. Many of Lao Tzu's exhortations (to become more attuned to the natural world, to practice thoughtful inaction [wu-wei] instead of thoughtless action, and so on) are aimed directly at Confucian principles.[70] So far as Shaolin is concerned, not much of Confucianism survives a Taoist critique.

Unlike the Buddha, Lao Tzu gives us no firm eightfold path to follow and the map he does provide is devoid of many specific place names and marked routes. Lao Tzu also differs from the Buddha in leaving much of his legacy to the "upper classes," those who will be leaders. Taoism was not formulated as an egalitarian doctrine, as noted by many passages urging the reader to follow certain principles of leadership, including leaving the populace ignorant. In chapter 3, the sage advises the ruler that in order to prevent theft "he should not value precious things himself. Thus the administration of the perfect sage is designed to remove the desires of his people. He supplies them only with suitable nourishment and lessens their individual ideas by strengthening the common physical health. He ever tries to keep his people in ignorance and desirelessness…" Such aristocratic language was easily transformed into a secondary Taoism, one with very distinct political and supernatural tones. Historically, many rulers have heeded this advice, but failed miserably to couple this yang element with its yin counterpart: "So long as [the ruler] governs his people by the principle of wu-wei (non-assertion, or non-compulsion), things naturally arrange themselves into social order."

In later years Taoism, like Buddhism, would acquire a peculiar theistic aspect. In Taoist theology, a major practice became "metaphysical" alchemy in which followers of the "new" Tao contrived to create an elixir of immortality (similar to European alchemists and their quest for the Philosopher's Stone).[71] Ardent Taoists engage in many practices in their quest for immortality, such as avoidance of solid food and holding of the breath,[72] which are no part of Shaolin. It is an irony indeed that a philosophy that was based above all on "going with the flow" of nature and the universe would produce a sect that tried so hard to "swim upstream." From this alchemical schism came another shift towards the dark side of human nature. Taoist magicians became robbers and murderers, and many were involved in overthrowing the government. Though these branches were never a part of Shaolin, they had profound influences on various non-Shaolin martial arts.

Within the temples, however, certain of Lao Tzu's teachings took incredible precedence. Indeed, many of the legendary accounts of Shaolin—from Chinese novels to television's *Kung Fu*—have stressed the Taoist influence. The television version went so far as to present a decidedly Confucian (!) temple in which the masters spouted Taoist sayings almost exclusively. The reality is that Taoism's sense of humility and naturalness was a fine marriage to Buddhism's search for clarity of vision.

Lead others by example, and when the work is done let the people say "we ourselves have done this." As was noted earlier, the leader in harmony with the Tao does not need special credit. This is Lao Tzu's message in chapter 17. To a Shaolin Buddhist, for whom results are important and seeking credit is seen as ego feeding, the words of Lao Tzu strike a familiar resonance. So too does the lesson "the Tao that can be named is not the true Tao." Buddhists do not accept that any answer is ever all-encompassing or of an ultimately definitive nature. After all, as Buddha taught, "truth is different for every sentient being." Even in the application of a martial technique the Shaolin adept is guided by Taoism: "Be in harmony with that around you; do not seek or strive, but become one with the whole."

The pinnacle of Shaolin's relationship with Taoism was reached at Wutang Shan Temple. For reasons lost to us, Wutang Shan residents were more worldly than their predominantly Buddhist counterparts. Perhaps it was Lao Tzu's influence, in that his writings spoke at length about how one should interact with the world. In any case, the monks at Wutang did two things that would effectively separate them from the rest of Shaolin: they would train specifically to become warriors, and they would develop the three traditional internal gung fu styles known as Pa Kua, Hsing-I, and, most famous, T'ai Chi Ch'uan. (Chow and Spangler have presented very accurate analyses of these styles with respect to Taoist philosophy.[73]) Wutang monks and their students were a major force behind the Boxer Rebellion and the subsequent termination of the imperial Chinese government. More recently, their kind were featured in the highly stylized and fanciful film *Crouching Tiger, Hidden Dragon*.

Unlike the majority of Shaolin schools, the Wutang school was very active in promoting and teaching its arts. By virtue of the focus on their internal aspects, the Wutang gung fu arts were widely dispersed and found their way into mainstream Chinese culture in a way that most other arts did not. Though Pa Kua and Hsing-I are readily available to students in many locations around the world, it was T'ai Chi Ch'uan that became truly famous. Parks in China and Chinese communities around the world are filled with T'ai Chi Ch'uan practitioners each morning. The slow, graceful, and gently stretching movements make the style practical for even the very elderly, and the ch'i circulation benefits have been credited with extending both the duration and quality of senior life. So many practice this art as gentle exercise that many practitioners are unaware that it is martial in nature. We have met several instructors who have expressed surprise, and even denial, that their New Age health program was in fact an efficient mechanism for self-defense.

In summing up the Taoist influence on Shaolin, we can link the teachings strongly with the Temple's governance, for in Lao Tzu's suggestions for ethical leadership are many ideas that have held the Order together through very tough times. The specific influences also provided the philosophical basis for the great rift between the mainstream Shaolin and the Wutang schools. When the *Tao Te Ching* was written over 2,400 years ago, the author left us with words and perceptions that are startlingly appropriate even today. In Chapter 57 Lao Tzu warns us:

The more laws and restrictions there are, the poorer people become.
The sharper men's weapons, the more trouble in the land.
The more ingenious and clever men are, the more strange things happen.
The more rules and regulations, the more thieves and robbers.

In the main temples of the Order, Lao Tzu's warnings were taken seriously, and governmental structure and rigid rules were kept to a minimum. At Wutang, however, the blend of Confucian and Taoist ideals led to a situation that widely diverged from the Buddhist-heavy foundations of Shaolin.

The Parable of the Empty Cup

There is *only* the tea.

In chapter 11 of the *Tao Te Ching*, Lao Tzu says that when we make a cup from a lump of clay, it is the empty space within that cup that makes it useful. This parable, which almost certainly predates Lao Tzu's Taoism, has been modified and expanded to the point where it has become one of the best-known Chinese (and Japanese[74]) folk stories in the West. Not surprisingly, it has also been largely misunderstood.

"The usefulness of the cup lies in its emptiness," goes the simplest version.[75] Some recent authors, mainly tournament martial artists, have dismissed the saying by claiming that the cup is useful when it is full, not empty. Here is where we must philosophically and semantically examine the two positions in order to get a decent bearing.

First, a cup is useful *because* it is empty. The fact that it is empty means there is a place within which something else, other than the cup, can be contained. One does not seek an already filled cup when one wants to pour tea from a teapot, but instead chooses an empty cup. By the same token, holding tea is the reason we have a cup at all, and we cannot drink anything from an empty cup. Therefore, we must distinguish the cup being useful *because* it is empty from the cup being useful *when* it is full. This metaphor is about cause and effect or, more appropriately, between yin and yang concepts.

In later versions, this story is embellished with a young martial artist seeking to study with a sage. As the sage explains facets of his training and philosophy, the student frequently interrupts with "Oh, yes, I know that." At one point, the sage is pouring the student tea, and keeps pouring until the cup generously overflows. The student jumps up before the tea scalds him, and demands to know "How can such a great master spill tea like that?" The sage stops pouring and replies, "If you wish to sample *my* tea, you must first empty *your* cup."

The cup's usefulness as an empty vessel is a repeatable experience, implying that we may reform ourselves into blank canvasses many times in our lives, and in so doing we may gain clarity, insight, or new knowledge. The greatest tea cannot be tasted from an already filled cup, so it becomes incumbent upon the student to provide the blank canvass.

The circularity of this journey, from total emptiness to accumulation of knowledge, with returns to at least some degree of emptiness, is reflected in the colored belt ranking system of the Okinawan and Japanese martial arts, in which beginners wear a white belt. At the highest degrees (11th and 12th dans), the black belt is exchanged for a double wide white belt. However, because the return to such a sublime and pure state of blankness is seen as beyond the capabilities of a mortal, these ranks—actually codified in Judo and some Karate systems—have never been awarded. Chado, also known as the "Way of Tea," is a method of Japanese Zen training which brings many arts together in an effort to still the mind's striving for dualism.[76] Given the fascination for tea shown in Japanese culture, it is not surprising that the tea parable has been partially incorporated into the ranking system.

The Teachings of Tamo

Mind is the path.

Tamo

As Shaolin priests we have mixed feelings about the way our tradition has been portrayed in magazines and on television. Perhaps most glaringly absent has been a focus on the heart of Shaolin, the philosophy of this unique sect of secular Buddhism. Though Shaolin has become famous for the gung fu styles and abilities of its monks, the foundation and spirit of the Order are actually much more centered in the Buddhist teachings of Dharma Master Bodhidharma. Bodhidharma/Tamo is the Indian monk credited with bringing Ch'an into China and revitalizing Buddhist practices. To begin, we shall examine how Tamo perceived Buddhism and then explore his contribution to Shaolin, including written teachings that have survived.

In Tamo's life and teachings there are numerous suggestions that the "trappings" of being Buddhist were inconsequential. Tamo ate meat, wore robes of his choosing, and did not shave his head or beard. He practiced his own individuality instead of adopting a "uniform" and "expected" appearance. "Listen to the *message*," he was proclaiming, "and ignore the messenger." His was a radical approach in a time of nearly omnipotent emperors and kings, when Confucian teachings, with their great emphasis on class and obedience, were widely accepted in China. It is no wonder that the Theravadin head monk at the newly constructed Shaolin Temple kept the Indian monk outside for so many years. In eventually accepting Tamo the head monk was also rejecting the class and societal order of imperial China. This was no simple decision.

When the fang chang (abbot) of the Temple relinquished spiritual authority to Tamo, it ushered in a very new phase of Buddhist philosophy. Tamo did not invent Ch'an—the practice of using meditation to achieve enlightenment—but he did extend its applications considerably. Tamo believed that the meditating mind should be supreme in a highly developed individual, that a person in harmony is a person always in a meditative state. To Tamo, all action was meditation, be it washing dishes, doing laundry, reading, or sitting in thoughtful contemplation. In a parallel concept to the Greek "sound mind, sound body," Tamo insisted that monks practice physical arts as part of their meditative training. This physical activity would make the body stronger, and thus allow the mind to grow stronger (i.e., it takes a strong mind to control a strong body with advanced reflexes and coordination).

We must remember that Tamo came from central eastern coastal India (or Iran), and that he walked (for at least a substantial distance, if not the whole way) on his trek through Tibet and into China. Along the way he encountered numerous physical hardships, attack by animals or people, and a wide variety of climates. His teaching of physical skills was no idle attempt to change a curriculum; it was born of practical experience of how hostile the world is to a human body. It should therefore not come as any surprise that Tamo's central physical teachings would evolve into the Shaolin martial arts.

Tamo did not invent gung fu; his martial training was a combination of classical Indian styles mixed with things he learned in his travels. His goal was to teach motion and dexterity that would promote the flow of prana (ch'i) through the body. Unimpeded ch'i flow was crucial to attaining full enlightenment. In time, Shaolin efforts would focus first on training the body to be strong, second to develop and master ch'i, and finally to attain enlightenment via a combination of moving and still meditations. It would be more than a century after the passing of Tamo before the Temple's physical training centered on the new martial arts its practitioners would develop.

To almost anyone familiar with Buddhism—including nearly all practicing Buddhists—the practice of martial arts by this one sect must seem contradictory to the Buddhist doctrine of non-violence. To actually *use* these skills must seem a major violation.[77] To a Shaolin practitioner, however, there is no conflict. A Shaolin does not enter combat—a competitive activity—in any circumstance. Contrary to movies and legends, he does not prepare for a fight or look for trouble. But when an opponent appears and initiates violence, the Shaolin merges with the activity so he may reflect it like light from a mirror. His action is a refusal to accept violence, to return it from whence it came. Even in his mind there is no conflict; does a shadow contemplate the actions of the person who casts it? If an opponent dies in combat with a Shaolin, it is perceived as, in essence, a suicide, for he has only received back the energies he cast at someone else. Historians and martial scholars manufacture all manner of hypotheses to "explain" or "justify" Shaolin martial practice, but the truth of the matter is simple, and (we hope) made clear here.

Look at this important issue another way. Anything given to us unsolicited is a gift. We often receive unwanted gifts, hence those long lines at department stores after Christmas. To a Buddhist, even an action is seen as a gift. Thus, if someone takes us to a theater, we may welcome the gift. If the same person throws a fist at our face, we may decline that gift. The monk who values life is free to refuse any gift, including the "gift" of violence. Thus, there is no conflict with Buddhist teachings in using a self-defense action to refuse violent aggression. While we must acknowledge that there is pain in life, we are not obliged to accept all the pain that life has to offer! In fact, the point of following a Buddhist path is to develop a life with a minimum of pain and suffering.

This point is central to the sect called Shaolin. No person has the right or authority to harm any other through an act of aggression. There are no exceptions. In using our martial arts, we are returning incoming aggression back at the attacker, *not initiating violence ourselves*. The practitioner may **not** do *whatever it takes* to avoid injury. For example, doing "whatever it takes" might include blowing up a building to kill one person who offers a real threat to one's safety. This would not be acceptable. Shaolin does not condone hurting the innocent or non-aggressive. Shaolin allows the use of combat to neutralize a person who would do us harm, just as we condone the use of medicine to kill a disease. Though we acknowledge that there is evil in our world, we are not knights or police to fight such forces. Following Tamo's individual-focused practices, we believe that we can only truly fight evil by keeping it out of our selves, and in so doing inspire others to follow suit. Once we initiate an action to change someone else's behavior, we have crossed the line that takes us off the path towards enlightenment. The ultimate path to nirvana does not involve such control of other people. Ultimate knowledge comes from control of one's self.

Tamo left few direct writings of his interpretation of the Dharma (or principles) of Buddhism, but through written and oral history, Shaolin has maintained his legacy. Much of that legacy rests in our particular mode of operation and tradition (for instance, our combination of Buddhism and martial training, as just discussed), but there are a few historical records of Tamo's teaching. Tamo became somewhat renowned in later Buddhist histories for spreading the teachings of the *Lankavatara Sutra*, yet a discussion of that work is beyond the scope of this one. We shall present here a lesson in the Shaolin interpretation of its own spiritual roots and principles, based upon Ch'an writings on Tamo's teachings.

Two translations of Tamo's major teachings have been published, *The Zen Teaching of Bodhidharma*,[78] and *The Bodhidharma Anthology*.[79] The translator of the former work, Red Pine, wonders why these basic teachings have not been more widely circulated. We pose the same question, and suggest the following possible reasons:

First, Tamo's message is simple: The mind is the Buddha. Tamo prescribes meditation and an elegant interpretation of Buddhist practice, focusing upon the bodhisattva ideal, as the core reality to seekers of enlightenment. These are simple enough concepts, but Tamo places the entirety of becoming (or rather *recognizing* the state of being) enlightened on the individual. In a sweeping gesture he urges self-motivation, self-awareness, and self-recognition at the expense of hierarchical "orders" of monks and token ceremonies. Cut the extraneous, he goads, ignore illusions, and go for the core that is already there. Certainly such a philosophy is anathema to practices that perpetuate the illusion that someone else can enlighten you.

Second, Tamo left the disciple considerable latitude in how to live, as did Shakyamuni Buddha himself. He did not require monks to be celibate, fast, or perform rites of asceticism, nor was the "priesthood" restricted to males. Quite the contrary, he embraced the human condition as the starting point from which all "higher" revelations would spring. Shaolin remains nearly unique (especially among Chinese Ch'an schools) in allowing its members this degree of freedom (and thus being more like Methodist ministers than Catholic priests). In Tamo's message of simplicity, he limits the more embellished aspects of sectarian religious practice and organization—which is why Ch'an does not characteristically include elaborate rituals, bureaucratic hierarchies, and opulent temples.

Finally, much of Tamo's influence was largely circumvented by the plethora of Buddhist scriptures, scholars, and sects. As with most original thinkers, there is more commentary written *about* him than *by* him. The *Two Entrances* (the *Erh-ju ssu-hsing lun*, or *Treatise on the Two Ways of Entrance and Four Practices*) was recorded by **T'an-lin** (or "Armless Lin," as he was known), a student of **Hui-k'o**, the 29th patriarch. T'an-lin may have actually studied with Tamo himself, the historical record is uncertain. What is certain is that T'an-lin was a Sanskritist not held in high esteem by most Ch'an masters of his day.[80] He was considered "too scholarly," due to his extensive work on the *Shrimala Sutra* and work translating Sanskrit scriptures into Chinese. But the fact that we have access to Tamo's teachings today is partly to the credit of this scholarly monk. Here is an annotated review of Tamo's teachings as embraced by both Buddhist commentators and the Shaolin Order during its 1500-year history. Tamo's message (a concise version of the *Two Entrances* based upon the mentioned translations by Red Pine and Jeffrey Broughton) is **bolded** and our interpretive notes are in standard text.

Two Entrances

Many roads provide an entry to the way, but these reduce to two types: recognition and practice. By recognition is meant that the teachings reveal the truth that all living things are identical to True Nature, a nature concealed by the veils of illusion.

By "many roads," Tamo points out that enlightenment is reached by different minds in different ways; these may include the various seated and moving meditations. Such means are termed yogas, gung fu, and sudden self-realization. However, all of the possible routes reduce to either recognition, an awakening (based on the teachings) to the single nature that Ultimate Reality shares with all beings; or practice, meaning the four practices (discussed below). Recognition of the fact that all of life is connected spiritually is essential to waking up (becoming enlightened).

For one who shuns illusion for reality and meditates on walls, then self and other become identical, as do common man and sage. If without shifting you abide in firmness, after that you will not follow the written teachings—this is how to recognize Reality. It is nondiscriminative, quiescent, and inactive; it is entrance by recognition.

Reality and what appears as reality are difficult to separate, especially if one looks to outside sources (which may themselves be illusions). Wall-meditation is the inward focus of the mind on itself, extinguishing the illusion of duality, and is generally performed in peaceful surroundings. The Tibetan tantric schools of Mahayoga and Atiyoga interpreted wall-meditation, not as sitting cross-legged facing a wall, but as "an analogue of tantric teachings on all-at-once perfection."[81] Shaolin, through its close association with Tibetan sects, may have been influenced by this interpretation, as our Order does not place any emphasis on literally staring at walls but *does* place emphasis on something like the "great perfection" of Tantrayana. Such a meditating mind must cut through illusion and realize that duality is also an illusion, as is the ego specifically. We are mortal and sage; we are self and all else. Once this Ultimate Reality is *seen*, written teachings such as the sutras drop away from us, much as a child discards his bicycle's training wheels as soon as he develops confidence.

By practice is meant the participation and acceptance of the four all-inclusive practices: requiting injury, adapting, non-seeking, and practicing the Dharma. First comes requiting injury. When followers of the way suffer, they should recall that in the countless previous incarnations they have been deterred from the path, sometimes becoming trivial and angry even without cause. The suffering in this life is a punishment, but also an opportunity to exercise what you have learned from past lives. Men and gods are equally unable to see when a seed may bear fruit. Accept this suffering as a challenge and with an open heart. In recognizing suffering for what it is, you begin to follow the way.

This is a lesson in karma: that we are ultimately responsible for our actions (karma is also known as the universal law of cause and effect). If we can learn from a punishment and attain true rehabilitation, we rejoin the path and move ahead. Because the first noble truth recognizes that "there is suffering in life," an adept is expected to know suffering as both a condition of being alive and as a disease that can be treated. Tamo's words enjoin us to contextualize adversity in our lives through an understanding of karma. When we act upon an intention motivated from hate, delusion, or craving, or even possess such intent without acting upon it, we accumulate karma. We "sow the seeds," so to speak. Later, perhaps even during a reincarnation, that karmic "seed" may bear "fruit." The message is simple: the effects of our intentions will always follow us, whether we can make the connection or not. By accepting suffering with an open heart and no ill will, we begin to take responsibility for our actions at the highest spiritual level. Consider a child who hits a ball through a window, chooses to approach the appropriate house, knocks on the door, and apologizes for her carelessness. In requiting all injuries, we accept this kind of responsibility, but on a higher level. We are not always capable of rationally understanding or seeing the link between "hitting the ball" and the angry neighbor. Indeed, we likely won't even remember hitting the ball. We will simply and suddenly face a ranting neighbor. Tamo's words do not merely constitute a lecture, however, but also suggest right action. In your day to day life, when you are faced with a "ranting neighbor" whose motivation is unclear to you, do not let excitation get the better of you. Exercise compassion and understanding.

Second, adapt to your conditions. Sentient beings have no self, and are whirled all around by conditions. All we experience depends upon surroundings. If we reap a reward or great boon, it is the fruit of a seed we planted long ago. Eventually, it will end. Do not delight in these boons, for what is the point? In a mind unmoved by reward and setback, the journey on the path continues.

In essence, Tamo says that we shall all have good days and bad days, the "goodness" and "badness" depending on circumstances or viewpoint. Accept what comes, knowing that both good and bad will pass, and stay focused on the important points of the Dharma. Be adaptable. Just as you requite injury with equanimity, accept honors and rewards with equanimity.

Third, do not seek. Worldlings delude themselves. They seek to possess things, always searching for something. But insightful people wake up and choose Reality over habit. They focus on quieting the mind and inactivity; and accept that their bodies, and all things, change through the seasons. The world offers only emptiness, with nothing worth desiring. Disaster and Prosperity constantly trade places. To live in the three realms is to stay in a house on fire. To have a body is to experience suffering. Who can attain peace? Those who see past illusion are detached, and stop both thoughts and seeking. The sutras teach that to seek is to suffer, to seek nothing is to have bliss. In seeking nothing, you follow the path.

Buddhism is notorious for its non-attachment. There is an apparent logical discordance in Buddhist practice: the seeking to not-seek. For now, consider Tamo's core point as follows: seeking and trying to avoid seeking are both desires/intentions (and hence causes of suffering). By neither seeking nor not-seeking, one reaches a state of "mindless bliss," or the "one-point." Suffering is the disease that binds us to rebirth, and attachment—especially for life—is the tether that keeps us suffering. We all experience ups and downs, and these are transitory. To attach to any feeling is to drop an anchor in the fleeting moment that quickly becomes the past. Accept what comes, even enjoy (or loathe) it, then *let it go*. This is how to seek not. Reflect on Tamo's words: "The world offers only emptiness, and nothing worth desiring."

Elsewhere, Tamo has more to say on this state of "mindless bliss", or no-mind (also known as "wu-hsin"). In the Tun-huang manuscripts, which contain the *Two Entrances*, the following exchange is recorded:

Again, the monk asked, "If the attached mind creates karma, how can one cut it off?"

Bodhidharma replied: "Because of wu-hsin, there is no necessity to cut off [karma]. This mind does not arise and is not destroyed; the reason is that erroneous thinking produces dharmas."[82]

So volition creates karma—in fact, *any* intentional activity produces karma, even actions taken to try to eliminate karma! The solution to this mess is found in attaining the state of wu-hsin: "a state in which there are no *ego-centered* thought-constructions or conceptual overlays to inhibit a spontaneous and total response to life situations."[83] The importance of wu-hsin to all Buddhists, but especially to Shaolin Buddhists, cannot be underestimated. A mind that has extinguished the ego generates no karma; such a mind has fully awakened to its own buddha-nature. For Shaolin, combat acts as an *expedient device* to teach the student wu-hsin, as does forms training. Lee, describing wu-hsin as the "non-graspiness" of mind, also emphasizes its importance in combat, especially against multiple opponents.[84] Meditative martial arts practice pacifies the grasping nature of the unsettled mind. And at a certain stage, improving martial skills absolutely requires no-mindedness. The Shaolin focus upon combat is seen to aid the disciple in awakening, or relinquishing attachments. In order to cultivate no-mind from a more philosophical foundation, Nagarjuna and other Prajnaparamita philosophers employed the idea of emptiness, or shunyata.[85] Hence, another way to look at Shaolin gung fu is as emptiness in motion. To engage in this emptiness in motion, working towards attaining a state of no-mind, is truly to travel a Shaolin path.

Fourth, practice the Dharma, the Reality of intrinsic purity. All illusion is dropped. Duality does not exist. Subject and object do not exist. The sutra says the Dharma is free of the impurities of sentient beings and self, hence there are no sentient beings in Dharma, and there is no self in Dharma. Those who understand this truth wisely follow the path. They know that True Reality contains nothing worth begrudging, and so freely give of their bodies, minds, and spirits. They share material and immaterial things in charity, with gladness, with no vanity or thought of giver or taker of the gift. In this way they teach others without becoming attached to characteristics. This allows them to progress on the path, but also to help others see and enjoy the path to enlightenment. When they are truly charitable, the other five virtues follow; and in practicing the six virtues to eliminate delusion, they practice nothing at all. This is what it means to practice the Dharma.

This passage contains several important concepts, and it would have been nice of Tamo (or Armless Lin) to elaborate more fully. Buddhism appears in conflict with many other philosophy-heavy religions in denying duality. For example, many schools teach the dual nature of reality as positive/negative, hot/cold, male/female, and so on. Buddhism teaches that duality is an illusion. Of course, reality may manifest positive/negative/neutral, hot/warm/cool/cold, or male/female/sexless (as in many microorganisms). Consider the cliché "fight or flight." The implication is duality, either run or attack. A third possibility is also readily apparent: freeze and do nothing. Many misconstrue even the sacred Taoist concept of "duality," missing the point: there are not merely yin and yang, but also both together (Tao) *and* the possibility of neither. Yin and yang are best thought of as a "oneness;" those caught up in the idea of yin being opposite of, and separate from, yang miss the point.[86]

But not all possibilities are even dual or triple in nature, so Buddhism seeks to free us from seeing the world through the blinders of a philosophical model. Creating a philosophical "system" is a real threat to Buddhist practice.[87] This is a narrow case of the more general phenomenon of conditionalizing the Buddha's teachings. The true mind, according to the Buddha, is not the discriminating mind. When Ananda attempts to apply his discriminating mind to understand Shakyamuni's message in the *Surangama Sutra*, the Buddha employs a metaphor to illustrate Ananda's mistake:

It is like a man calling the attention of another man to the moon by pointing his finger toward it. The other man ought to look at the moon, but instead he looks at the finger and by so doing, not only misses the moon but misses the finger, also. And why? Because he has taken the finger to be the moon. Not only that, he has failed to notice the difference between darkness and brightness. And why? Because he takes the dark finger to be the moon's brightness. That is why he does not know the difference between darkness and brightness. Ananda, you are just as foolish as that man.[88]

The Buddha's final admonition to his cousin is a loving one; he wants Ananda to be sure to understand the problem. This problem of "missing the point" is also touched upon by Bruce Lee in the 1973 film *Enter the Dragon* where Lee employs the same metaphor, which serves to illustrate the emphasis he placed upon the Buddhist heritage of the arts.

The practice of Dharma refers, in part, to following Buddhism's eightfold path to enlightenment. This path is central to all sects of Buddhism, though there are varying interpretations of its meanings. The central elements are: right views, right resolve, right speech, right action, right livelihood, right effort, right attention, and right meditation.

The Dharma also includes a few other core Buddhist teachings, such as anatman (no self), shunyata (emptiness), and pratitya-samutpada (conditioned arising). For Mahayana Buddhists, anatman is characteristic of all existence. Applied at the individual level, this means that each of us does *not* have a permanent "self" or "personality" that is persisting and unchanging. No thing does, and so anatman gives rise to shunyata, or emptiness. All phenomena are empty. They are simply mental representations.

The Buddha's concept of emptiness implies that what exists *for us* simply is representation. That which is truly real (all that which has no-essence: anatman) contains nothing worth begrudging, at least in part because there is no one (no-self) around to begrudge. A rough understanding of concepts like anatman and shunyata should help shed light upon Tamo's posits about the Dharma being free of sentient beings and self. Reflect on Tamo's remark that practicing the Dharma is practicing "nothing at all."

The teachings include room for sharing (as a direct result of ideas like shunyata and anatman), mainly as a benefit to one's self in following the path, but also as a benefit to others by helping them find and appreciate the path. Actions taken to help such souls are seen as highly important to followers of the path. Indeed, those who become enlightened and later choose to undergo another rebirth into this world are seen as saints, foregoing nirvana to help others reach liberation. Such noble souls are bodhisattvas. Indeed, Tamo's comment about practicing the "six virtues" refers to the paramitas (Sanskrit for "that which has reached the other shore"), six virtues that are to be perfected by one striving to become a bodhisattva. The paramitas are charity, selfless kindness, humility and patience, perseverance, tranquility, and wisdom—these paramitas are elaborated upon in the *Lankavatara Sutra* and the *Diamond Sutra*. (Chögyam Trungpa's *Meditation in Action* explains the paramitas with great clarity and insight.[89]) The idea, analogous to the practice of the eightfold path, is that these six virtues are organically interrelated. A perfect practice of charity will be automatically followed by a perfect practice of the other five virtues.

Will the Real Tamo Please Step Forward

Jeffrey Broughton argues persuasively that T'an-lin modeled the *Two Entrances* upon the *Shrimala Sutra* with which he was so familiar.[90] The structure of both texts is the same, as is the vocabulary. The recognition and practice polarity, Broughton argues, was simply T'an-lin's way of making sense of Tamo's message—which was not especially susceptible to analytic treatment. Further evidence suggests that the *Two Entrances* is an excellent and concise primer on Mahayana Buddhism, but that it does not capture much of Tamo's new way of teaching. Broughton points out that the four practices discussed in the text are simply a pithy summary of the Mahayana creed, capturing essential concepts like shunyata, non-attachment, and the bodhisattva ideal. And sayings more reliably attributed to Tamo diverge a great deal from the nature of the *Two Entrances*.

Ch'an scholar Ch'i-sung (1007-72) corroborates this conclusion.

Ch'i-sung remarked that T'an-lin was not considered capable of grasping Tamo's deeper teachings, and so Tamo employed an expedient device with respect to teaching T'an-lin. What this means is that Tamo, much like Shakyamuni Buddha, used ideas and concepts that would be useful to his specific audience. The Buddha did not lay the four noble truths on everyone he met. They were reserved for those who (1) had open minds and (2) the Buddha felt were capable of grasping his teachings.[91] Shakyamuni was a true master of employing expedient devices for sharing his message. Ch'i-sung's point was that Tamo taught T'an-lin at the latter's level of Ch'an understanding, but also that Armless Lin's grasp of the way was weak.[92]

If Broughton and Ch'i-sung are correct in thinking that the *Two Entrances* is more T'an-lin than Tamo (and we think they are), then the oral tradition of the Shaolin Order and assorted recorded sayings attributed to Tamo become crucial if we wish to form the most accurate and holistic view of his teachings. Tamo's influence on the traditions and perspectives of our Order is discussed earlier, so here we will briefly consider further teachings from the historical record.

Ch'an Master Kuei-feng Tsung-mi (780-841) wrote a compendium of Ch'an literature that is lost to us, but the introduction survived. He begins the introduction by saying: "At the beginning I will record Bodhidharma's one thesis."[93] Other such comments by ancient Ch'an scholars, in addition to remarks that Tamo's teaching was profound and mysterious, support the notion that the *Two Entrances* does not represent the heart of his message. A document entitled *Method for Quieting Mind* was in circulation ca. 800 that was attributed to Tamo and his circle of disciples. This work shows significant signs of being heavily influenced by Nagarjuna's *Middle Verses* and the *Vimalakirtinirdesha Sutra*. Both of these texts were important in the early Ch'an tradition. Nagarjuna's work emphasized shunyata; the *Vimalakirtinirdesha Sutra* stood out as placing equal value on lay and monastic life (as well as transmitting lessons about emptiness). The *Method for Quieting Mind*, called "Record I" in *The Bodhidharma Anthology*, contains many sayings either directly attributed to Tamo or to his students. Here are a few:

> When one does not understand, the person pursues dharmas; when one understands, dharmas pursue the person. When one understands, consciousness draws in forms; when one is deluded, forms draw in consciousness. The non-production of consciousness due to forms is called not seeing forms...

> If there were no who, then it would be unnecessary to cultivate the path.

> To awaken according to Dharma, to awaken to the fact that there is nothing to be awakened to, is called Buddha...

There is neither an awakener nor something to awaken to. If one awakens according to Dharma, when one truly awakens there is no self-awakening at all. Ultimately no awakening exists. The perfect awakening of all the Buddhas of the three times is but a conceptual discrimination of sentient beings...

People of sharp abilities know that mind is the path. People of dull abilities seek everywhere for the path but lack knowledge of its location. Moreover, they do not know that mind from the outset is unexcelled, perfect enlightenment...

Forms are not forms. They are constructed in the manner of an illusion by your own mind. If you merely realize that they are not real, then you will attain liberation.[94]

Notice the tremendous *dissimilarity* between these statements and everything appearing in the *Two Entrances*. Shaolin, like other Ch'an sects, follows the four practices. They are fundamental to the Buddhist ethos. But the above statements attributed to Tamo and his students more soundly mesh with Shaolin traditions. "The mind is the path...there is nothing to awaken to...[realizing that forms are not real] you will attain liberation." These sayings capture the Shaolin focus: "being here now," realizing that our original nature *is* buddha-nature, and seeing that duality is an illusion.

So how are we to reconcile the *Two Entrances* with these other teachings? There isn't really any difficulty here. The *Two Entrances* contains nothing antithetical to Shaolin, and it may actually represent the manner in which Tamo transmitted his message to T'an-lin. We consider it an excellent text expounding an accurate Buddhist message. But these other teachings probably had a more fundamental role in influencing early thought within the Shaolin Order. There is a strong argument for the contention that the *Method for Quieting Mind* is one of the oldest pieces of Ch'an literature available to us.[95] One piece of evidence, which we will defer examining in detail to another time, is how much the *Vimalakirtinirdesha Sutra* affected the thought of the Bodhidharma circle. This sutra, with its equal emphasis on lay Buddhist (versus monastic) practice, may *help* explain why the Shaolin Order differs so much from many other Ch'an schools. For now, reflect on Tamo's words, and seeking nothing, be a person of sharp abilities.

Ch'an is really the method of no-method.
There is no bridge provided, because there is no river. If you let go
of your attaching mind, at that very moment you are enlightened.

Ch'an Master Sheng-yen

The Nature of Truth

[The two truths are] like the simmering of heated air.
Deluded people see the air waving due to the heat and understand it as water,
but it is really not water. It is the simmering of heated air.

Tamo

Philosophers have debated on the meaning and nature of truth for millennia, and a uniformly accepted definition remains elusive. With respect to truth, let us consider the controversial topic of euthanasia: imagine that you are slowly dying on a hospital bed, and that your life is being artificially prolonged by machinery. What is the best thing for you to do? Shaolin, unlike some religions that maintain a single answer applies to all, holds that it will be different for different people, but for each person *their* truth of what is best is true. As a healthy individual, you may have an inkling of what you would do in such a situation, but you don't really know, as you aren't actually in that kind of situation. Let us assume that you *do* find yourself lying on that hospital bed. You will need to make your own investigation and assessment of your predicament. You may conclude that "pulling the plug" is the best course of action; it is the truth that this course is the right thing for *you* to do. The person next to you, though, may have a combination of beliefs and situation that lead him to decide that his life should be prolonged as long as science is capable of doing so.

This example is *not* an attempt to argue that all truth is relative in any sense that would allow you to justify any belief by making an ad hoc argument for the "truth" of that belief. The Buddhist conception of truth does not allow you to murder innocents because you feel it is the "truth" that doing so is the best thing for you to do! Nagarjuna emphasized a doctrine often referred to as the "twofold truth," where there are two different ways of looking at truth. (Please bear in mind that this teaching is an expedient device, and that these two truths are not exhaustive of all truths in the world.[64])

The Ultimate Truth for a Buddhist is that "everything is conditioned and relative" —it's a thesis about impermanence that can *only* be seen (not known through rational faculties, as mathematics or history are known), and this *seeing* leads to the cessation of suffering. A buddha, then, can say, "Everything is relative," and mean precisely that in a very literal sense. (From the perspective of Nagarjuna's Madhyamika philosophy, the Ultimate Truth is closer to a statement that all things are shunyata, or emptiness.)

But there are also the truths of the world, truths which are like convenient rules that allow us to function in the world. The laws of physics classify as this latter kind of truth. And certainly, the four noble truths are oft considered by Buddhists to be true in this way, just as the eightfold path is seen as a valid means of working towards enlightenment. But these claims can be tested! And that is precisely the point of the euthanasia example, that you must probe and test experience to discover worldly truth, and that such truth has perspectival elements. Buddha impressed upon his disciples not to accept a truth merely because it is in a book, or some great person uttered it, or because it is a tradition. Rather, test each "truth" for yourself and establish its validity. Buddhism is thus an Asian precursor to the West's scientific method, but also something more, because it applies to the spiritual as well as the scientific.

So there are two basic kinds of truth in Buddhism: Ultimate Truth that can only be seen, not rationally known; and worldly truth. An ancient sermon by Ch'an Master Pai-chang elegantly states the difference:

> The spiritual light shines alone, far beyond senses and objects; the essence reveals true eternity. It is not captured in words. The nature of mind is stainless, fundamentally complete and perfect in itself; just detach from false conditioning, and you merge with the Buddha of suchness as is.
>
> All verbal teachings are just remedies to cure illness. Because illnesses are not the same, therefore the remedies are not the same. That is why it is sometimes said that there is a Buddha, and sometimes it is said there is no Buddha. True words are those that cure illness; after the illness is cured, all of them are untrue statements. True words are false words insofar as they produce opinions; false words are true words insofar as they stop people's delusions. Because illness is unreal, there are only unreal remedies to cure them.[96]

Take a few moments to consider Pai-chang's meaning before reading onwards. The following story well illustrates Shaolin's simple and pragmatic notion of truth:

A young disciple named Mei Weng was considered to be the finest practitioner of light weapons and unarmed combat among her peers. Yet month after month went by and her master did not prepare her for advancement befitting her skill level. Finally her patience wore thin and she spoke to her *training master*, the famous nun Ng Fut-lei.

"I do not understand why others advance whose skills I exceed," the disciple began as the two sat near a small round pond in the meditation garden at Fukien Temple.

The master sat stolidly, and let the disciple gather her thoughts. Disciple Mei became uncomfortable by the silence, and at last continued.

"I have studied hard, Master," she went on carefully. "No student of my age can best me in combat. The texts of Buddha and Tamo I can recite as well as a master." She licked her lips, then went ahead. "Why, then, am I passed for advancement over others lacking my skills?"

The master continued to sit peacefully, her gaze fixed at some point in the distance. This time the disciple did not interrupt her teacher's thoughts. An hour passed, then another, and the sun began to sink behind the western hills. Afternoon turned into twilight, and the master began to speak.

"It is true, my disciple, that you are highly skilled in our physical and mental lessons. But your mind is too much like the paper of a scroll. You have recorded all we could teach you, yet that same teaching has closed you into a meditation cell." She paused and closed her eyes, apparently listening to something in the far distance.

"Do you hear that sound coming from beyond the swamp?" she asked Mei Weng. Mei listened, and heard the sound that resembled the plucking of a stringed instrument.

Mei nodded.

"What is that sound?" Master Ng inquired.

"It is said that the wood nymphs play the reeds as a maiden plays an instrument," the younger said.

"Do you doubt this explanation?" asked Ng.

Mei thought this over, and then answered. "Perhaps. I do not know. But how is this important?"

"The Buddha told us to always see with open eyes and allow our vision to pierce the veils of illusion," Master Ng explained. "A master must see with clarity. So far you have learned that which we know, but you have not learned how to see things new; you have not imagined things unimaginable. When you can do these things will you be ready to become a master.

"Go from here and beyond the swamp. Find a wood nymph and bring it back here, to play the midnight music at our temple."

The younger woman thought this an odd request, but being Shaolin had taught her that odd requests were the norm. She rose, bowed to her mentor, and left for the swamp.

The next morning, Master Ng found her disciple doing her long-staff training in a courtyard. The younger woman stopped her exercises, approached her teacher and bowed.

"Good morning, Disciple Mei. Did you find a wood nymph for our temple last night?"

"No, Master Ng, I did not," the young woman replied. "Instead, I found a small frog who lived among the reeds."

Ng nodded slightly. "I see. And was this frog a large frog, so he could make such a loud noise that we could hear so far from the swamp?"

"No, Master. In fact, it was a tiny frog I found, smaller than the frogs I usually see when I walk along a lakeside or pond. It was barely the size of the tip of my thumb."

"Then surely it had large, strong arms with which to pluck music from the reeds on which it lived!"

The disciple shook her head. "Indeed, it had only thin and frail limbs. It made music not by plucking, but by blowing through a big globe it made from its own throat."

"This globe, then, it surely was huge?"

"No, Master, though it was nearly half as big as the frog itself."

The master nodded and smiled. "So instead of a delicate wood nymph strumming music from the reeds, you found the evening sound to come from a tiny frog blowing air from its own body."

The disciple now nodded.

"This is a lesson in finding the nature of truth that you must remember," the master explained. "It is easy to create an answer, or accept an answer that has become widely accepted by others. It takes a much more skilled mind, and vision to see through illusion, to walk the path of a buddha."

The disciple thought about this a moment, then asked: "Why is knowing that frogs sing important to a Shaolin? Of what use is such knowledge?"

"Ah," said the master, smiling, "That is the essence of all knowledge. At what point does a good story replace truth? In what ways might good stories hide or distort truth? Truth builds on itself, like each brick in a house. Each depends on the ones beneath and beside to provide support. If one brick is bad, how much weaker the structure? How many weak bricks can a house stand before a wall collapses?

"In Shaolin we strive to seek truth. But as Buddha taught, truth is not always easily seen, it is not always fully exposed to all eyes. It is our challenge to learn to recognize truth when we see it, and to do this by seeing it for ourselves."

Chapter Five

Inside the Shaolin Temple

There is no there there.

Gertrude Stein

The famous front gate to the Shaolin Temple of Honan Province is practically a trademark. Though the façade is familiar to Buddhists and martial arts students the world over, the original gate was destroyed and rebuilt many times since the Temple was founded. In general, the front gate was used only for important ceremonial occasions, and was not the "front door" so frequently depicted in the movies. Above the gate is a sign stating simply: "Shaolin Temple." The gatehouse is a narrow edifice that has two front-facing windows, and is joined to the Temple walls on either side. Inside the gate is a plaque with a brief historical description:

It was first built in the 13th year (1735) of Emperor Yongzheng's reign of the Qing (Ch'ing) Dynasty and was renovated in the 11th year (1872) of Emperor Tongzhi, a reign of the Qing Dynasty. In 1974 it was rebuilt according to the old model. Above the lintel there is a horizontal board inscribed with three Chinese characters—Shaolin Temple—handwritten by Emperor Kangsi himself. Outside this main gate there are two stone side gates which were built during the reign of Emperor Jiajing of the Ming Dynasty in 1544 and 1555 respectively.

Omitted from this history is the account of the Temple being destroyed by feuding warlords in 1928 (Warlord Shi You-san, to be specific), and the subsequent razing of the ruins by communist forces in 1949. Today the mountain gate, once used only for masters and high-ranking guests, is now the entrance through which tourists from around the world enter. The Temple, which had been a series of ruins as recently as 1980, has been restored and expanded as the tourist potential was recognized.

Tourism will certainly bring in the revenues and notoriety needed to restore the Temple physically and perhaps prevent another destructive episode when political tides turn again. Because of the martial arts aspect of Shaolin Ch'an Buddhism, the Temple was the subject of military actions many times in its history. The most recent destruction by the communist regime was an effort to eradicate both the martial and religious presence of the legendary order. As part of the Maoist rebellion (and later the Cultural Revolution), all symbols of religion, organized non-communist groups, schools and scholars were systematically destroyed, imprisoned, or forced into exile. So long as the symbolism of the main gate is lost to visitors, the Temple grounds cannot be considered venerable or, as Americans put it, official.

Once inside the gate, a visitor passes through a brick archway that leads to the Garden of Visitors. Here, the stone-floored courtyard contains old trees and commemorative stones that record notable visitors and patrons from over the centuries. These visitors were the people of high enough stature to be allowed access through the main gate.

If you enter the Garden of Visitors and go off to the left, you will face a long wall with another arch—this is the entry to Gung Fu Hall. It was in the courtyard and small rooms surrounding the court where Shaolin monks taught and practiced their martial arts. The new area was constructed in 1984 and encloses an area of 850 square meters. The small study rooms are now filled with excellent life-sized models of Shaolin monks and students in 14 representations of life in the Temple and Temple history. Included are exhibits of sitting meditation, different aspects of martial arts training, the founding Shaolin monks building the Temple; when they supposedly used their hands as tools to cut wood and form blocks as part of discipline training; monks being called to meditation, the legendary 13 monks rescuing Emperor T'ai-tsung of the T'ang Dynasty, Monk Hsiao-shan leading an army, Shaolin monks fighting Japanese invaders, and a variety of Wushu exercises. It is to the credit of the builders of the new Temple that the historical reconstructions are very accurate, though few of the inscribed plaques tend to include any mention of the government actions against the Order from 1949 onwards. A casual visitor could easily believe that nothing of importance occurred here between 1949 and 1984.

The inner courtyards of the Temple are beautiful and characteristically Chinese, with little to distinguish the architecture from other Buddhist or Taoist compounds. Even Shaolin had its guardian fu dog, and the hilly terrain made it necessary to install dozens of stairways around the vast compound's grounds.

Temples at Fukien, Kwangtung, Omei Shan, and Wutang Shan were constructed along similar lines as the Honan Temple, though the terrain around each was quite different. Fukien was built in a forest on flat ground, and Kwangtung was built on a flat expanse on a low cliff near the ocean. Omei Shan Temple was atop a steep mountain while Wutang was built along a cliff face overlooking a valley. Despite these drastic distinctions, the buildings of each temple were very similar. Honan and Fukien had a main gate with the Shaolin logo and round windows. All had a large central bell tower and several classroom-lined courtyards. Universally there is a Buddha Hall for ceremonies and special occasions, and a Hall of Ancestors for contemplation and meditation. It was important to have distinct places for training, meditation, holding classes, and hosting ceremonies. There was also a Hall of Wooden Men ("dummies") at Fukien and Honan where a disciple would take the last test before becoming a Shaolin master.

A temple was both home and school to many people, so there were typically a number of additions that made life more pleasant. Gardens were ubiquitous, and included both agricultural plots and ornamental gardens. Fishponds were also built, and provided a place to observe some of the local wildlife up close. Each temple also had an elaborate and well-kept library. Omei Shan's library was particularly noteworthy as it contained nearly every medical manuscript ever written up until that temple's destruction. Other libraries were well stocked with texts on Buddhism, Taoism, astronomy, meteorology, biology, art, music, philosophy, mathematics, and other learned subjects. A Shaolin monk could not advance to higher disciple or master levels without the equivalent of a solid liberal arts education.

Living quarters for students were spartan, but this was partly because so many *novices* would fail to stay on at a temple. Some did not pass their tests, and others left because they could not take the workload. Usually, a student would have a small cubicle of his or her own, a room about 10 feet by 10 feet. The cubicle would be furnished with a sleeping mat and a small table that served as an altar. All a novice would keep were robes, a food bowl, a pair of shoes, and perhaps one personal possession from her family. Two candles were allowed each week, and writing and reading materials provided as part of lessons.

Disciples and masters shared similar quarters. Their rooms were larger, and included a place for meditation, a small wardrobe for different robes, and a desk and bookcase. All rooms had windows, and a recess for water basins. Even the abbot used such quarters. If guests were being entertained, they would be hosted in ceremonial halls and allowed to room in a monk's cubicle (several were kept available for visitors). Not surprisingly, members of the imperial household were very rarely visitors at Shaolin.

In contrast to the spartan living quarters—which were actually only used for sleeping and dressing—the other chambers were quite elaborate. The meditation halls had rows of pillows upon bamboo rolling carpets, so monks could sit in comfortable meditation. Walls were adorned with detailed murals depicting important events in the life of the Buddha, Tamo, and the Temple. Smaller objects such as incense holders, Buddha statues, and *mandala* art, were generally gifts brought by visiting monks from other orders. As for the meditation pillows, they were often payment for items that a temple produced, usually for rice, wooden bowls, or teaching. The pillows sometimes were elaborate silken designs, but as often were simple cloth. One day a master might sit on a silken pillow, the next a mere novice. No status was given to material objects—except books—in the Temple.

Books were a main feature within the Shaolin temples and alone among material objects held special value. Why, one might ask, was there this exception to a seemingly universal Buddhist doctrine? The answer is simple: books are products of the minds of people, and as such allow each person and each generation to know more than the previous generations. Books record where we might successfully wander, and where pitfalls or dead ends await. They help each generation become more intellectually advanced without requiring each generation to "reinvent the wheel." Thus, to Shaolin at least, books are truly sacred knowledge; the surviving essence of humankind after the flesh has come and gone. There are no bad books: even *Mein Kampf* serves as a lesson about the mind and potential dangers latent within anyone.

The Shaolin libraries were well-built structures, always on stilts to keep manuscripts safe from possible floods. Books were usually kept individually wrapped in silk or cloth sacs, and stored on shelves. The storage areas (racks) were kept away from light; in fact, only the front wall of the library had windows. There was no reading room, but rather books would be taken to a monk's room, the garden, or another hall to be read. The majority of Buddhist texts at Honan were gifts from our Tibetan cousins.

Shaolin temples, naturally, also had many areas set aside for gung fu practice. There were outdoor courtyards, indoor classrooms, and designated training fields outside a temple. Novices had punching bags of reeds bound in cloth, or wooden posts around which had been tied pads of silk. Other striking aids were made of simple wood, usually sanded or polished. Few trees outside a temple's grounds were safe from kicking practice by experimenting disciples.

The Shaolin Order holds its temple grounds in great reverence, for these temples were the wellsprings of who we became. Nevertheless, the Buddha taught that it is the heart and not the shell that is the real substance. Without true Shaolin, the rebuilt temples, no matter how splendid, are nothing more than embellished postcards. They may recall the past and bring it alive in our minds, but so far as we can tell they remain like Hollywood sets inhabited by actors (at worst) or genuinely Buddhist, but not traditionally Shaolin, temples (at best). Many new "Shaolin" schools, most aimed at teaching children Modern Wushu, have sprung up around the Honan Temple, and the classical setting has helped recruits set aside any question of authenticity about what they are learning.

Temple Lifestyle

The roots of Confucianism, arguably China's most influential philosophical school, are manifested in the Shaolin lifestyle in several ways. Rituals were an important part in the life of the monks. They had special rituals for the burial of their dead, for the recognition of members who advanced to higher levels, for marriages, passing seasons, academic honors, and other events. To some degree, strict observance of ritual allowed a member of one temple to recognize someone from another temple in his sect. Salutes were the commonest means of such recognition. They were often based on a common model (fist into open palm) and added elements that were style, school, temple, or rank specific.

The class structure and family system that were central elements of Confucian philosophy did have a place in the Temple. Shaolin had a limited class structure with four major levels: students, disciples, masters, and grandmasters. At the base was the student class, which held the most individuals and was most often utilized. Members of this group cooked all the meals, washed clothes and performed other routine housekeeping and grounds keeping chores. The tasks were aimed at teaching them humility and respect: humility came from understanding that all living things are bound by several "base" needs—eating, cleaning, sleeping, eliminating waste—and respect came from learning to take proper care of one's self and environment. These students might one day be entrusted with devastating martial abilities and could not be allowed to harbor or encourage thoughts of an arrogant or boisterous nature. At this stage they would develop benevolence (*jen*) and uprightness (*chih*) through a rigorous course of practical and academic training. Benevolence encompassed skills in dealing compassionately with people and working to perform deeds that made positive (or "good") contributions to a community. Uprightness was practiced by being ethical and true to one's expressed values—in other words, sincere avoidance of hypocrisy and guile. Moreover, since new members were like the youngest daughters and sons in a family, they were expected to perform such duties out of filial piety (hsiao) to their "older brothers," "uncles" and other "relatives" who composed the ranks of the Shaolin. One who entered before you and was still in your class was an older brother. A disciple would be an uncle to a student or an eldest brother. Masters of a temple fit into the role of the father. The grandmaster fulfilled the position of the head of a family like a grandfather or a great-grandfather.

Hsiao as a separate Confucian virtue is not especially prized in Shaolin, but respect and courtesy are important in cultivating an environment that accords with the Tao. And although the Confucian virtues of li (propriety in all things) and yi (righteousness) had some influence in the temples (they were in *China*, after all), they were always superceded by Ch'an and Taoist pragmatism.

Students who had proven themselves worthy of learning the martial arts of a temple would be placed under the guidance of a master and become designated as disciples. Upon elevation to this level, they would spend some two to four years in the exclusive study of the Shaolin martial arts and essential principles of Buddhism, Taoism, and the role of a monk in society. As students, they had learned the foundations of Shaolin ethics. As disciples, the time had come for them to live a life based on those ethics, becoming examples for others to follow.

Governing the activities of a temple were the masters, the fully ordained monks of that temple. The title of master had been bestowed upon them because they had learned both the philosophical background to be a monk, and a system of martial arts. They were the dispensers of knowledge to the students and disciples, master-teachers as well as monks. From the earliest times, it was the Order's policy to limit resident masters to thirteen. Other monks could come and go, but the number of residents was fixed. Each temple would have an abbot (or head monk), a sub-abbot, two additional grandmasters, four masters of red-sash (ordained) rank, and five training masters of gold-sash rank (see ranking chart, below).

Titles for Shaolin practitioners at different levels. Terms are given in the Cantonese dialect. (Mandarin is also acceptable.) Sash colors are the traditional ones used by the Order from about 1845 onwards.			
Level of Practitioner	**Male**	**Female**	**Sash Color**
Junior Student	si di	si mui	White
Senior Student	si hing	si jei	White
Disciple	sisuk	sigoo mui	Black
Instructor (Disciple)	sifu	sifu	Black
Senior Instructor (Disciple)	sibok	sidigoo	Black
Master	sigung	sipoo	Gold or Red
Style Founder	sijo	sijo	Red
Grandmaster	sitaigung	sitaipoo	Red

At the top of the class structure were the grandmasters. These masters governed the overall activities and functions of a temple, setting policy. All Order activities were coordinated by the grandmasters, from the admission of new students, to promotions and other activities. Whereas a monk needed only to master one or a few of the Shaolin systems, as befitted his or her age and ability, an abbot (normally also a grandmaster) of a temple was a master of all the knowledge that was conveyed in that temple. In this light, he would be likened to a great-grandfather, whose great age and vast accumulation of knowledge made him the one who was sought when advice was needed. Let us reinforce a key point: grandmaster is not a rank, as are student, disciple, and master. It is merely a special term for a master practitioner who has taught disciples to the rank of master. Other very traditional Shaolin-infuenced Chinese schools (such as that of Ark Wong) use the terminology in this way as well.[97] Red sash level masters are only addressed as "Grandmaster" (or "Si Tai Gung") if they have such credentials as teachers. In Shaolin, then, "grandmaster" is used as an honorary title for a teacher of masters.

The sash colors also have a history. A white sash was given to a student after being accepted into a temple's initial training program. For most students, this took place six months to a year after being brought into a temple for evaluation. The sash represented a blank page, for paper was valuable and one was careful what would be written thereon. Advancement to disciple level meant that pages had been filled with great quantities of important information, so they wore the ink-black sash. In the north (Honan Temple), masters traditionally wore a gold sash. The wisdom associated with understanding more than just written words on pages was supposed to develop into sorting facts in new ways, even though they were not specifically linked or taught as such. This process is symbolically reflected in the light of a clear dawn on a new day. The dawn is "dawning consciousness" moving closer to enlightenment, and the new day is the event of having mastered the teachings one has received. This dawn light is symbolized as gold. The southern temples (Kwangtung and Fukien) used a red sash for mastery. Red blood is the fluid symbol of life, and as Buddhist practices emphasize becoming a "better" living creature in concert with all living creatures, the red of blood was interpreted as the most tangible common bond.

In the 1850s, when northern and southern temples sorted their various differences into a more coherent entity, the northern gold sash was re-designated the symbol of a weapons master, one who had completed all the martial training of a style but was still mastering Buddhist spiritual precepts. The "weapons" aspect of this title denotes the martial aspects of Shaolin training, and not specifically *weapons* in the sense of sword and staff. The rank was termed "training master" and these monks oversaw all martial training at a temple. The red sash was awarded to monks who became priests or priestesses, signifying that they had been ordained in the Shaolin Order.

The Dharma be your light.
The Dharma be your refuge!
Do not look for any other refuge!

Shakyamuni Buddha

Setting the Record Straight on Women and Sacred Objects

Shaolin is not a deistic religion as understood in the West. Buddha is not a god, but a mortal man who found a path to enlightenment. Tamo (Bodhidharma) is not a deity but a rather feisty and fanatical Buddhist monk. Shaolin does, however, acknowledge the historical lineage of deities and **the significance of deity characters as symbolic of important universal ideas and principles**. Thus, *Shiva* (borrowed from Hinduism) is not a god in a specific sense, but a thought-image that represents qualities historically associated with Shiva. Shiva the Destroyer is not a vengeful warrior, but the Destroyer of Ignorance, a Remover of Impediments to the gaining of knowledge and enlightenment.

As part of preserving the venerable past and the symbols from which Buddhist philosophy grew, Shaolin monks would make and keep a variety of sacred objects and commemorative art. Much of this art has been lost, destroyed, or badly damaged over time, but many pieces have been restored or created new so they can be displayed at Honan.

Contrary to the beliefs of some Buddhists, the Buddha admonished his followers not to make and worship statues in his likeness. Not only was he clear and repetitive in so warning, but he also made it clear to his followers that such practices were counterproductive and in direct opposition to his teachings. As a man, and a man *only*, Shakyamuni Buddha had discovered the path to enlightenment. Anyone who would pray to him or worship his statue was in effect looking outward for the path, and Buddha was adamant that the way lay in looking inward. When Shaolin meditate before the image of Buddha, the image serves only to remind the meditator of the Dharma path.

The role of women in the Shaolin Order is another area of our tradition which has been commonly obscured. The priestesses of the Order were as highly trained and knowledgeable as their male counterparts. The Wing Chun and Dragon styles (both the early Dragon movements developed in the 7th century, and Southern Dragon developed in the 16th century) were primarily created by female Shaolin. Snake, or large parts of Snake, has been heavily influenced by female practitioners; and even though Southern Tiger was initially codified by a man, most of Tiger's *ch'in na* techniques were developed by a woman. After Wing Chun was developed, about 70% of the female monks learned it from female instructors and the abbot. Women Shaolin, too, sometimes shaved their heads. Sometimes, when mistaken for and addressed as men, their failure to reply precipitated arguments and they were forced to defend themselves. Shaolin priestesses were also branded with the tiger and dragon marks upon graduation from formal training. Women who remained celibate, usually the strictly Buddhist-influenced ones, kept their heads shaven.

More traditional Shaolin women, with Buddhist, Taoist, and the unique Shaolin martial training, allowed their hair to grow back. Female Shaolin disciples of instructor level are addressed as "Sifu," just as male disciples are (or "Sifu, MA'AM!"). "Sifu" is an appropriate way for laity to address both male and female Shaolin monastics, in general.

As with some Tibetan orders, Shaolin makes no prohibition against fraternization between male and female monks. Relationships within some Tibetan orders are not formalized however, and both begin and end due to mutual choice. Relationships could be of this sort in Shaolin, but formal marriages were (and are) also allowed. To those who are only vaguely familiar with Buddhism (or whose notions of Buddhism have been influenced by Theravadin sects), this may seem contrary to Buddhism itself. This is not so; one concept Shaolin has always shared with our Tibetan comrades is that human beings are a part of the natural world. Shaolin temples were one place in dynastic China (one of the only places) where women were treated no differently than men. There was no "affirmative action," or quota system, however. It was simply a matter of each person being assessed based upon skill, with no regard shown to gender. The requirements for women were just the same as those for men. This egalitarianism is amply reflected by the many achievements of our female monks.

Most Shaolin were men, however, and only two female abbesses are recorded. They served the order at different times and were installed after burnings reduced the Order and forced it to rebuild. The first was the Ng Mui who is credited with founding the Dragon style. (This oral history, that Ng Mui served as chief monk after a temple burning, appears to strengthen the likelihood that the Honan Temple did indeed experience some upheaval around 1570, as mentioned in Chapter Two.) Throughout the history of the Order, there have been numerous masters of the feminine persuasion.

Student

Admission is free but you pay at the door…

There were many reasons why a youngster would try to gain admittance to a Buddhist temple. The monk's life offered shelter, education, and a livelihood that were not available to many of the orphans or poor people of China. At a specified time every three years, the temples would evaluate children for entry into the Order. Relatives would bring children, aged five to ten, or children would find their own way to a temple, and sit outside the Novice Gate. From that time onwards, masters and disciples would carefully scrutinize the children. Their first tests were to evaluate manners, for life in the Temple was very orderly. True, the monks would teach the students many things, but they required students to display and practice good manners as a first requirement. (Another basic requirement had long been that new students must be Chinese. By 1870, though, this requirement was relaxed, the then-guardian successor having decreed that such racial discrimination was anathema to the Buddha's wish that the spiritual path be open to all sentient beings ready to walk it.)

One of the more accurate sequences depicted in the movie *Kung Fu* is the screening process for children wishing to enter the Temple. They were expected to wait patiently until selected. Those who played games, started fights, or ran from the rain were disqualified. Those who ate or drank before the senior monk present or failed to say "Please," "Thank you," or call a senior "Sir" or "Madam," were disqualified. Those few who were selected were then taken to have their heads shaved (a sign of membership, both for the student and to others, the symbol indicating that the child was under Temple protection). From this point onwards, Shaolin life departs radically from the television series' portrayal. (For one thing, almost every platitude of wisdom depicted in the series derives from Taoism, not Buddhism. The general absence of women in the series' depiction is also faulty.)

After having his or her head shaved, the new student would be introduced to a disciple who would act as "older brother" or "older sister" and direct every aspect of the student's life. The disciple would escort the student to the bathing area where students would scrub thoroughly, then be issued the clothing of a student. This clothing usually consisted of simple baggy black trousers and a long-sleeved jacket.

Training in Shaolin philosophy and gung fu lasted (typically) for a traditional thirteen years. Students would enter the Temple when they were 5-10 years old, and begin their lives as monks by learning the basics of all the Shaolin arts. This included tackling housekeeping and grounds keeping duties, dishwashing, learning to read and write, and learning *stance* work. Shaolin students were also often taught acting, mime, make-up, costuming, and ventriloquism skills as part of their liberal education, but also so that they could blend in anywhere. Honan beginners were taught a blend of several northern styles, while southern temple students would be trained in different ways depending on the year of training. In essence, the particular master assigned to teach determined much of the curriculum. Students were supposed to ask seniors for lessons. The student did menial work so the teacher was reimbursed for his or her teaching time and could have time to perfect his own learning. The worthiness of a student was gauged by how he or she did more mundane tasks—and also gave a teacher an idea of what kind of focus that student could bring to bear on studies.

Students were matched with instructors based on rapport, body type, temperament, and other factors. Each priest or priestess was responsible for his or her own students and disciples. There was little formal organization except for the abbot and his administrative duties. The abbot approved all graduations and promotions.

Students who worked hard were introduced to the core styles. Those who did not were dropped from the Temple (if they did not meet Shaolin standards). During years two through eight, a student would be taught at least one form from each representative Temple style. At some point, the student and master would agree on a "major" style, one that suited the body, kinesiology, and temperament of the student. By the tenth year, most of the kuen (forms) of that style would have been shown to the student.

Some small temple (at different points in our history, a variety of temples served as part of the Shaolin network) rank symbols prior to 1860 consisted of the following:

> Students after 6 months: yellow sash
> 3 ½ years: blue sash
> 4 ½ years: green sash
> 6-8 years: red sash (until 1850s)
> 15 years: gold sash (until 1850s)

Honan and Fukien Temple rank symbols:

> Students after 6 months: shoes
> 1 year: white sash
> 4 years: black sash
> 8 years: gold sash
> 12 years: red sash

The number of years associated with each rank is an approximation for a full-time Shaolin student—every student proceeds at his own pace. Once a student had been in the Temple for a month, he would be required to take vows of admittance. (Presently, these vows are normally taken sometime between the third and sixth month of study.) These vows are:

1) A promise to obey all seniors, without question, within the Temple;
2) A promise to perform all chores and exercises to the very best of their abilities, striving always for perfection;
3) A promise to honor, learn from, and study the path to enlightenment.

(2) and (3) are straightforward enough. Regarding (1), seniors are those within the Temple with direct responsibility for a student, such as masters, disciples, and perhaps very senior students (who might be assigned to teach a novice on occasion). Given the fairly relaxed Shaolin hierarchy and our focus on the Buddha's admonition to "always test a thing for yourself" before accepting it, it may initially seem strange that we require such a strong vow of obedience from students. But consider that students are often taught dangerous martial skills, and that even a practice session with a student incapable of following directions could result in a fatality. Given this degree of responsibility on the part of a teacher, student obedience becomes necessary for everyone's safety.

But there is more than this. Furuya, in his *KODO Ancient Ways*, relates an insight that nicely captures the importance of obedience:

> If the teacher says this piece of white paper is black, then, to the student, white is black. This is not just a game of obedience, this is spiritual trust between the teacher and the student. When I say this trust must be 100 percent, I see students begin to squirm. No one likes to hear this. It sounds too suspicious. However, without this 100-percent trust, the dynamic, profound interaction between teacher and student can never take place. Nowadays, students say, 'Sure, I'll say this white piece of paper is black, but what do I get out of it?'[99]

In our very materialistic and frank culture, students always question; but as Furuya points out, they often ask the wrong kinds of questions. (Furuya, as a Zen priest and a martial artist, shares many profound lessons in his book, and a serious student of the Shaolin path would be well advised to study them.)

A Shaolin teacher not only provides martial instruction, but also acts as a spiritual guide to Shaolin Ch'an. Without the deepest trust between teacher and student, martial *and* spiritual progress is constrained. Critically related to these issues of trust and obedience is a master's authority (and sometimes responsibility) to expel any of her students at *any* time up to the point where a student becomes a master himself. There is no appeal.

To not value one's teacher and not cherish the raw goods—
Though one had great knowldedge,
he would still be greatly confused.

Lao Tzu

Disciple

You never get good.

Kensho Furuya

A young student was curious about why some wore the black sash and others did not, though both showed similar martial prowess. The master was approached, and the questions presented to him. His answer was lucid.

"What is a black sash? By now you know that it means entry into discipleship, one who has proven himself over a period of rigorous training. Disciples are dedicated, loyal, knowledgeable, and above all, trustworthy. They are entrusted with so much, in fact, that they alone in the organization have a rank which automatically expires annually unless they prove they are still worthy.

"It is not an automatic award; there are no specific physical requirements to be met for all. The number of forms is irrelevant. Intangible elements are the most important elements in this promotion, such as: taking responsibility for one's life and actions; the ability to respect a trust; the ability to be friend, counselor, sibling, or training companion. Out of the nearly 3000 students in this school, only a very few have been awarded the black sash.

"They do more than what is asked of them, seeing tasks not as duties but as challenges to learn from. They sacrifice time and effort. Rather than neglect work or school, they learn to cultivate each with their gung fu.

"They are competent in their chosen field, and use this knowledge to enhance that competence. They do not forget the philosophical principles after each class; they live them. And they persevere, even—*especially*—when things get rough.

"They lead, not through intimidation or rank, but through compassion and respect. They are models, and people openly and genuinely respect them. And they learn, always."

The student pondered this answer for some time. He watched the senior students and new disciples work out, then he watched them during non-training time. In time he saw the difference between those acting with full awareness of their actions, and those desperately fighting a flow from outside. Finally he understood the whole point of the structure of Shaolin ranking, as it were. You could not be made into a worthy one, but rather you acknowledge that you are by being one. How subtle! How Shaolin.

Year seven was the crucial year for students, as they had to demonstrate gung fu proficiency against a variety of opponents and weapons, under different conditions. They would also have to explain a variety of uses for each technique in each kuen. It was at this stage that the student would move from rote learning to a level of comprehension that indicated potential as both a master and a future teacher. Successful completion of the tests at this level elevated the student to disciple status. The usual age range for disciples was from 15-25. (These days—with students beginning study in their teens, twenties, and thirties—the age range for disciples is more like 20-40.)

By this stage, too, the disciple will have learned that the true goal of gung fu is not about fighting an enemy or winning some contest, but rather about defeating the conflicts within you. Gung fu is practiced as much as an exercise to defeat the ego as to keep the body in top physical condition. The Shaolin, indeed the Buddhist, path is one of self-development.

Discipleship within the Order is rather different from the discipleship tradition in most civilian gung fu lineages. Becoming a disciple in most pais entails acceptance to the "inner circle" of the master, and often involves formal rituals binding the disciple to the master and the school. Shaolin administers a formal test for discipleship, yet no corresponding Confucian rituals are performed. Shaolin discipleship is less about hierarchical relationships, and more about level of skill and ability to live Shaolin ideals.

A Shaolin practitioner lives by a set of rules aimed at helping her stay on the eightfold path and contribute to the good of sentient beings. At some temples, monks would take vows to live by these rules in a single formal ceremony (usually around the 2nd or 3rd rank). Sometimes a disciple would subscribe to one or two at a time over the course of training. These rules included the following:

Avoid conflict. Since you cannot combat worldly conflicts, strive to overcome conflict within yourself. A wise man does not contend and therefore cannot be conquered. Yield and overcome.

Learn. Truth is unbounded. My truth may not be your truth. Obey principles without being bound by them.

Treat all with courtesy. If an elder is at fault, do not let him lead you into the fault of disrespect. Do not lower your values to be compatible with the narrow-minded.

Be open to new ideas. Accept information as it is given. Doubt inhibits— learning must be a tool to an uninhibited mind. Weigh evidence, and *then* form an opinion. Hear, test, then decide.

Be assured of unity. No matter your problem, the combined efforts of the Order and all of its members are here to help you. Membership is granted pending adherence to this concept above all others. The success and well being of the Order is dependent upon the success and well being of each practitioner.

Be like Shiva, and destroy ignorance wherever and however you find it. Ignorance causes fear, and fear leads to darkness and violence. Beware the demons that attend Ignorance: Greed, Poverty, Subjugation, Hatred, and Fear.

Be always compassionate. Buddhism is the practice of *mindful* compassion.

Master

> The ancient masters were intelligent, subtle, profound, and spiritual.
> Their thoughts could not be easily fathomed.
>
> *Lao Tzu*

By year ten or eleven, the disciple was a competent martial artist—by any standard an expert—and would renew studies in philosophy, nature, anatomy, and other subjects essential for a fully trained priest or priestess. It was also at this time that a master would introduce his student to both advanced applications of techniques (meditative and martial) and intensify the disciple's ch'i training. By year thirteen, historically, the disciple was expected to graduate. In other words, the youngest age for ordination was twenty-one. It was more usual for a disciple to become a master in his late twenties or early thirties. (Again, the culture of the modern world has generally delayed this. Because modern-day Shaolin have more demands upon their time than their 18th and 19th century counterparts, the rank of master is now usually conferred during a disciple's thirties or forties.)

"Graduation" from a temple is a little confusing, as different temples managed the process in varying ways. The process differed between the Honan and Fukien Temples, but then was made uniform in the 1850s. Ordination requires the complete mastery of two martial styles, in addition to other requirements, but the rank of master typically follows upon the mastery of a single style. Pre-1850s at the Honan Temple, receiving the brands and setting forth to wander meant graduation from the Temple as a *master*; ordination, if ever, occurred later. At Fukien, the trademark brands were received at ordination and not before. We also know that, at some point in our history, monks left the temple for 3-5 years at what we now call 3rd rank (Green Dragon). The following description is of graduation at the Fukien Temple, becoming a fully ordained Shaolin priest.

Eventually a disciple has mastered two styles of Shaolin gung fu and is expert in at least three others. He or she has lived, and can explain the meanings of, Buddhist teachings, can meditate effectively, and has demonstrated compassion for all sentient beings. The disciple has learned a variety of skills (some practical, others academic) that allow for increased learning and compassionate interaction with other people. Upon recommendation by the senior monks of the Temple, the candidate is now ready to take the final Shaolin examination.

Step one began with taking the vows of priesthood. These are the same three basic vows taken by all Buddhist monks (and all Buddhists): **I take refuge in the Buddha, I take refuge in the teachings, and I take refuge in the Order**. (The Triratna, or Three Jewels, of Buddhism are also often listed as the Buddha, the Dharma, and the Sangha.) This triple vow is referred to as the "Refuges." Disciples normally take the Refuges once they determine to make a lifelong commitment to the Order, but taking them again at this point is an important reaffirmation.

By taking refuge in the Buddha, the monk affirms that he is dedicated to working towards enlightenment and has recognized the reality of suffering. Perhaps more importantly, the monk knows (with his thinking mind) that his own original nature is his buddha-self, though he may not yet intuitively grasp this. So by taking refuge in the Buddha, the monk is also affirming his commitment to awaken to his own buddha-nature. Taking refuge in the teachings (Dharma) means that the monk will follow the eightfold path and the Buddhist principles upon which the Order was founded. Taking refuge in the Order (Sangha) means that the monk subscribes to being part of Shaolin, and will help its members when needed, and will freely seek help from the Order when needed. There is also a fourth vow that Shaolin monks take: **I take refuge in myself**. This vow comes from the Buddha's frequent teaching that a person must find truth for herself, and that discovering this through direct experience, not blind faith, was essential to following the path. This fourth vow also served as a strong reminder to take full responsibility for one's own actions, and to listen to one's own heart.

Taking the Refuges is but the first aspect of ordination, however. There is also the matter of taking the master's oath. The term "oath" is generally held to mean a vow taken to God or a supernatural deity whose authority is seen as strong enough to enforce compliance with the oath. Shaolin monks take a sort of oath, though they do not address a supernatural being but their fellow monks and the sentient beings that they will serve. The wording of this *Master's Creed of Conduct* has varied from time to time and temple to temple. We do not know whether it was Abbot Li's innovation or an older Shaolin tradition, but Shaolin priests in America have written their own, individual ordination vows. This serves to ensure that a priest's vows are personally relevant, and brings the Buddha's words to mind: "Better your own truth, however weak, than the truth of another, however noble." This oath is a basic example of how an oath might read.

Master's Creed of Conduct

I freely and willingly make these promises in recognition of my responsibilities to myself, my teachers, fellow monks, and sentient beings everywhere.

First, that I respect and honor all life, and will not kill. In Buddha's name I take this vow.

Second, I shall dedicate my life first to my spiritual development, for I know that I only have the power to change myself. If I cannot achieve a spiritual union with my buddha-self, I shall be unable to guide other beings to their buddha-selves.

Third, I will strive to do no harm, abstaining from stealing and illicit sexual behavior.

Fourth, I shall be a warrior only against the forces of ignorance — by learning, teaching, and compassionately interacting with other sentient beings. I shall oppose any restrictions that block a sentient being, myself included, from walking the path towards enlightenment. In this one domain I shall act in a way that may shape society.

Fifth, I shall at all times hold the principles of compassion, mercy, wisdom, and kindness as the greatest of treasures that a sentient being may bestow, and bestow them with frequency.

Sixth, I honor the secret teachings of the Temple and Order of Shaolin, and shall neither demonstrate nor divulge such teachings except in manners prescribed by the Order's grandmasters.

Seventh, I vow to always strive for the highest levels of physical, mental, and spiritual control to which my faculties may reach. To this end I shall refrain from the taking of intoxicants, medications, or any other substances that would alter my control of my body and mind.

Eighth, I vow to follow the Dharma to the best of my abilities, hold to my beliefs and ideals in the face of adversity, and do that which I believe is correct and just regardless of consequences. I will share the teachings by living them every day. I will speak truthfully.

I acknowledge that the secrets of the Temple and Order of Shaolin are sacrosanct because of their power and potential for corruption. Therefore, I act as a guardian to these teachings, revealing only those that I am permitted by the grandmasters and tradition to share. Should I violate these vows; by unauthorized teaching, by joining a force intent on violating any of these vows, or by revealing the names of (or other information about) my fellows, students, or masters without their permission; I agree that I shall be removed, by death if necessary, from the Temple and Order of Shaolin Ch'an for all time.

In taking such vows, the monk would also take (or sometimes be given) a symbolic name, to be used only among other Shaolin. The next step has become legendary: entry into the Hall of Challenge. This hall was a long room in the temple that contained many booby-traps that tested the all-out martial skills of the candidate. These traps could seriously injure or kill a person, and included arrows, darts, swinging clubs, false floors, and other devices. Some of these traps were purely mechanical, and were set off by trip wires or floor plates, while monks on the other side of the walls operated others.

The successful candidate would emerge at the far end of the hall fully intact, and would face the final test. An iron urn stood blocking the door leading outside. The monk had to lift the urn out of the way in order to leave. Complicating the task was the fact that the urn contained about 300 pounds of burning coals, bringing the total weight to over 400 pounds. It had to be moved by using the forearms. On the sides of the urn were raised animal designs, a dragon and a tiger, which would be branded on the inner forearms of the successful candidate. With the urn moved and the forearms branded, the monk had become a full priest or priestess of Shaolin (at the Fukien Temple). The Order used the brands to represent a permanent "diploma," having suffered the loss of all physical objects many times in their history. No one could survive the test to obtain these brands unless he or she had truly earned them. Masters of the first four temples had the brands of the tiger on the left forearm and the dragon on the right forearm. (Some authors have mistakenly reversed these.[100] And many non-Shaolin authors writing about the "myths of Shaolin" claim that the tradition of arm branding is a martial arts fairy tale because they have never seen such brands, or because these brands aren't historically documented. No matter. The tradition stopped around 1900, so few people living today would have even had an opportunity to see them.) Masters of Omei Shan Temple had the mantis and the crane on the right and left forearms. These represented the dominant martial style (Praying Mantis) and that temple's central role as a hub of medical and healing arts (symbolized by the crane). We have no intention of ever resurrecting the branding practice, as in today's culture it would only serve to inflate the ego.

Once outside the examination chamber, senior monks would care for the new priest. They would apply healing salve on the burns, and present the graduate with the saffron robes and red sash (pre 1860—it was gold at Honan post 1860) of a master of the Order. On the next day the new graduate was expected to leave the Temple and join the outside world for at least three years before returning. The time for such activity was variable, and it could take a decade for a priest who might return to the Temple as a teacher. Others would remain as permanent wandering monks. The option was a matter of personal choice, as Shaolin Ch'an puts individual will in a very high place in its discipline. Some monks did return and became *fut doo*, the monks who remained in the Temple, while others only visited periodically. Many remained "outside" and used their skills to help other people as best as they could. If a priest decided to return to a temple, it was no guarantee that he would be assigned to teaching and mentoring duties. Before being entrusted with new students, the potential teacher would be put through rigorous tests of methodology, techniques, and, of course, Buddhist teachings. Upon being accepted as what was in effect a faculty member, a new teaching master would (post 1860) be made a "training master."

As has been mentioned, there were some differences in becoming a master at Honan Temple versus becoming a master at Fukien Temple. The ceremony which ended in having one's forearms branded, at Honan, meant that one had "graduated" as a master from the Temple, but was not ordained as a Shaolin Buddhist priest. The Honan monk would go forth for at least three years, and if he returned, might become a training master. Ordination, if it ever occurred, came later. Since the Order's closest guarded secrets were reserved for priests, one important consequence of this practice was that those secrets wouldn't be lost by masters who "graduated" but never returned. At the Fukien Temple, the branding ceremony was an adjunct of becoming ordained. For Fukien Shaolin, one went into the world for three years upon becoming a full priest. (Much of the discussion here has centered upon ordained masters [priests] only.)

As an interesting aside, these differences between Honan and Fukien tradition reflected two very distinct environments. Shaolin at Honan tended to work with closed fists longer (both literally and figuratively). They were closer to the dynastic political arena and were imperially monitored, to a degree. There was a greater hesitancy in the North to pass on high level technique, which explains why monks went forth into the world for awhile before being ordained and entrusted with the secrets of the Order. This sojourn formed a sort of test. Did the graduate become involved in politics, or otherwise stray from the path? At Fukien, there was a greater ratio of masters to students and more openness in training. The politically remote location played a salient role. This attitude is reflected in the training of certain styles. Northern Snake practitioners, for instance, worked more with the *leopard fist*, whereas the southerner Snake stylists preferred more advanced open handed technique, such as the *snake hand*.

For Shaolin everywhere, the master ranks (or degrees) are named for different dragons. (Disciples also hold dragon ranks.) Seventh degree is called "Sapphire Dragon," and is the terminal level for formal training. The levels above are based on personal development, contributions to the Order and sentient life forms, and other less tangible factors. The eighth degree, or "Emerald Dragon," is awarded by senior monks based on an overall assessment of a candidate's record. Ninth degree, or "Silver Dragon," is awarded to abbot/guardian heirs while the those priests are still alive. The guardian successor, or "Gold Dragon," is the head of the Order. Abbots/style guardians are also Gold Dragons. By definition, there is only one guardian successor per generation, and no more than six silver dragon ranking monks (one per Gold Dragon). Likewise, there were never more than six gold dragon ranking monks, which included the guardian successor and five guardians/abbots.

Shaolin Ranking

In an interesting case of "yin-yangedness," the individual-based and liberating Buddhist philosophy of Shaolin incorporated a hierarchical system that is something of a cross between academia and the military. Though specifics of the ranking and uniforms varied over the centuries, certain features remained fairly constant, such as use of saffron robes for the masters and black sashes for disciples. This section reviews the ranks, their most recent uniforms, and a very general overview of requirements for each level.

As in most other ranking systems, Shaolin has its upper and lower levels of distinction. The lower levels, containing the students, are ranked by grades. In the academic world we have grade school and high school diplomas, while in the military we have enlisted ranks. These roughly correspond to Shaolin's student grades, which go from 1st grade (probationary novice) through 5th grade (senior student). The grades all fall under the traditional designation of white sash, thus contemporary sash colors are arbitrary. In a monastic environment, students were simply students and everyone was familiar with everyone else's level of skill. In the modern world, students are still students, but the different sash colors help students set goals and discern whom they might ask for help.

Beyond student grades comes the rank level, roughly equating to university degrees or military officer ranks. In Japanese styles (familiar to many people), the degree is designated by the word "dan" in combination with the level. Thus a second dan black belt is a nidan while a tenth degree is a judan. Shaolin degrees or ranks are much like levels in collegiate subjects, however, as time in grade has no bearing on promotion. In Shaolin, we often use the term "rank," as in "2nd rank" and "5th rank." The use of numbers and ranks in this fashion is a recent development, yet these ranks are based on Dragon titles which have been used among Shaolin masters for hundreds of years. Traditionally, disciples, masters, and priests of different levels were accorded special titles. Moving from one of these levels to another is not like a promotion (such as in the military or at a job), but is rather a recognition (like an academic diploma) of a person's Buddhist attainment and martial skill.

Student Grades: White Sash
A student's uniform is all-black, with open-bottom trousers.

Novice, 1st grade: All novices are assigned the 1st grade and are considered probationary students. The sash is white and never carries any additional markings.

Student, 2nd grade: Awarded after the first set of examinations are passed and under sifu recommendation. Knows basic protocols and procedures of Temple life. Understands basics of self-defense techniques, stances, breakfalls, and simple punching drills. Is now a member of the Shaolin Order.

Student, 3rd grade: This is a middle range student with a background of three to five basic forms, several self-defense applications done to effectiveness, and passing a basic history and philosophy examination. 3rd grade students must be proficient in all fundamentals.

Senior Student, 4th grade: Students are awarded this grade when they have completed prescribed requirements of basic gung fu, a set of some ten defenses against weapons done at combat speed, solid knowledge of their style, its history, and Shaolin history. A student at this level must also display a firm grasp of Taoist philosophy.

Senior Student, 5th grade: To reach this level, students must learn at least one form from three styles other than their "major" style, so they have some breadth of understanding of martial techniques. A sound understanding of Shaolin Ch'an is required. They also generally need at least six months' study of a non-Chinese martial art, the intent being to give senior students a fuller understanding of combat and other teaching philosophies and methods. There are additional requirements, such as knowing and being able to functionally perform at least three defenses for each move of a set number of forms, displaying competence in sparring, and possessing useful knowledge of using at least one weapon. These additional requirements are set by the primary sifu. Again, all of these grades are arbitrary and requirements are altered to fit the individual.

Disciple Ranks: Black Sash

At this level the uniform may consist of black or gray trousers and a gray jacket.

Probationary Disciple, Black Dragon (1st rank): Earning a black sash has several universal requirements, including a) advanced knowledge of Taoist philosophy and its relationship to Shaolin, b) effective unarmed defenses against two knife-wielding opponents, c) expert performance of all forms to date, with at least four uses demonstrated for each technique, d) blindfolded defense against one unarmed opponent of equal rank, e) demonstrated knowledge of major martial artists, styles, and their histories (that is, the disciple must be able to distinguish, say, Tiger from Aikido, and know who Masutatsu Oyama, Gichin Funakoshi, Ng Mui, Pak Mei, etc. were), and f) fulfill protocol and etiquette evaluations by the main sifu and senior masters. There are other general requirements as well, in addition to individual requirements based on style: for example, Tiger and Praying Mantis stylists must each be able to demonstrate expertise in one staff form, while a Wing Chun stylist must be able to use sticky hands to practical effect. The 1st rank may wear a solid black sash with a single gold or (if instructed by a master teacher) red ¼-inch stripe parallel to the sash tips and three inches from the tip.

Disciple, White (2nd), Green (3rd), Blue (4th), and Red (5th) Dragons

From this level upwards to senior disciple (4th rank), the promotion requirements are based on advanced knowledge of multiple styles, defenses, sparring, philosophy, history, applications, and other materials that are style specific. Each additional rank through 4rd rank earns an extra ¼-inch gold or red stripe located above the original stripe. A 5th rank's black sash will have ¼-inch stripes edging both the upper and lower borders of the sash, but no tip bars. A 5th rank may also be awarded the rank of training master. Whether or not a 5th degree Shaolin wears a black or gold sash is decided upon by the senior monks. Without getting caught up in the details, it may be useful to think of the black sash with double longitudinal stripes as a half-promotion to the rank of master.

Training Master Ranks: Gold Sash
The uniform may consist of a yellow or saffron jacket and either gray or black trousers.

Training Master, Red Dragon (5th rank): Earning a gold sash entails true mastery within a particular style of gung fu as determined by qualified senior masters, but also requires demonstrated ability to pass along the arts and philosophy of Shaolin. Remember that the Order has repeatedly been reduced to very few individuals in the past (and present!), so being able to rebuild the Order is a major concern. The training master earns this rank by showing that he or she possesses the knowledge and skill to pass it to a new generation. This teaching may be by direct instruction, through writings, or by other means deemed appropriate by master examiners. An "unarmed monk," a basic style master who is something more experienced than a disciple but less qualified than a full-fledged master, also might wear a gold sash. For such individuals, the sash distinguishes persons of experience from the younger disciples. A 5th rank wears a plain gold sash and is entitled to be called "master" or "si gung/si poo." Note: because this rank equates with mastery of the arts, there is no sex-designated title in English, meaning female masters are *not* called "mistress."

Training Master, Ruby Dragon (6th rank): A training master is awarded the 6th rank upon completing a period of time, usually not less than five years, as an actively teaching training master. The knowledge of Shaolin, Taoism, Buddhism, martial arts, basic psychology, natural history, teaching methods, and other subjects is expected to be at equal levels of mastery, such that the primary qualification for promotion is belief by masters that this candidate has the likelihood (and not merely "potential") to become a priest of the red sash levels. The rank wears a gold sash with a ¼-inch ruby red stripe along the upper border.

Master Ranks: Red Sash

The uniform may be either all saffron, or a saffron jacket worn with black trousers.

Priest, Sapphire Dragon (7th rank): The awarding of a red sash means that the candidate has achieved highest honors and mastery of all materials—often including a Ph.D. or equivalent education—along with full mastery of a second gung fu style. The Sapphire Dragon is a fully ordained Shaolin priest. There are numerous tests to be passed for this level, including a) blindfolded unarmed defense against two armed opponents, b) use of three weapons in self-defense, c) highest level knowledge of the history and philosophies of Shaolin and other major martial arts, d) expert knowledge of comparative religions and philosophies, e) demonstrated knowledge of all eight basic Shaolin styles (Crane, Northern Mantis, Dragon, Snake, Tiger, White Eyebrow, Southern Mantis, and Wing Chun) to at least 1st rank proficiencies, f) acknowledged mastery of an academic discipline apart from martial arts or Shaolin history/philosophy, g) demonstrated expert ability to perpetuate Shaolin teachings, h) demonstrated adherence to the philosophical foundations of Shaolin, and i) undergoing an official ordination. A 7th rank wears a ruby red sash and may wear a ¼-inch sapphire stripe along the upper edge.

Priest, Emerald Dragon (8th rank): Requirements for this level are determined individually by the senior masters, much as a doctoral committee sets the requirements for each individual Ph.D. candidate. The red sash may bear a ¼-inch emerald stripe along the upper edge.

Priest, Silver Dragon (9th rank): Award of this rank is similar to that of 8th rank with the added stipulation that the 9th rank holder is designated the successor to a particular style within the Temple, and will become a 10th rank upon the stepping down or death of the present 10th rank holder. The red sash bears a ¼-inch silver stripe along its length.

Priest, Gold Dragon (10th rank): This is the terminal rank for a head of a style (also appropriately called a "guardian," style masters were often also abbots) or the founder of a genuine new style. It is awarded upon one of three conditions: 1) the death of a 10th rank automatically promotes the 9th rank designated successor to 10th rank, who then wears a ¼-inch gold stripe along the sash's upper border; 2) a living 10th rank no longer feels able to fulfill his responsibilities and thus "retires," allowing the 9th rank successor to become the active 10th rank (while the retiree becomes the ancestral 10th rank; the new 10th rank wears the ¼-inch gold stripe and the emeritus 10th rank wears a ½-inch white stripe); and 3) a council of masters determines that a new style has been created and acknowledges (but doesn't actually award) the 10th rank status of the creator, who also carries the title "sijo." This last case may choose a non-standard marking to be worn on the red sash.

Priest, (Gold Dragon) 11th rank: Like the U.S. Army rank of general of the Army, this is a "wartime" rank only, used only if *all* of the following conditions exist: a) the Order is sufficiently large to warrant such a rank, b) a person who is master of all Shaolin styles and requisite arts exists, who holds a 10th rank, and who can run the Order, c) the guardian successor sees need and justification to designate an alternate/successor for the Order, and d) the senior masters of the Order (9th ranks and above) concur and confirm the awarding of this rank. Furthermore, should the living guardian successor feel the need to step down for any reason, then the designated successor (who generally would go from 10th to 12th rank: see next paragraph) may become an 11th rank, though this has never yet happened within the Order. The rank (actually its equivalent) has only been awarded three times in history, so there is no currently accepted sash.

Priest, (Gold Dragon) 12th rank: This is the designation of the guardian successor, or single head of the Order. Award of this level is made by the prior guardian successor, who confers with his most senior fellow monks before announcing the successor. Generally, promotion is made from 10th rank to 12th upon the passing of a guardian successor, without an intermediate step to 11th rank. A 12th rank wears his/her 10th rank sash, but may wear any modification of the sash desired. There may be only one living 12th rank in any generation. In earlier times, 12th rank was only invoked when the Order saw a need for it (e.g., the Order was particularly small, there was only one individual with the knowledge necessary for the post, etc.); when the Order was at "full strength," the guardian successor held the 10th rank, just as style masters did. Today, however, Temple protocol has evolved, and the guardian successor is a 12th rank. Finally, recognize that these numbered ranks, and even the more ancient dragon titles, are merely tools. Even the clergy/laity distinction is a tool, with a specific degree of usefulness. We've included this exposition for general interest and completeness, but these things are not essential to the path.

There is, of course, a special set of ranking marks that indicate to the inner circle precisely what the background of a particular monk might be. Just as military uniforms contain badges and ribbons that tell an informed observer a great deal about the training and history of the wearer, so too does Shaolin have special markings used on ceremonial articles. In addition to sashes, abbots wore necklaces of precious stones that functioned as their badges of office.

There are additional sash markings as well. All master-level sashes may bear ¼-inch diagonal silver stripes near each tip to represent time within the Order. Each stripe represents ten years, though at the 50-year mark masters often drop the many small silver stripes and replace them with a 1-inch silver stripe. Additional decade stripes would again be ¼-inch, and placed above the 1-inch stripe. Some ceremonial sashes also bore longitudinal stripes indicating the style in which a wearer had primary mastery (or teaching responsibility). Regardless of the number of styles mastered, only one style stripe was worn, inside (below) the longitudinal rank stripe. These stripes are only worn on gold and red sashes. The colors representative of Shaolin styles include:

Style	Stripe Color Worn on Sash
Black Crane	black
Choy Li Fut	tan
Cobra	emerald
Drunken	orange
Five-Formed Fist	yellow
Five Immortals	white
Leopard	light gray
Lohan	saffron
Northern Dragon	black and brown bars
Northern Praying Mantis	brown
Snake	very dark (Kelly) green
Southern Dragon	emerald
Southern Praying Mantis	medium green
Tibetan or non-Shaolin White Crane	pale blue
Tiger	red
White Crane	white
Wing Chun	pale green

White Eyebrow is studied within the Shaolin Order, but is not honored or recognized with its own color.

To be a Priest or Priestess

What is of all things most yielding can overwhelm
that which is of all things most hard.

Lao Tzu

The Shaolin priest seeks to be as water: impossible to grasp, flowing around and engulfing any object in its path, and conforming to its surroundings. When met by force, the monk yields to it rather than meeting it with force. After all, an attacking force is generally stronger than the entity it attacks. The result is two forces that combine into one larger force that is under the control of the person who yields. By blending his ch'i with that of his foe and yielding, he overwhelms the enemy.

Water in little drops is harmless, but few forces in nature can rival the awesome power of a tidal wave. A monk who can become like water is virtually invulnerable. One cannot grab him; yet when he strikes it is like the onslaught of a wall of water. Looked for, a Shaolin priest was not seen…because he acted just like any other Buddhist monk. Today, in normal contexts, the person in the street has no way of telling a Shaolin priest from anyone else. Felt for, a Shaolin priestess cannot be touched…because she isn't *there* when the strike arrives.

The monks of the Shaolin are peaceful men and women who wish only to be left in peace to pursue their paths to enlightenment, and to help other beings. "What is most full seems empty." This phrase describes the monks of Shaolin. In order to avoid confrontation with those who sought to gain a reputation as great fighters, the Shaolin often put up the façade of being weak and harmless. In this way, the Chinese counterparts of western gunslingers of the nineteenth century would not injure themselves by challenging a monk to ritual combat. If a man could not force a Shaolin to fight, he could not build his esteem by defeating them. The result would be that no one would be hurt.

Shaolin priests and priestesses are people who recognize that martial arts are only one of several means to an end, and are to be employed as a last resort. A Shaolin priest is first and foremost a teacher with a broad background including academic and practical disciplines. Masters of our Order have included agriculturists, gemologists, zoologists, teachers, economists, engineers, philosophers, writers, botanists, entrepreneurs, doctors, intelligence operatives, and chemists—to name just a few livelihoods. Even five hundred years ago, Shaolin monks did not sit around meditating all day. Our brand of Ch'an places considerable emphasis upon the balanced development of the entire individual. And our priests' greatest duty is to act as guides for others who seek this holistic path.

Chapter Six

Shaolin Instructors and Public Perception

When the student is ready, the teacher will appear.

There will always be interest in learning the Shaolin arts. This is because the arts are often considered mysterious, highly spiritual, and impressive, and because achieving the status of a Shaolin is thought of by many people as an elite achievement. There is also considerable truth to these assumptions, though mastery of the arts will require the practitioner to abandon any possession of pride or elitism, as taught by the Buddha. Desire to walk this path is not easy to fulfill, in no small part because there are very few true Shaolin masters from whom you may study. There are so many myths flying about that a Shaolin master is "like this" or "does that" that we offer here an explanation of what you should expect when seeking a genuine instructor. Students beware, though, as many con artists can present a most convincing front; sadly, this is a widespread problem in the martial arts.[101]

In the guidelines that follow, we frequently urge the potential student to "avoid" this or that kind of school or instructor. By this, we explicitly mean that such a school is not traditional Shaolin, and that if it is your intention—as indicated by the title of this chapter—to find a Shaolin instructor, then you must look elsewhere. If, however, you seek tournament experience, or wish to learn something different, then these alternatives might be more appropriate. There are many excellent non-Shaolin martial arts and martial artists; we are only warning the student against being conned into buying something that is not actually being offered. These guidelines are meant to help the student who is looking for a sifu deeply rooted in Shaolin's spiritual, as well as martial, heritage.

Guideline One: avoid a teacher who is loudly proclaiming to the world that he is Shaolin.

A Shaolin master is not typically going to be wearing traditional saffron robes to the grocery store. By leaving the temples and China, part of the new role of a monk is to blend into his or her new surroundings, and that means wearing the normal attire of the region. This does not mean that our monks have abandoned their vows, but they avoid the robes that would advertise their presence (we do not wear monastic attire in public). It is not important that the world know who we are; rather, it is important that we survive to pass our arts and philosophies to the next generation.

Guideline Two: avoid sport and tournament based classes.

If you find a source that calls itself Shaolin, go visit a class. Shaolin does teach forms, but our focus is split between meditation and self-defense. A room displaying many trophies is a room that is loudly telling you it is not an authentic Shaolin *kwoon*. Part of gung fu power comes from keeping techniques secret, so we would not display them at a tournament, nor learn to fight using the very artificial rules of sport. Shaolin practitioners **may** perform formwork in exhibitions, but this will never be a major focus of training.

Guideline Three: expect compassionate, Buddhist-style teaching in a friendly and comfortable atmosphere.

Shaolin classes are about teaching moving meditation via gung fu. In watching a class, true Shaolin will not start with calisthenics, "shock aerobics," or ballistic stretching; for the formwork provides plenty of warm up, stretching, and conditioning. Teachers will not treat students like recruits in boot camp, and will not yell or demand push-ups as punishment for minor infractions. Classes will be run more like meditation sessions or even games, using positive reinforcement and gentle encouragement in place of shouting and bullying.

Guideline Four: a smorgasbord is fine in a Swedish restaurant, but not in a Shaolin school.

Do not expect a Shaolin instructor to be advertising a host of martial arts as if they were column choices from a Chinese menu. Avoid schools with signs listing "Karate, Kung Fu, Tae Kwon Do," or something similar. These instructors use familiar names to lure students into taking classes in the one art they teach, which is rarely even Chinese in origin. We have seen many storefront schools capitalizing on the fame of "kung fu" because of the television program by that name. Such stores advertise "Kung Fu Karate," an insult to Chinese and Okinawan martial artists, and to the prospective students who, before their first lesson, are already being cheated by the unknowing. Choose your sifu carefully!

> ### Guideline Five: carefully assess the "what and where" of what you will be paying for.

Wherever possible, check on background. A martial arts school in a Chinatown is more likely to be authentic (or used to be), but many non-Chinese schools, knowing this, have set up shop in Chinatowns. Often, classes are held in parks, community centers, or even in the instructor's home. A Chinese (style, not ethnicity) martial artist is unlikely to have signs on the window proclaiming they teach "Karate, kick-boxing," and a host of other arts. Lesson fees, unless for private one-on-one sessions, are not expensive.

> ### Guideline Six: any instructor selling himself as teaching Shaolin "warrior" arts or emphasizing "warrior" aspects is not teaching more than a tiny part of Shaolin.

We are scholar-teacher-monks, not warriors, and anyone advertising otherwise is not offering an authentic Shaolin curriculum. In fact, though many Shaolin arts left the Temple to become warrior arts, no genuine Shaolin practitioner would want to be associated with the term "warrior," so such word usage is a good guideline to watch out for. (Recall right speech!)

> ### Guideline Seven: if the instructor seems too concerned with his or her rank, and especially your awareness of that rank, you may want to look elsewhere.

Shaolin masters are Buddhists first and martial artists second or third. They are therefore generally humble folk who have conquered their egos and will not use or expect someone from outside their school to call them anything but "Sifu" or "Teacher." They neither need nor desire public acclaim, and are only addressed as "Master" or "Grandmaster" by students of their own school or style.

> One who brags about himself gets no credit;
> One who praises himself does not long endure...
> These things do not bring happiness.
> Therefore followers of the Way avoid them.
>
> *Lao Tzu*

Guideline Eight: a Shaolin master will not do a demonstration for you, nor let you watch his or her practice time.

Perhaps most important, and most difficult for western consumer-based students to understand, is that a Shaolin master's job as a teacher is to teach and as a student you must, after an appropriate time, judge if what you are learning is worthwhile. To expect a sifu to "show you something" is seen as a sign of great disrespect. Just as many great coaches were modest players, many great masters are no longer great performers. Besides, as a matter of traditional protocol, the teacher evaluates students and not vice versa. Likewise, a Shaolin teacher will not boast about her lineage, and may not even share such information with beginners.

It is useful to understand what we consider good teaching (and good sifus) to be. Participate in a few classes, judge the usefulness of the material to your needs, and then choose your school. Iyengar, in discussing the traditional Asian master-student relationship, provides a description of a guru which is equally applicable to that of a Shaolin sifu:

> The guru does not enforce discipline with strictness, but builds an awareness of it in his student, allowing the latter to build an inner discipline. A wise guru does not lay down codes of conduct, but motivates the disciple by precept and example.
>
> The guru does not demand attention, he commands it. In the process of teaching, he creates total confidence in his disciple, and helps him or her develop the will power to face all circumstances with equanimity. The guru constantly improves on his teaching techniques, opening the disciple's eyes, improvising where necessary to create new dimensions in his teaching. The guru is compassionate, but does not expect emotional attachment from his disciple, nor does he become emotionally attached himself.
>
> The guru should be confident, challenging, caring, cautious, constructive, and courageous. The clarity and creativity of his teaching should reflect his devotion and dedication to his student…[102]

Iyengar offers such a concise and powerful description of the spiritual teacher—we suspect that it applies just as well to spiritual teachers from many other religious traditions. Along the same lines, but pitched especially to the martial arts, is Lee's excellent description:

A teacher, a really good teacher, functions as a pointer to truth, but not a giver of truth. He employs a minimum of form to lead his student to the formless...being able to enter a mold but not being caged in it...Above all, a teacher...studies each individual student and awakens him to explore himself, both internally and externally, and ultimately to integrate himself with his being. Such teaching, which is really no teaching, requires a sensitive mind with great flexibility and adaptability, and it is difficult to come by nowadays.[103]

Shaolin uses martial arts to promote a spiritual journey of discovery within each practitioner. When choosing a teacher, set and maintain high expectations, and consider yourself fortunate if you find a gung fu teacher who fits the mold described by Iyengar or Lee.

Particularly salient to Shaolin instruction are the roles played by the animals themselves, given that Shaolin places so much emphasis on the study of nature. There are many reasons for the study of so many animals and their defenses, but the central reason is that each creature offers something of interest or value to different people. A person might study T'ai Mantis because of its high *stances*, unusual sweeps, or its vague similarity to the predatory insect. Similarly, it is hard to think of oneself as a 98-pound weakling if you are also adept at Tiger gung fu. The mental associations between creature and practitioner must not be dismissed.

But on another level we must acknowledge that each style offers different approaches to combat and defense, methods that appeal more to one personality or body type than another. True, a short, stocky person can learn White Crane, but is also less likely to benefit from that style's peculiarities than would a leaner and longer-limbed practitioner. By studying nature's variety, Shaolin methods provide a great range of techniques and tactics to a wide variety of human body types. By the same token, personality types will influence how and how well a person may perform a particular style. A retiring soul will not be comfortable with the aggressive nature of Tiger, nor an introvert with the dramatic and theatrical Monkey. A good instructor finds time to study a student in order to match appropriate animal techniques to the body *and* spirit of the student.

Though a few contemporary practitioners of Buddhism and many martial arts instructors claim lineage to authentic Shaolin roots, consider the foundations Tamo laid for the Order before accepting the very "orthodox" Buddhist practices of many monks. (As well, many schools of gung fu teach nothing of the eightfold path while loudly proclaiming "Shaolin" heritage.) Tamo's face was not clean-shaven, nor did he shave his head. In fact, many contemporaries considered him a rogue because of his appearance, but he knew that Buddha was not concerned about appearances. One's appearance, he observed, does not enhance enlightenment. He also eschewed the traditional saffron colored robes of most Buddhists, wearing blue or gray. By the standards of his time, he was not wearing clerical but contemporary lay garb. He also ate meat and practiced unconventional forms of meditation. In Tamo's message lay his cornerstone teaching legacy: the path to enlightenment lay not in ritual, appearance, or blind following of a doctrine, but in the careful cultivation of practices that relieve one of the ego and transcend the illusory perceptions of the world. This path was difficult for most people to understand—especially in a highly regimented society such as Confucian China—for which reason Shaolin always remained among the smallest and most controversial of Buddhist sects. (Consider that at many points in Chinese history, tens of thousands of Buddhist temples operated throughout that land, and their clergy numbered in the millions.[98] Shaolin only ever had a few temples.)

On the other hand, just because a particular instructor is not Shaolin does *not* mean that they have little or nothing to offer! There are so many martial arts styles and schools precisely because people are different, and what appeals to one may not matter to another. The caveats here are not about disparaging non-Shaolin instructors—far from it! Many highly dedicated and proficient martial artists abound in a variety of schools and styles, and a student would learn valuable lessons from these sources. Just as an Australian soldier once wrote "all officers are gentlemen, but not all gentlemen are officers," we might paraphrase this sentiment as "all Shaolin are martial artists, but not all martial artists are Shaolin."

Also keep in mind that most martial traditions coming from Shaolin dispensed with Shaolin's particular Buddhism. There are many excellent teachers of Shaolin arts who are not Shaolin monks! In fact, this describes the vast majority of good sifus out there. Part of our motivation for publishing this text is to make the Shaolin Ch'an *philosophy* available to those who are studying Shaolin-rooted martial arts, but who also wish access to the Buddhism of our order.

Finally, if you wish to pursue an alternative martial arts environment for whatever reason (after all, there are very few authentic Shaolin instructors around, and not all are easily located), keep in mind your goals as to why you want lessons, what you hope to accomplish, and also what you expect from a school. Without clear goals, you are unlikely to find a match with which you will be happy. (Chow offers sound advice in the "Personal Philosophy" section of his book on how to become a proficient practitioner while also revealing some of the hallmarks of a good teacher.[104]) Studying martial arts is a multi-year commitment, so you want to start in an environment and with a teacher that you can see yourself still being happy with in ten or twenty years.

> The Way of Heaven has no favorites,
> It's always with the good man.
>
> *Lao Tzu*

A Haunting Question

Caveat Emptor.

"Is it still possible to study the Shaolin arts under a genuine priest at the Shaolin Temple in China?" This is a question we expect will be asked with increasing frequency in the coming years. We shall attempt to provide some answers without being polemical; however, there will always be those who take offense at any assertion at odds with their own beliefs. Our intent with this book is to present an accurate portrayal of our tradition which does not mislead the spiritual seeker. This is a challenging task given the volume of Shaolin misinformation in print.

Unfortunately, the Shaolin temples were all destroyed by 1931. Much later, the Chinese government decided to begin refurbishing the Temple at Honan. While martial arts are studied in the vicinity of Song Shan today, this is a recent re-emergence into the arts. Members of our order who have visited the Honan Temple in 1985, 1988, 1998, 2000, and 2004 report that what is taught is mostly Wushu and T'ai Chi Ch'uan.

"Wushu," in the sense employed here, is not meant to refer to martial arts, but rather Modern, or Contemporary, Wushu. This Wushu was created as a sport in the 1950s, based on Long Fist and a few other styles, to emphasize athleticism and "fighting spirit." It was expressly *not* designed for self-defense or combat, as per the requirements of Chairman Mao. The Chinese State Physical Culture and Sports Commission drew up the first set of Wushu competition rules in 1958. And since the early 1980s, Modern Wushu has been heavily promoted by the PRC. Some colleges in China currently award masters and doctoral degrees in Wushu. In an effort to break the master-apprentice relationship customary in gung fu training, Wushu instructors are now called "coaches" and certified by the government. (The master-apprentice relationship, especially in spiritual contexts, threatens any system of government that requires that a citizen's first and highest loyalty be to the state.)

The Chinese government has pursued a relentless and international public relations campaign to promote Wushu, to the point of drowning out the history of traditional gung fu. The People's Republic has good reason for obfuscating or simply remaining silent regarding the history of traditional gung fu. First, martial history is closely tied to Buddhist and Taoist traditions. Second, almost all successful revolutions in China have taken place with the aid of the empire's martial artists, unified behind the overthrow.[105] The communist government has always been concerned about putting too much power in the hands of the people. Hence, within the PRC, martial arts have been largely replaced with performance arts.

We have only admiration for Modern Wushu as a sport and performing art, and think it's an excellent means of exercise for young people. The Song Shan region attracts many young people, most coming from within China, to study Wushu. During the 1990s, especially, worldwide popularity has made Wushu training a viable career path for young Chinese. It is sad, however, that the PRC covers up the history and rich wealth of Shaolin arts and philosophy by claiming that this new Wushu is Shaolin. Chow and Spangler comment on the replacement of traditional gung fu with Modern Wushu, accurately capturing the feeling of many "old monks" in our sect:

> The old monks would have been deeply saddened by the extremes to which their honored art has been taken. They would have been very distressed that their Kung Fu "way of life" was being drained of its philosophical essence, emptied of its "emotional content," and was being used strictly for physical "sport" development in their homeland.[106]

Even the Smithsonian has partaken in this covering up and rewriting of history, claiming that the Wushu schools near the location of the Honan Temple teach the "kung fu techniques practiced by the ancient Buddhist order of monks that have lived here...for 1500 years."[107] These schools confusingly call their forms by names such as "Dragon," "Eagle," and "Praying Mantis." The Smithsonian magazine further reports that boys at these schools endure a "punishing training that leaves muscles bruised and joints sore. Yet even peasants pay a king's ransom of $20 a month so their children can become policemen, soldiers or even movie stars."[108]

"Shaolin monks" at today's temples do not practice the Shaolin tradition we are familiar with—some observers state that they are all government employees.[109] There is a burgeoning tourist/pilgrimage business, and just outside the main gates you can refresh yourself with dim sum and Shaolin Cola. Our contacts who have visited the Temple beginning in 1985 believe it is more a trendy tourist spot than a real effort to restore the arts and the Buddhism outlawed by successive Chinese governments from 1901 up to the present. The tourism business must be booming, since three more "Shaolin Temples" have recently been built. Fukien Province now boasts Shaolin Temples at Putian, Fuqing, and Quanzhou (this last site likely never served as a Shaolin temple). In 1991, the Honan Temple even sent a delegation of martial monks to the Putian site to teach their brand of martial art to the Putian staff.[110] Finally, regarding the debate about the location of the "true" Southern Shaolin Temple: over the centuries more than one site has served as the southern headquarters. In fact, at various times, dozens of different temples fell under the Shaolin umbrella.

Jon Funk, a well-known and highly adept practitioner of Northern Praying Mantis, has written a controversial article entitled "The Shaolin Temple Hoax."[111] Because there are so many questions about "the return of Shaolin Masters" to the tourist-dedicated, refurbished Honan Temple, we feel obliged to publicize his laudatory effort. (Many other practitioners have noticed the truth about the "restored Shaolin Temple," but Funk's article probably had the most impact.) Funk is spot-on about the complete absence of anything even remotely akin to imperial era Shaolin arts being taught at the Honan Temple today. None of the traditional Shaolin styles are taught there, not to mention the apparent absence of Ch'an Buddhism (although this is hopefully changing). As a part of the Wushu movement, the PRC has taken a myriad of southern styles such as Hung Gar and Choy Li Fut, with their focus on infighting and low stances, and turned them into a single, generic conglomeration called "Nan Ch'uan," or "Southern Fist." Some people now seem to maintain that versions of "Southern Fist" and Long Fist predate the founding of Honan's Song Shan Shaolin Temple in the 6th century.[112] Were this true, it would lend credence to the PRC's strange claim that the current martial mélange practiced at the Honan Temple is authentic Shaolin Chinese boxing. Yet it is a doubtful hypothesis that versions of *any* of today's styles actually existed in recognizable form prior to the 6th century. (Snake *might* have existed this early, yet we are skeptical that even this ancient style predated the founding of the Shaolin Order in a recognizable form.)

Because so many people believe that the Honan Temple is now offering traditional Shaolin arts and Buddhism we quote a short, but important, part of Master Funk's article:

> The Chinese government, it should be remembered, is communist, and doesn't want a religious group generating any ideas that don't conform to the party line.

Consider, for example, the intensity of the Chinese government's efforts to outlaw and punish participants in the recent Falun Gong movement (not to mention what has occurred in Tibet). So far as we can tell, Right Speech is permitted by Chinese authorities just so long as that speech isn't critical of those authorities. The PRC has attempted to recreate the "Shaolin master;" yet their new version is based on Wushu showmanship and notions of Buddhism borrowed from *other* Chinese Ch'an sects, which vary significantly from Shaolin. Common misconceptions abound. We occasionally hear that genuine Shaolin monks: cannot be women, cannot eat meat, cannot marry, must have a shaven head, and must *always* wear red and yellow robes. Imagine our surprise.

There is always going to be a (large) gullible audience for "too-good-to-be-true" claimants. A variety of independent sources have now corroborated our assessment of current activities at the Honan Temple. Prominent martial artists in various forums have also noted that the re-emerged "Shaolin warrior monks" are not practicing the traditional arts, some pointing out that these reopened temples are populated with actors, not priests.[113] (An important note: some of the martial arts practiced at Shaolin today *do* indeed appear descended from traditional village arts, just not traditional *Shaolin* arts.) It is a sad commentary on the state of the international martial arts community that numerous teachers are flocking to loudly affiliate themselves with the PRC-endorsed Shaolin monks at Honan. However, some people may be genuinely interested in the Modern Wushu, Long Fist variants, and newly created arts practiced there.

We do wish to clarify that those people living on the actual Temple grounds may be sincere Buddhists, as well as very outstanding martial artists. We are in no position to judge those things. We are in a good position, however, to assess whether the martial and spiritual training bears any resemblance to the pre-1900 Shaolin tradition as it has been transmitted through our sect. Students may find good training opportunities at today's Temple, although that seems unlikely given the cultural and economic purposes our once venerable grounds have been put to. Real training opportunities are more likely found in nearby schools.

Since non-attachment lies near the core of our Buddhism, we feel, not outrage, but a certain amusement regarding the current affairs of the Honan Temple (especially with respect to recent attempts to somehow trademark the word "Shaolin"). Although the heart of our particular branch of Buddhism appears to have vanished from mainland China, the spirit of Shaolin philosophy survives in the hearts of human beings, and not in any worldly place. The Honan Temple *was* a Shaolin Buddhist religious site that now stands as a shrine to other things. There is a constant stream of customers to Song Shan—and a smaller stream of martial artists who wish to be somehow "certified" by the government-appointed "Shaolin abbot."

The Chinese government believes that the mere presence of martial arts instructors at the Honan Temple makes the Temple authentic. The same government was also responsible for the "removal" of the Dalai Lama's choice for the reincarnated Panchen Lama, substituting their own child in the role. Yang remarks that, in the late 1980s, the PRC actually attempted to search out and revive some of the Chinese martial traditions with a special committee, but that so many traditional masters had been executed during the Cultural Revolution, and that most living masters did not trust the communists' intentions.[114] These were civilian masters. Where did this onslaught of young "Shaolin monks" in China come from?

We believe that today's Shaolin tradition in the PRC traces back to Shaolin students and disciples who returned to the Temple grounds after the temples were evacuated. These people could very well have been Shaolin Buddhist monks, in a technical sense. Yet the loss of vast amounts of Shaolin knowledge in the PRC indicates that the last of Shaolin's priests either fled the country or were killed during the civil strife of 1900-1931. (This was also directly related by three Shaolin abbots.) We do not point this out in a spirit of competition, nor out of meanness. Our philosophy is rooted in cooperation, and we have no wish to damage tourism in China, an industry which provides crucial material support to many people. Our goal is to preserve our particular Buddhist tradition for those present and future beings it is meant to serve—against a propagandism which obscures the message, historical methods, and intent of Shaolin Ch'an Buddhism.

Shaolin Performing for Money?

Just as yellow leaves may be gold coins to stop the crying children, thus,
the so-called secret moves and contorted postures
appease the unknowledgeable martial artists.

Bruce Lee

The ascendance of the Honan Temple in the 1990s has given rise to traveling "Shaolin" stage acts which purportedly showcase amazing *Ch'i Kung* skills. The first of these tours, staffed by monks from the Honan Temple, came to the United States in 1992. That tour was very simple, compared to more recent tours, and simply demonstrated a series of forms and Ch'i Kung feats. More recent tours are equal parts martial arts, gymnastic flamboyance, and Broadway show. The common thread running through all of these shows is that the supposedly genuine feats of internal strength are, in fact, magic tricks. Leung Ting, with the help of Cheng Kai Ming, superbly documents how these tricks are performed in *Skills of the Vagabonds II: Behind the Incredibles....*[115] From the preface of that manual:

> ...more and more martial art or chi-kung instructors are staging performances of miraculous feats and using them for promotion...This is a very damaging "education", because these people are obviously trying to mislead others (including their own students) to believe that they have "super powers". Unfortunately, these so called martial artists or chi-kung experts and their so called "Incredible martial art/chi-kung demonstrations" have nothing what so ever to do with [r]eal martial arts or chi-kung. For them, "martial arts" or "chi-kung" is just a cover—[j]ust like magicians who use wands, top-hats and cheese-cloths. They serve, only, to distract watching eyes while the magician's deft hands go into action.[116]

Perhaps you've seen someone bend iron re-bar with his throat? Or extinguish a candle flame from ten feet? Or use a sword to slice through a melon resting on someone's stomach without injuring the human melon-stand? Or take hard blows across the belly, arms, or back? Or lay on a bed of knives? Or break concrete blocks on someone's head? Or be driven over with a car? All these supposed Ch'i Kung feats are elaborate magic tricks. We don't mean to denigrate these tricks. Performing them correctly requires a tremendous amount of training and skill, and can be quite dangerous if not done properly. Magic is an amazing and respected trade; consider the fame and accolades heaped on Houdini. But these touring shows hypocritically pass off their magic tricks as genuine Ch'i Kung, and they are nothing of the sort. (We discuss basic Ch'i Kung later in the text.)

Because western audiences are unfamiliar with these tricks, and because of the way these shows are advertised, people are being duped in large numbers. The fact that these shows are advertised as "Shaolin" misinforms an ignorant public about what Shaolin really is. As Buddhists focused on our own individual paths, we have no interest in putting on shows to wow audiences. We eschew demonstrating *genuine* supernormal skills (as well as magic masquerading as Ch'i Kung) because we believe this behavior to be detrimental to the spiritual development of those in our sect, as explained by the Buddha in the *Kevatta Sutra* and elsewhere. A Shaolin monk does not "wail and flail to make a sale." This perspective is not shared by the Shaolin tradition which appeared with the PRC-sponsored refurbishing of the Honan Temple.

Leung Ting points out, "Stupidity has no limits." Well, perhaps it is not stupidity outright, but rather that—as P. T. Barnum once noted—people *like* to be humbugged. If you should ever happen to attend one of these performances, recognize it as a fantastic deception and enjoy it for what it is. But do not mistake the artistry you witness as having anything to do with a *martial* art or with the cultivation of genuine internal power. (Something is *intentionally* amiss with the photograph below. See if you can figure out what it is.)

People like to be humbugged.

P. T. Barnum

Part 2:
The Martial Arts of Shaolin

Control is the mark of a superior man or woman. As one learns more about self-defense, one has a greater repertoire and the training needed to control rather than hurt; hurt rather than maim; maim rather than kill. Involvement in a *martial* art is something of a sacred trust. Your skills should never be used lightly, never be misused to frighten, and never be employed because you "lost control." Loss of self-control is a defeat much worse than merely taking a beating, for in such an action you betray your art, your teachers, and yourself.

a Shaolin monk

Chapter Seven

Gung Fu

One may conquer in battle a thousand times a thousand men,
Yet he is the best of conquerors who conquers himself.

Shakyamuni Buddha

China is a country of much greatness. It is a large country, with a large human population, the largest architectural structure, and the largest variety of martial arts. These martial arts range from the intellectual exercises of scholars…to the military strategies of generals…to the plundering tactics of warlords…to the unarmed combat we call "gung fu" today. Few people already familiar with the term "Shaolin" are unaware of the Order's intimate association with contemporary martial arts. Many schools of Asian martial arts claim some association with the famous temples and their arts.

"Gung fu" means hard work, or skilled effort, and was originally used in reference to the grueling years of practice that were necessary to achieve mastery of a style. Over the years, Chinese martial arts have been known as *ch'uan fa* (fist arts), *kuoshu* (pronounced "gwo-shoo", it means "national arts"), Chung-kuo ch'uan (Chinese boxing), wu kung (effective use of martial force), ch'uan shu (fist arts), and wushu (fighting arts), the latter made popular during China's ascending Communist Period (1949-1971). It is true that one can be a gung fu chef, gung fu painter, even a gung fu gardener. In Shaolin etiquette, therefore, we tend to link the style and the term gung fu as a single entity, as in Tiger gung fu or Wing Chun gung fu.

There can be little doubt, after examining firsthand the structure of gung fu, that mastery of it is indeed mastery of a fine art form. It requires a tremendous amount of background, in the way of both tacit and demonstrated skills, which would shame our liberal-arts students. The

133

priests of old were adept in: medicine, music, art, weapon-craft, religions, animal husbandry, cartography, languages, history, and of course, gung fu. The artist had to be more than a fighting machine, he had to know how, where and why to enter a fight, and even of greater importance, how to avoid conflict. Only with the "unbeatable" ability of the priest was one secure enough not to need to fight.

The power of the gung fu practitioner lay in his ability to defend himself against seemingly impossible odds and situations—be they physical or mental in nature. After years of diligent practice, Shaolin monks became more than merely adept at the ways of survival. But the initial acceptance to be one of the chosen few was difficult. After all, knowledge, once imparted, cannot be recalled.

As youngsters, the applicants for priesthood were made to do the most menial and difficult work related to the upkeep of their temple. Their sincerity and ability to keep the secrets of the Order were severely tested for years before the finer aspects of the arts were revealed to them. But, upon being accepted by the elders of the Temple, entry into gung fu practice was to open fantastic new vistas. Students would work long hours training mind and body to work together in a coordinated effort. They would learn the principles of combat, the way of the Tao, and the Buddhist lessons, and together these teachings would ensure the student's way to peace.

Within the Temple, priority was given to training in unarmed gung fu. In principle, any weapon can be taken from a practitioner and used against him. Superior knowledge of unarmed combat includes extensive training in disarming opponents. For this reason, the forms of Shaolin are generally referred to as kuen or "fist sets." During the first six months to one year of gung fu, a student would only learn the wide horse stance. The stance training not only strengthened their legs, but encouraged concentration and perseverance, absolute essentials before martial arts techniques would be taught. Students who failed to master the stance, or cut corners on training were dismissed from the Temple, for it is a Shaolin belief that "all strength starts with a solid foundation."

The next phase involved learning basics of eye and hand coordination. Under the supervision of a disciple, students would learn to make and throw a proper straight fist. Shortly thereafter, students would be given access to a set of three stout bamboo poles, on which were padded targets. One was just above eye height (from a horse stance), one at face height, and one at abdomen level. The disciple would call out "high, low, low, high," for example, and the student had to quickly punch the appropriate pads as quickly as she could. This training would also last about six months, and would be supplemented with learning additional stances, basic stance walking, and a few simple *blocks*. Only after these basics were well ingrained could a student begin working on the first kuen.

The choice of when a form would be taught, which form would be taught, and which version would be taught would be the supervising master's alone. After evaluating the student and conferring with teaching disciples, the master would either offer a general form or, for more gifted pupils, a basic form in one of the styles. General forms came from simple Choy Li Fut, Black Crane, the generic Five-Formed Fist sets, or a non-Temple style. The goal in teaching a general form was to give a student additional material with further subtleties of movement and combinations so that a further evaluation would be possible. Some students would never move into one of the elite styles, and though they would continue to train in gung fu, would not typically be considered candidates for eventual master's rank. Some were encouraged to join other orders.

Three types of Chinese forms are taught to students: drill type, simulated combat, and encyclopedic. Drill forms are much like calisthenics, exercises to strengthen the body, improve coordination, and teach basic techniques. Simulated combat forms train the practitioner to respond to opponents without thinking while drawing on an increasing variety of techniques. Contrary to popular belief, these forms are not taught as preparation for actual combat (in which an opponent is an unpredictable variable) but as ways to increase speed and transition from one technique to another. The drills increase speed and coordination skills needed in combat, and so remain a part of Shaolin practice. Encyclopedic forms usually begin on the left side and do the same moves to both sides, acting as an encyclopedia of movements. The latter two types are at the same level of difficulty. Of all forms, soft sets were generally practiced in the morning and hard sets in the evening.

Forms normally have three levels or versions. The basic level, taught with moves that may be extremely general (you can learn a straight fist or snap kick from many sources) or merely difficult (to serve as a training tool); an intermediate level, in which more of the true meaning and subtlety of the moves is revealed; and the advanced version, which the masters themselves practice. Often kicks are eliminated or kept low in the advanced versions. In part, this acknowledges that some effect of aging might reduce the mobility of an elderly practitioner, a concept embodied in an old Shaolin saying: "Don't practice now that which you will not be able to do better when you are eighty."

Upon completion of the student stage, the practitioner became a disciple, who would be taught the higher secrets of the arts and philosophies. Use of weapons of all descriptions would be taught as weapons of attack and defense. The monk would perfect his movements to coincide with his breathing. Lessons aimed to meld the mind with the realm of meditation known as mindlessness. From this training students would learn to harness their ch'i.

Ch'i is a concept of such magnitude, so alien to many western minds that we shall deal with it throughout this text in many different lights. For now, suffice it to say that ch'i is the power governing life. Only by harnessing such energy can a person of mild stature learn to break bricks with their bare hands, or learn to sense the movements of an opponent in the darkness.

Essential to movements in gung fu are ch'i-controlled actions. The essence of ch'i-controlled action may be illustrated by comparing a karateka with a gung fu stylist. The karate movements are principally linear, hard, and distinct from each other, while gung fu moves often follow circular paths, look soft and graceful, and blend subtly into each other. Gung fu techniques have few clearly distinct "start" and "stop" points. The two broad approaches are as different as a sledge hammer and a bullwhip.

Ch'i, properly coordinated, allows for fluidity. Consider a single drop of water. Alone, it is harmless, gentle, and powerless. But what on earth can withstand the force of a tsunami? The concept of ch'i is the same. By tapping into the universal energies, one increases one's abilities manifold. How can an opponent damage a gung fu practitioner when he is unable to strike and injure a body of water?

Therefore, we come full circle. The principles guiding the practitioner have become carefully guarded secrets, which even today cannot be bartered for with mere money. One must want to learn, and above all have the wisdom and attitude to control the tremendous power that control of ch'i confers.

The Illusion of Martial Dualism

Deluded people do not understand and through false thought see maleness or femaleness, but this is an illusory maleness and an illusory femaleness, ultimately without reality.

Tamo

The concepts of hard/soft and external/internal are not easily described. In terms of styles with which most people are familiar, Karate would be an example of a hard style and Aikido or T'ai Chi Ch'uan examples of soft styles. A hard style is generally considered one where force is used against force; a block is used to deflect an incoming strike by meeting it either head on or at a 90-degree angle. A soft style does not use force against force, but rather deflects the incoming blow away from its target. There are uses for both hard and soft techniques. A practitioner may wish to break the attacker's striking arm with the block. On the other hand, a much smaller opponent would not be able to accomplish this, so instead may wish to deflect the incoming attack.

An external style is one that relies primarily on strength and physical abilities to defeat an opponent. In contrast, an internal style is one that depends upon ch'i and timing rather than power. Aikido (at the master's level) would be an internal style,[118] while most Karate systems are external.

However, the concepts of hard/soft and internal/external are finding fewer proponents among senior martial artists. Both conceptual twins are impossible to separate in reality, and masters will generally acknowledge that any distinction is largely only a matter of subjective interpretation. Novices and philosophical dilettantes, ignorant of the inseparable nature of opposites, often wage arguments about the reality of the concepts. They see yin and yang as elements that can exist independently, while philosophical and physical reasoning demonstrate that they cannot. Without their union (Tao), neither can exist. Ergo, a "hard" technique such as a straight fist is guided by the soft power of mind and the internal component of ch'i. Equally, the softest projection of Aikido requires the "hard" element of physical contact and movement, coupled with actively redirecting the opponent. In short, preoccupation with distinguishing soft from hard and internal from external is a distraction from learning martial arts and moving towards a unifying technique and mastery.

"Robert's Rules" of Combat

Many of Shaolin's lessons are aimed at practical matters, as is the following philosophy of self-defense. While there is no doubt that the likelihood of any particular person getting attacked by another is statistically small, our modern society is seeing that percentage rise annually. In practicing self-defense, consider four rules put forth by an imaginary sifu, let's call him "Robert," which should be in a practitioner's mind when working on self-defense drills. These gung fu equivalents to "Robert's Rules of Order" are:

An assailant is physically stronger than his intended victim.

It is a rare thing to be assaulted by a significantly smaller or weaker person, though an armed opponent uses the weapon to make up the size and power differential. Practice your skills as if your attacker was going to be the Incredible Hulk. Face reality—short, skinny attackers don't ambush linebackers. In the (highly unusual) case of someone trying to commit suicide by picking on a bigger person (only on television), the aggressor will be sure to attack someone he at least feels superior to. Recall here periodic press coverage of the "victim mentality" which includes rodent-like posture and movement, clutching a purse for dear life, and quick, worried glances. Fear can reduce your strength in many ways, and actually turn a physically superior person into a weak victim.

The way of least resistance is easiest, fastest and most direct.

Keep your practical self-defense techniques simple, direct, and—obviously—practical. Complicated moves tend to be slower and less devastating than simple ones. If your opponent is stronger than you, you must rely on ease of technique rather than strength. You must complement his motion to borrow his attacking force, and you must make your first strike count.

Murphy's Law must always be considered a reality.

If anything can go wrong, it will tend to do so, and at the most inopportune time. Practice your skills with a "Plan B" for every technique. You never know when you may slip on dog doo or ice, or have to dodge a car on the street, or even be hit by your opponent. Be prepared for something to go wrong and know how to recover. You might be one of the top ten martial artists in the world but the opponent might be in the top five. Your footwork and balance are perfect in the kwoon but that dog litter in the street may ruin your balance. You can outrun your assailant and lock yourself in your car…but not if you can't find your keys. It may be the case that, right now, *you* are locked *out* of your car. Assume that Murphy is real and knows where you live; respect Murphy as if your life may depend on it!

Simple things are hard to learn because we seek to find the "magic" which makes them simple.

It may be hard to believe, but because of the phenomenal mystique of martial arts, many people fail to see a simple technique for what it is. Instead, they seek magic or "oriental mystery" in place of logic. Remember that a punch is really just a punch. In our ever more technical society, we often mistakenly equate "simple" with "horse and buggy." In the few seconds that span a life or death encounter, you must be fast, and that means you must keep your response simple. Don't worry about stance, shifting, hand formation, chambering; just sight your target and shoot, period. Accept the simple as simple for that reason. Don't look for hidden micro-maneuvers in every technique or you'll never master any of them.

The secret principle of martial arts is not vanquishing the attacker
but resolving to avoid an encounter before its occurence.

Funakoshi Gichin

Fundamental Techniques

Stances: The Foundation of Gung Fu

It is increasingly fashionable to teach novices forms and combat techniques from their first days in class. However, the traditional approach to teaching was based more on the idea of moral and ethical development than the need for an instructor's salary. In the Shaolin temples, a student would only commence gung fu training after a probationary period that allowed instructors and disciples to evaluate the character of the student. The next phase involved teaching the bedrock foundation of martial arts—proper stance work. The novice would be introduced to the classical *horse stance*, in which he or she would be expected to stand for at least thirty minutes each day.

A proper stance will develop leg and lower back strength, improve posture, and provide a solid yet mobile platform for the martial artist. Avoid the major pitfalls: arching the back, sloping shoulders, allowing your heel to leave the ground when inappropriate, and failing to bend the knees enough. An ancient rule of thumb remains true today: if you are a novice and your stance isn't painful, you are almost certainly doing it incorrectly! A proper stance has you stand with your back and head straight and in vertebral alignment, with legs bent and supporting your weight gracefully. The feet are in proper position. You breathe in and out through your nose, and you relax your shoulders so your breath is not forcing your ch'i and balance center upward.

To perform a classical *horse stance*, or *ma bo*, spread your feet so they are shoulder width apart. Your feet should be parallel to each other, toes pointing straight ahead. Now bend the knees until you are almost in a sitting position. DO NOT allow your feet to shift position. This is *horse stance* version one.

Doing a very similar stance, but with your feet twice your shoulder width apart, the knees should bend until your thighs are parallel to the floor. This is the *deep horse stance*, or horse stance version two. For most of the history of the Temple, a student would train in nothing but the *horse stances* for six months. This would develop incredibly strong legs, focus attention on overcoming discomfort, and demonstrate worthiness to learn additional material. This usually involved learning a basic *straight fist* and its variations coupled with learning the remaining stances. Stances are divided into four categories as follows: horse, forward, low, and high. (Regarding the stance illustrations in this part of the text, the hand positions are arbitrary—"stance" here refers foot position and weight distribution *only*.)

Deep Horse Stance

Scissors Stance

Horse stances include the two versions described above, plus the *scissors stance, cross stance*, and *X stance*. The *scissors stance* is done by rotating the torso 180 degrees from a *horse stance*, twisting the body so that the lead leg is still bent with the thigh parallel to the floor and a flat lead foot, but the rear leg has the shin almost parallel to the floor and is only on the toes and ball of the foot; the knees do not touch. In the *X stance* (*lau ma*) you cross one leg behind the other as you bend both knees so that the knees touch (the rear knee is in light contact with the rear of the front knee). In the *X stance* the heel of the rear leg may be raised, depending upon the style. The *cross stance*, mainly used by Tiger styles, crosses one leg behind the other, but with only slight bending of the knees (they may lightly touch).

X Stance

Cross Stance

Forward stances are those in which the practitioner is facing the opponent with one leg in the lead (where the torso is facing) and the other in the rear. Most familiar is the *bow and arrow stance* (*chin kung hao chin ma*, or simply *kung bo*) where the lead leg is bent so that the knee protects your groin and your foot is at a 45-degree angle between your opponent and your groin. The rear leg is nearly completely straight. The feet are parallel to each other and the torso is twisted to face directly towards the opponent. In the similar *hill climbing stance*, or *forward stance* (*teng shan bo*), the body parts are in about the same positions, but the body is more erect, very similar to a person in the midst of taking a pacing step. The *cat stance* (*ding bo*) is a shift of weight from a *forward stance* backwards, so that about 65%-80% of the weight is over a bent rear leg. The front leg is bent, with the ball of the foot touching the floor (in some versions, only the toes touch). It may be used as a high, medium, or very low stance. Shaolin also uses a *low cat stance*, with 90% of the weight on the rear leg, which is bent lower than a sitting posture level. The front leg would be nearly straight, and bear just 10% of your weight. The *back stance* is a *forward stance* with the leg positions reversed, so the lead leg is straight (but the knee is not locked). Finally, the *rear-leaning stance*, or *seven stars stance*, is similar to the *cat stance*, but is rarely executed as a low or very low posture. The rear leg is slightly bent, the lead leg is straight, with only the heel touching the floor. This awkward-looking footwork is a very effective way of checking an opponent's lead foot.

Hill Climbing Stance　　　*Bow and Arrow Stance*　　　*Back Stance*

Cat Stance　　　*Low Cat Stance*　　　*Seven Stars Stance*

High stances are typical of Crane and Snake styles. The *standing stance* is the one used in Wing Chun as well as many other styles. It is a *horse stance* in which the knees are only slightly bent with the knees arched inwards. The *white crane stance*, or *hanging horse stance* (*tu ma*), is a single-legged posture, with one leg drawn high along the centerline. Technically, the *crane stance* has the toes pulled *up*, so they face the opponent, while in *hanging horse* the toes point towards the *floor*.

Standing Stance

Hanging Horse Stance

Dropping Dragon Stance

Snake Stance

Low stances are generally preludes to low kicks, sweeps, or rolls. Again, these are typical of Crane and Snake, but also common in Northern Praying Mantis. Among these is the *snake stance* (known as "*snake creeping down*" in T'ai Chi Ch'uan), which resembles a low reversed version of the *bow and arrow stance*. In this case the lead leg is straight and nearly parallel to the floor, while the back leg is completely bent with the foot flat on the floor. This stance is used in many ways, including as a prelude to a sweep, an evasion, or as a linear takedown. The extreme version of the *standing stance* is the *dropping dragon*; the feet are two shoulder widths apart, toes pointed forwards, with the knees touching along your centerline.

Hand and Elbow Weapons

The number and variety of hand and arm techniques could easily fill an illustrated volume of hundreds of pages. There are a finite number of basic bodily weapons that will be discussed here, giving the reader a sense of the scope of such methods in Shaolin styles. Additional techniques are described under different style sections of the following chapters, and some more esoteric techniques are not included in this text. Though the number of weapons that the human body can form is quite finite, the ways in which those weapons can be used is truly astronomical. That is why there is so much more to mastery of gung fu than simply learning "all" of the techniques.

Hand techniques include finger, hand, and fist strikes. Fist techniques require less finesse and training to use so they are taught first. Most basic is the *straight fist*, in which the final posture has the hand palm down, using the first and second knuckles as the striking surface. This most universal of strikes—used by almost every kind of gung fu, Karate, and other Asian martial art—is a weapon for smashing and deep penetration into the body of an opponent. This is generally the first technique taught to students for the purpose of breaking boards. Practice the *straight fist* by assuming a *horse stance*, and placing each fist palm up at your waist (the chambered position). Extend your arm and rotate it so that your fist is facing palm down just prior to the time you contact your target. Begin by practicing in the air, but move quickly to punching a padded target. Keep your fist tight, aim at a point along the target's centerline, and *do not* move your shoulders; *do not* lean into the punch. Other fist techniques are practiced in a similar manner: use a solid stance, punch towards the centerline, and do not move the shoulders towards the target.

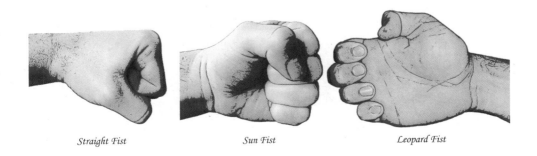

Straight Fist   *Sun Fist*   *Leopard Fist*

The *sun fist* uses the first three knuckles, and is delivered when the fist is thumb side upwards. Upon contacting the opponent, the lower part of the fist is snapped upwards, with the goal of lifting an opponent's center of balance. In delivering a *corkscrew punch*, the fist is rotated 180 degrees upon contacting the opponent, thus striking and twisting flesh simultaneously. This particular fist is primarily used when the intent is to cause debilitating pain without necessarily causing severe or permanent damage. Twisting flesh from underlying bone causes massive superficial hemorrhaging.

If you hold your hand flat, then flex the fingers so the first segment touches the third, you have formed a *leopard fist*. It may be used to strike with the joint tips, or rake laterally. This fist must be delivered with great speed—the velocity helps the narrow strike penetrate deeply and cause maximum damage to your opponent. If your enemy has massive muscles, which could cushion him against a *sun* or *straight fist*, the narrow aspect of the *leopard fist* might work much better. A *leopard fist* is really a multi-edged weapon, using the leading knuckle ridge, the backhand knuckles, or the flesh edge of the hand (similar to a Karate "chop"). The *mantis fist*, or *phoenix fist*, is a *sun fist* with the index finger extended and braced with the thumb, providing either a gouge or pressure point strike. Southern Praying Mantis practitioners use it almost exclusively. When used lightly against pressure points, the opponent is likely to feel numbness or pass out; when used with greater force, this strike can be lethal. In the similar *dragon fist* it is the middle finger that is extended by one joint and braced with the thumb. Both strikes use the joint between the second and third finger segments as the striking surface. This fist, too, is used against pressure points, but always with more force than the *mantis fist*, and almost always against targets on the torso and back of the body. (The striking point on the *dragon fist* may also be braced by placing the thumb across the knuckles of the first and third fingers.)

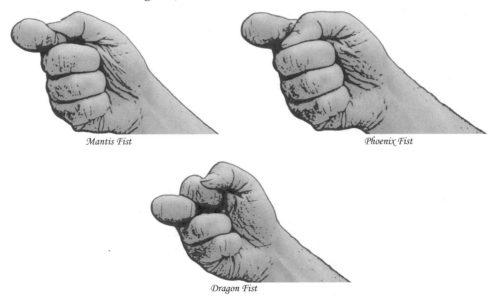

Mantis Fist   *Phoenix Fist*

Dragon Fist

Mantis Claw

The single striking index finger is the *mantis claw*, used in hitting soft pressure points such as eyes, throat, or the armpit. Using the index and middle fingers is the similar *spear finger* or *viper finger* strike, also to soft targets. Use of all four long fingertips is the *spear hand*, and it can be used against fairly solid targets once it is properly learned. If the *spear hand* is delivered with the palm perpendicular to the floor (thumb upwards) it is known as *thrusting fingers* or *dragon's tail*, and is typically delivered with a sudden swift downward strike after the fingers contact their target. (*Dragon's tail* splays the fingers while keeping the thumb tucked.) If delivered in a palm down motion, it is called a *snake hand*. All of these "soft" techniques must be done with maximum speed because their power is generated by the speed at impact, much as the power of a whip comes from the speed of the striking tip. These kinds of strikes are often employed to lethal effect, though a skilled martial artist can use them to induce unconsciousness or paralytic numbness in a limb.

Viper Finger

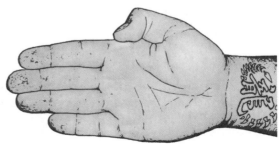

Spear Hand

The next group of techniques contains those that are used almost exclusively for lethal strikes or strikes that cause permanent physical damage to the opponent. A *tiger claw* is formed as if you are holding a gallon jug by the rim, all fingers and thumb tightly flexed inwards. *Crab claws* are formed by flexing the thumb and index finger, while *eagle's claw* flexes the thumb and first two fingers. All are techniques for grabbing to tear, gouge, or grapple with an opponent. Use of the thumb to brace the hand while allowing the index and middle fingers to gouge into pressure points is called a *viper's bite*. It differs from the *eagle's claw* in that the middle and index fingers are separated by 2-3 inches; in the *eagle's claw*, the fingers are pressed together. The *viper's bite* strike is a **dim mak** technique, used only against lethal pressure point strikes, and only as a last resort. *Dim mak* is the legendary "*delayed death touch*" technique that allows a practitioner to touch an opponent during a single encounter, with death resulting days, weeks, or even months later. (This topic is discussed in later sections about the Snake style and ch'i.)

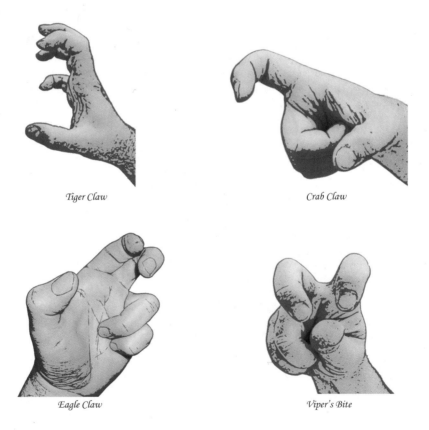

Tiger Claw

Crab Claw

Eagle Claw

Viper's Bite

To practice any of the above clawing techniques: begin by getting a small burlap sack or a gym sock and fill it with BBs or small ball bearings. Toss the sack into the air in front of you with one hand, then thrust the opposite hand as a claw to grab and then squeeze the bag. As your grip increases, get larger sacks and add more BBs, until you can easily grab and hold at arm's length a 15-pound sack. Tiger stylists will also enhance the grip with the water jug exercise. Get a one-gallon jar (preferably plastic) with a wide mouth lid. Add one cup of water to the jar, then grab the jar's rim with a *tiger claw* technique. Slowly lift the jar until your arm is straight out in front of you, and then slowly lower it. Do this three times a week, lifting the jar twenty times with each hand. Add another cup of water each week and repeat the drill. Once you can lift the full gallon jar, replace the water with BBs, starting with 8 pounds of BBs and adding one-half cup of BBs each successive week. At this stage, you should lift the jar both straight up in front of you, and then do drills lifting it to each side. This exercise will help you develop a strong grip and shoulder muscles.

Among the most powerful, in the sense of "hard", hand techniques are the *palm heel* strike and the more subtle *star of palm* strike. In the former a practitioner strikes with the base of the palm below the thumb with a battering ram like force. In the latter, the empty hollow of the palm is used, the trapped air forming the majority of the striking surface. Improperly applied, the *star of palm* can be dangerous to the practitioner, for the delicate carpal (hand) bones are easily fractured. The commonly employed *knife hand* is identical to the familiar "Karate chop," and uses the fleshy outer edge of the hand. These strikes are used as broad, hurting weapons, sometimes used to break through tough defenses such as shields, walls, and strong attacks including forearm and leg blows. A *palm heel* aimed at the knee of an opponent's kicking leg can break the knee or, at least, lock the kneecap and cause severe pain in the aggressor. All of these lateral strikes should be practiced against a solid, and initially padded, target. Lateral strikes are among the fastest in your repertoire, and they and palm strikes are excellent tools for breaking bricks and boards (which are both focus and confidence exercises).

Knife Hand

Palm Heel

The Shaolin Grandmasters' Text

Elbow techniques can deliver incredible striking power. Many gung fu styles use elbow strikes though only a few use them as major portions of their repertoires. *Forward lateral elbow strikes* are delivered from outside to centerline, using the outer surface of the lower arm near the elbow. A *rear elbow strike* is the result of a chambering (returning) fist, the elbow striking backwards and slightly upwards. The *reverse elbow strike* swings the elbow backwards and laterally, horizontal to the floor to hit an opponent at your side. The tip of the elbow is the striking surface. The *crane's wing* is a strike using the middle of the forearm as it arcs slightly upwards and forwards. When practicing these strikes or performing them in form work, the elbow is typically slapped into the open palm of the opposite hand; that is, the right elbow gets slapped into the left open palm. These are all heavy, hard-hitting blows used at very short range and with tremendous force on contact. They should, like knife hand and punching techniques, be practiced on solid, initially well padded, targets.

Blocks and Parries

Shaolin is famous for feats of seemingly superhuman strength and power, including the formidable ability to break boards and bricks with expertly executed blocking techniques. It will therefore surprise many readers that in traditional Shaolin, blocking techniques are only taught to student level monks; by disciple level the Temple styles abandon blocking and substitute either evasion or *parrying*. To better appreciate this, we must move the terms "block" and "parry" beyond confused semantics and give them clear definitions.

Blocking is an action that aims to negate an incoming attack by interception and deflection against the direction of the attack. Consider this example: you face an opponent who throws his right fist at your face. Using your left arm, you arc from right to left to intercept his forearm and deflect it to your left. Why would Shaolin eschew such a technique? First of all, it pits force against force, with the result that the defender may still be injured. Blocking is nothing less than a strike at an attacking weapon, so the blocking arm stands to sustain some degree of injury. These minor, cumulative injuries still tire and weaken a defender, sapping strength while increasing vulnerability. Second, few attackers pick on bigger, stronger victims. Recall that force equals mass times acceleration. If a big attacker throws a power punch at your face, you simply may not be able to generate enough lateral force to neutralize the attack, and you'd get hit anyway. Third, blocking simply feeds your adversary more energy. Isaac Newton's third law of motion states that "for every reaction there is an equal and opposite reaction." Translation: you block his right arm, giving him energy with which to twist and deliver a faster left counter strike. Blocking helps a savvy opponent use your own energies against you!

Parrying is the use of a motion to neutralize an incoming attack

by meeting, accelerating, and deflecting the incoming force by keeping it moving in its original direction. Consider the same opponent described above throwing the same right punch at your face. A simple parry arcs from your left to your right, meets his outer forearm, accelerates it while pushing it (gently) further to your right. The opponent has difficulty overcoming the inertia of the increased speed (Newton again) and the minimal energy you added to push the strike more to your right than your head! There is no bruising (to either party), very little energy expenditure, and the parry neutralizes the attack without giving the opponent an immediate counter opening. Furthermore, most parries open the opponent to vulnerable counterattack. Virtually any strike may be used as a parry. The essence of a parry embodies 3 elements: a) proper interception, b) motion complementary to the incoming attack, and c) minimal use of force/energy. Moving from mere proficiency to mastery, a properly executed parry will also set the defender up for an immediate counterstrike that uses mostly force from the deflected attack. To use our same example: the left to right arcing parry is delivered with a left *palm heel* strike. As soon as the attacker's trajectory has been altered to miss your face, your still bent left arm raises its elbow and counterstrikes the opponent's face, throat, or right ribs with a *knife hand* strike or *palm heel* strike. As a diver uses a diving board to spring higher, you use your opponent's arm to spring faster.

Beginners and intermediate students are taught a large number of blocking and parrying techniques and exercises. By the time a student moves into the disciple levels, this training is radically shifted because a strike can double as a parry. Few styles teach this simultaneous application of parry-equals-strike, notably including the Wing Chun style. Among the Shaolin there is a saying: "students block, disciples block and strike, and masters need not block at all."

Kicks and Sweeps

There is an old Chinese saying that has been used to distinguish two major martial arts divisions: "Kicks in the North, hands in the South." Like so many slogans, this one is a gross misrepresentation, for gung fu styles across China use both hand and kicking techniques. It would be more accurate—though not universally true—to say that northern styles are more likely to use high, flying, and long range kicks, while southern styles employ lower, grounded and medium to short range kicks. Southern Monkey and northern Black Crane provide examples of dramatic exceptions to both rules. Leg techniques fall into two general categories, kicks and sweeps.

Kicks are physical attacks equivalent to punches, delivered with the intention of causing direct physical distress to the opponent. Kicks may be delivered while you have one foot planted on the ground or while leaping through the air; they may be straight and snappy or arcing and circular. The table (opposite page) gives a breakdown of major kicking types and their most common uses. There are many variations within each kicking type, with aerial and ground-rooted, straight legged and snapping, chambered and crescent versions. This list is not exhaustive because it only enumerates the major, or basic, kicking types. For each basic type there may be four or more variations that are fairly distinct in their delivery and application. However, no martial artist will master a kick without first mastering its basic version. In all kicks, it is the foot that acts as the weapon, with the heel, ball, edge, whole flat, or top of the foot as primary striking surfaces. The power is generated so that the greatest velocity is in the foot, making the weapon the most difficult part of the leg to stop (as in blocking). In contrast, force above the knee, from thigh to hip, is negligible in even the most powerful kicks. So this thigh region is the weak point you would best target when parrying or blocking.

In general, any kick can be developed so it is a board-smashing weapon, but more typically the *snap kicks* are the ones used when you want to break the bones of an adversary. *Crescent kicks* will easily induce bruises and trauma, and are used to parry incoming attacks. Parrying an opponent's knife-holding hand with a proper *crescent kick* will simultaneously cause him pain, loss of knife, and possibly break his wrist.

Kicks are best practiced against targets such as padded bags. This is because kicking the air, while helping you to develop balance, does not allow you to learn about Sir Isaac Newton's contribution. When you kick an object properly, your thrust will cause energy to penetrate and thereby move the object, in this case the padded bag. Newton taught us that for every action there is an equal and opposite reaction. As your foot connects with the bag at considerable velocity (action), some energy will repel your foot and work to move you away from the target (reaction). People who only kick the air often find, upon their first strike against a solid target, that the reaction causes them to land unceremoniously on their rear ends! To truly learn kicking, you must practice accommodating reaction energy, and to do that you must kick a solid object with force.

Front Snap Kick

This chart lists some of the most fundamental kinds of foot techniques. There are numerous variations of these kicks, but these are the "basics." Some of the kicks are labeled "snap/thrust" to indicate that they may be thrown either as penetrating or as whipping techniques.

Basic Kicks		
Kick	**Delivery**	**Primary Targets**
Front Snap/ Thrust Kick	Knee is raised, then lower leg is extended to front of body. May kick with the instep, ball, heel, or toe of the foot.	Knee, shin, groin, bladder, stomach, solar plexus, throat.
Flying Front Snap/ Thrust Kick	As above, but performed while leaping into the air. Neither foot remains on the ground.	Solar plexus, heart, throat, head.
Side Snap/ Thrust Kick	Knee is raised, then lower leg is extended to the same side of the body as the raised leg. May kick with the heel or outer side of the foot.	Knee, thigh, bladder, stomach, solar plexus, throat, head, kidney.
Flying Side Snap/ Thrust Kick	As above, but performed while leaping sideways towards opponent. Non-striking foot contacts ground as striking foot hits opponent.	Head, throat, heart, kidney.
Inside Crescent Kick	The straight leg is swung out, up, and then in towards the centerline with the help of hip gyration. Striking surface is the heel or bottom of the foot.	Wrist, hand, fore-arm, bladder, heart, solar plexus, head.
Outside Crescent Kick	As above, but leg swings from centerline to outside of body. Striking surface is the heel or instep of the foot.	As above.
Back Kick	Knee is raised, then lower leg is extended to the back of body. The heel of the foot is the weapon.	Stomach, groin, solar plexus, head, kidney, bladder.
Dropping Thrust Kick	One leg bends to bring rear end almost to floor. Both hands brace the floor as other leg thrusts to back of body, strik-ing with the heel of the foot.	Shin, knee, ankle, groin, head (of opponent on/near the ground).
Hook Kick	Knee is raised, then foot is raised to nearly touch rear end. Lower leg is extended horizontally, using instep or ball of foot to strike.	Wrist, bladder, head, kidney, inside of thigh, groin.

Sweeps are low attacks that target the opponent's leg or legs, with the intention of throwing your opponent to the ground. A sweep is generally delivered like a kick, but the intention is not to "break" your opponent, but only to break his or her balance. In Shaolin there are only three types of sweeps.

The *kicking sweep* is nothing more than a low *snap kick,* arcing behind the opponent's lead leg to kick his knee forward (in the direction it is supposed to bend naturally) so quickly that he drops. The striking weapon is usually the top of your foot, as it is in the *hook kick.* This technique is found most commonly in the Northern Praying Mantis and Dragon styles.

The *crane sweep* (*forward sweep*) is done from a low *snake creeps down* posture with your hands on the ground. You use your hands to help pivot your body forwards, so your extended and locked sweeping leg uses the foot and ankle to lock and sweep your opponent's lead ankle. There is also a bit of hook and pull in your circular motion, so if the opponent doesn't fall quickly, he may be forced into a rapid and painful split. The *crane sweep* is an intermediate technique, a bit tricky to learn mechanically. However, the thin skin of the shin makes this technique potentially painful to the user as well as the swept. For that reason, *crane sweep* practice must include gradually increasing the number of shin strikes against solid — and again we add the word "padded" — objects. It may take a year or more to strengthen your shins to the point they can withstand actual contact with an opponent's leg while doing a *crane sweep.*

The third sweep is the *iron broom* (*reverse sweep*), which is simply the *crane sweep* done backwards, using the back of your leg's calf muscles as the striking surface. The *iron broom* is a more forgiving technique than the *crane sweep,* in that you do not strike with a sensitive surface such as the shin. Here, the bulky calf muscle — functioning much like a large pad — makes contact with the opponent's leg. The *iron broom* is also the most powerful of the sweeps because it is driven by the leg's larger, backside muscles.

Advanced stylists use sweeps sparingly, but with devastating effectiveness, often stringing multiple sweeps together in a bid to bring down an opponent. Surprised by a series of sweeping attacks, it takes a truly skilled exponent to evade a floor-height whirling dervish.

My conviction is that the fist and Zen are one of the same.
Together, this balance cultivates intellect ahead of strength.

Miyagi Chojun

Chapter Eight

Overview of the Styles

In this and subsequent chapters we shall provide some information on the major Shaolin styles and their distinguishing characteristics. Within each style may be sub-styles that show both similarities and distinct differences from the parent styles. For each style, we will list the *major* unarmed one-person forms (or sets, also known as "kuen") and any other peculiarities associated with the style and its practice. In most cases, we will also indicate the key form of a style, if such exists. Key forms contain much of the essence of a style with respect to technique, movement, positioning, principles and so forth. Many forms, drills, and training methods will not be listed, as this is not an attempt to comprehensively present the Shaolin styles. Neither is this text intended to be a learning manual. The sections on specific styles are very brief overviews, designed to acquaint the reader with the styles under discussion. Sections on styles function as a reference manual, with the caveat that our Buddhist approach significantly downplays lineal details—such as precisely who modified which styles and when. (For a good general book on gung fu that presents a fairly comprehensive treatment, see Hung Gar master Wong Kiew Kit's *The Art of Shaolin Kung Fu*. Also see the text by Chow and Spangler.[117])

Gung fu represents tremendous stylistic diversity with over 1,000 styles known or recognized. Draeger and Smith, in assessing the past and present of gung fu, lament that Chinese styles are afflicted by four shortcomings:

1. Some excellent methods have died because of the fetish of secrecy.
2. Some systems have been diluted by modifications.
3. Some contemporary types have borrowed the names of earlier types.
4. Some current methods are gymnastic rather than fighting in function.[119]

We would like to briefly situate Shaolin with respect to these concerns. We have fortunately not been strongly affected by concern (4). The Shaolin Order has maintained unbroken study of the styles covered in this text, and none of them have evolved towards the Modern Wushu model. Because of this, (3) has not been of too much concern—our naming conventions have been more or less stable. With respect to (2), whether a modification is a dilution or an improvement really seems to depend upon perspective. Shaolin gung fu has meditative and artistic purposes, as well as a martial purpose, and is not really *meant* to remain static throughout the ages. Modifications, provided they are made by masters with deep enough knowledge, serve as distillations and not as dilutions. The other concern evoked by (2) is the very common case of stylistic blending. Northern Praying Mantis is influenced by Monkey, Southern Dragon is influenced by Snake, Wing Chun is influenced by Crane, and so forth. Despite varying influences, these styles have maintained very distinct identities. In the case of many civilian style traditions, a style might borrow an entire form from a second style. But this does not necessarily dilute the first style—the borrowing may profitably serve to teach exponents of that style a concept not included in their native tradition. (1), the "fetish of secrecy," has been something of a concern for the Order. This book is largely intended to be part of the remedy for that problem. But with respect to most of these concerns, they only seem to be serious shortcomings from the perspective of academic study of Chinese martial arts. And so we have a situation where scholarly treatment of Chinese styles is rather trying...but where the prize is the amazing richness and variety of Chinese martial arts.

From gung fu came Karate (Okinawa and Japan), Escrima (Philippines), and most important, a way of thinking that became a code of life. From humanity's earliest efforts to fight using hands, feet, and crude weapons came many early martial arts. The Greeks developed Pankration (πανκρατιος), the Indians a complex style similar to Pankration and Karate. The Siamese invented Kickboxing (Muay Thai) and the southeastern tip of Asia became home to Silat (pronounced similar to "slot").

The proliferation of Okinawan and Japanese Karate systems reflects the gung fu systems and styles that were their ancestors. Goju-ryu combines aspects of White Crane, *Fu Jow* (Tiger), and Choy Li Fut, while Funakoshi Gichin incorporated ch'in na and Choy Li Fut into his Shotokan system. (Miyagi Chojun points out in his *Karate-do Gaisetsu* that Goju-ryu developed from Chinese arts which came to Okinawa from Fukien Province in 1828.[120]) The Japanese *Shorin* style is a direct, though significantly altered, form of Shaolin which places tremendous emphasis on its 600+ two-person drills ("Shorin" is the Japanese pronunciation of "Shaolin," and it, too, is a Buddhist monastic order—usually called "Shorinji Kempo"). There is some controversy as to whether Shorinji Kempo was truly inspired by Shaolin, especially given the clear influence of Japanes arts upon the style. We can neither confirm nor disprove the origins of this style.

Even early forms of gung fu were combat arts first and foremost. What Shaolin did for gung fu was to unite a very rigid ethical and philosophical code with a devastating assortment of martial arts. This is because combat and training for combat offer ample opportunities to put Buddhist beliefs into action, especially in a monastic (which was non-antagonistic and cooperative) environment.

Gung fu requires of the practitioner a strict code of physical and mental discipline, unparalleled in most western pursuits. It is only as a whole concept that gung fu can be discussed, and this entails more than fighting. To become adept, one must follow the Tao, the way or the essence of the philosophy and life of the originators of the arts. One cannot pay to learn this art; it is only acquired by the desire to learn, the will to discipline one's self, and devotion to practice. The complete martial artist is a true master, blending martial and artistic aspects into a unified and seemingly supernatural whole. This discipline also requires a finely tuned and trained mind, for the mind, after all, controls the body. As intense as Shaolin martial training is—and the legends on this count are not terribly exaggerated—the mental training, via academics and meditation, is even more demanding. No Shaolin master is a mindless fighter.

Consider two different approaches to learning foreign languages. The most common approach is to focus on developing fluency in a single language. Later, if desired, the student can study a second language. It is likely easiest to learn one language at a time. The benefit of this approach is that the student will be able to go to one foreign country and communicate well with the natives. The drawback is that the student will be hopelessly lost anywhere else. In time, this student will be able to get along quite well in a few different lands. A rather unusual approach is to simultaneously develop skills in many languages while proceeding to master a single language. The benefit here is that the student can buy food and shelter, find restrooms, and exchange basic information almost anywhere. The drawback is that this student cannot have deep, potentially enriching discussions with foreigners. Eventually, this student will be able to have those deep discussions in one or two countries, but will also still be able to "get by" anywhere else. This latter way is closer to the Shaolin approach to learning gung fu. It is not for everyone, and it takes tremendous mental discipline to succeed, just as it would to simultaneously master one language while learning the basics of many others. Shaolin martial training and mental training are closely interrelated.

Shaolin styles may be broadly divided into two large classes. *Centerline* styles are those that defend a line running through the practitioner's body, and defense and attack techniques tend to be short and linear. Circular styles are more active, involve greater mobility, and techniques tend to draw strength from circular motions that complement the natural joint motions of the human body. Part of the initial screening of potential students, once they have been admitted into the Temple, includes evaluation by masters as to which style or styles will most complement the body kinesiology and mental abilities of the student. Today's students choose a style and school because of proximity, availability, price, or because a style is "cool." In the traditional method, the style is chosen by qualified masters who put the student's best interests first.

Within the Shaolin Temple, several styles were invented or adopted and modified. Many styles are still practiced, while others are now lost to history. In general, Shaolin styles are named for animals or practitioners, though there are exceptions. Crane, Tiger, and Dragon are all Shaolin styles, but Monkey is not; there are styles named "Dragon" and "Tiger" that are not Shaolin. There are no rules governing style nomenclature, so there is no general way to determine if a style is a Shaolin discipline or not. The accompanying chart lists some well-known Shaolin styles and their origins.

Styles With Strong Shaolin Affiliation	
Style Name	**Place of Origin**
Black Crane	Honan Temple
Choy Li Fut	Kwangtung Temple
Cobra	Honan Temple
Crab	Honan Temple
Dragon	Several Sources
Drunken	Several Sources
Five Immortals	Wutang Temple (most likely)
Hung Gar	Fukien Temple
Leopard	Honan and other temples
Lohan	Honan Temple
Northern Praying Mantis	Honan Temple
Python	Kwangtung Temple
Snake	Fukien and Kwangtung Temples
Southern Praying Mantis	Fukien and Jook Lum Temples, and Hakka
Springing Leg	Wutang Temple
Tiger	Several Sources
White Crane	Fukien and Omei Temples
White Eyebrow	Honan Temple
Wing Chun	Fukien Temple

The Shaolin styles were developed from animal actions and were divided into *low styles* and **high styles**. The low styles of the Shaolin were Choy Li Fut, Crane, Cobra, and Tiger, styles that are largely—but not exclusively—"hard" styles that emphasize physical power. Low styles are so called because they rely on animal movements and defensive principles strictly grounded in mundane concepts. Stances are solid, strikes hard and piercing, and the creatures all common and easily observed. By "low" it is meant that the styles are earth-bound or near the ground, and are not generally dependent upon ch'i manipulation.

In contrast, high styles are founded on mythological creatures, subtle concepts (such as ch'i manipulation), and other subtle approaches. Strikes may be light, but aimed at sensitive vital points; stances are fluid and look flimsy, but allow great mobility and flexibility. The high styles of the Order were Snake, White Dragon, Black Dragon, Green Dragon, Blue Dragon, Red Dragon, Ruby Dragon, Sapphire Dragon, Emerald Dragon, Silver Dragon, Northern Praying Mantis, and the centerline styles of Wing Chun, Southern Praying Mantis, and White Eyebrow. The primary features that separate high from low are the fantastic economy of movement and the differences in application of ch'i in the high styles.

Gung fu has a repertoire of more styles and systems than anyone has actually counted. Within any given style, such as Tiger, may be dozens of individual systems, and some systems may have minor variations that warrant recognition. This lowest level of distinction usually follows when a system is distributed to different family groups, or *pai*, where one group may favor an open hand for attack X but another may favor a straight punch for attack X.

Non-Shaolin Styles

We present here a very general overview of some major gung fu styles practiced outside of the Shaolin Order. (For the prospective student who wishes to learn genuine gung fu, finding a qualified sifu teaching any of these following styles would be a boon.) You will notice that Choy Li Fut is listed above among standard Shaolin styles, and below, among other styles. Especially in the South, Choy Li Fut was taught in the temples, but it was primarily taught to non-Shaolin coming to the temples for instruction. So, today, the style is very widely dispersed, partially as a result of Shaolin propagation. Some form of virtually every Shaolin style has a corresponding lay practice; a Shaolin monk would teach a style (or a large part of a style) to a non-Shaolin family member or trusted friend. It is a testament to the Shaolin origins of the civilian versions of Southern Dragon, White Crane, and Hung Gar that they include strong ethical principles as a necessary component of their practice.[121] The following list of mainly non-Temple styles is by *no means* definitive, but serves only to give the reader an idea of the vast scope of fighting skills encompassed by the nearly meaningless phrase: "gung fu."

Buddha Hand (Fut Sao) is an open handed style that uses moves resembling a cross between Pa Kua and some Choy Li Fut. The style's name is not a reflection of a temple or Buddhist affiliation, per se, but rather because the palm strikes resemble the hand positions of monks in various types of meditation.

Choy Li Fut is a southern style that contains more forms than, perhaps, any three other styles combined. Chan Heung developed the style around 1836 and named it for his teachers Choy Fok and Li Yao-san ("Fut" is Cantonese for "Buddha", serving in this instance to refer to the Shaolin Temple's Buddhist influence upon the style). This style employs low stances and powerful punches. The *corkscrew punch* is a major weapon here, as is the low *snapping kick* and the *hook kick*. Choy Li Fut was based on a posture called a riding horse stance, so called because when adopted, one appeared to be straddling a horse. The movements are initially very stiff and hard, depending primarily on muscular power for adequate performance. Traditionally there are only three kicks in the entire system, all very low. Recent innovators have added aerial and spinning kicks, but these flamboyant techniques were not part of the original style. According to legend, Choy Li Fut was designed for use on the houseboats of the South where a stable stance and powerful hand techniques were necessary. Today, many varieties of Choy Li Fut exist, and these include extensive training with the 18 classical Chinese weapons. Some schools of Choy Li Fut now include as many as 136 forms in their curricula.

Drunken Style (Chui Ch'uan) mimics a drunken man's movements, but under strict control. The looseness of body and unpredictability of the direction of motion are major characteristics.

Drunken Monkey is a fascinating hybrid of Drunken and Monkey.

Eagle Claw (Ying Jow) is a clawing and grappling art that uses high stances and kicks as well as intricate floor work. It resembles aspects of Tiger and White Crane, and is a northern style of gung fu that utilizes a healthy amount of pressure point work. Like many traditional gung fu styles, Eagle Claw has likely disappeared altogether (or nearly so) from mainland China. American senior Eagle Claw practitioner Leung Shum reported not being able to find any traditional Eagle Claw in China in the early 1980s, and that only remnants of the style existed as a part of the new Wushu.[122]

Eight Drunken Fairies (Ts'ui Pa Hsien), according to Draeger and Smith, is a form of T'i T'ang (a kind of ground boxing).[123] Sometimes referred to as "Drunken Style," Eight Drunken Fairies relies on the appearance of limpness and lack of balance, and is tricky to learn.

Eight Immortals is based on classical deities of the Taoist tradition, with movements representing the virtues (or special powers) of the deities. The most prominent derivative of this style today is the Eight Drunken Immortals (or Eight Drunken Fairies) style. The Eight Immortals style is also an ancestor to the Temple style of the Five Immortals.

Five Element Fist (Five Ancestor Fist, Ngo Cho Kune, or Wuzuquan/ Wu t'su Ch'uan) was developed around 1860 and incorporated White Crane, Monkey, Lohan, Ta T'sun Ch'uan, T'ai T'su Ch'uan, and more.[124] The White Crane influence was strongest. Ngo Cho Kune had tremendous impact upon the development of Okinawan styles. This style should not be confused with the Five Immortals style, which was a Temple style.

Five Southern Family Systems (Hung, Lau, Choy, Li, and Mok) are five different family systems which appeared during the Ch'ing dynasty in southern China. According to Ed Parker: the Hung system employs low stances and long hand techniques; the Lau system is known for staff and short hand work; the Choy system employs foot movements modeled on the rat, and hand and body movements taken from the snake; the Li system stresses defensive stance shifting and short hand movements; and the Mok system is known for its kicking techniques.[125] Hung Gar is discussed in a later section of this text, specifically the section on Tiger styles. Lau Gar is mentioned in the present chapter (below). Some maintain that each of these systems was named for a Shaolin monk, although this is not part of our oral history. Another bit of trivia often repeated is that these five styles were the primary legacy of the southern Sil Lum temples. This may be true with respect to the civilian sphere, but of these five, only Hung Gar has any representation in the Temple curriculum. Many authors ape one another when they write "Southern Shaolin just *is* the five southern family styles." It's a little awkward when we read or hear this. Unfortunately, there has always been a problem in martial arts "scholarship" of ignorance— something we are undoubtedly guilty of as well.

Fut Gar (Sil Lum Fut Ga Kuen, or Shaolin Buddhist Family Fist) is a southern style formed from the influences of many different southern styles. It emphasizes tremendous speed, often foregoing stepping in favor of stance shifting, and training hand technique to match the planting of a solid foundation. As with many other southern styles, Fut Gar encourages rapid, successive striking.

Grand Earth (Ting T'ang Men) style revolves around ground fighting. Much combat in the style isn't exactly grappling, but rather fighting close to the earth. The style has six core forms and takes much of its inspiration from the ancient Snake style.

Hsing-I Ch'uan (Mind Form Boxing) is similar to Pa Kua but is linear in practice. The subtle movements of this style make it difficult to learn as a martial art except when taught by very well qualified instructors. See the glossary for more information.

Jeet Kune Do (Way of the Intercepting Fist): We've got news for some, it isn't a style.[126] We've nevertheless given this philosophy of combat an entry here for those who may be interested. See the glossary for more information.

Jow Gar (Chow Clan) was created around 1915 by Jow Lung from his training in Hung Gar, Choy Gar, and northern Shaolin (probably Long Fist). These "combination" styles are very common in Chinese boxing, as is the name "Jow," sometimes also written as "Chu" or "Chow." We're aware of several very different styles which may legitimately be called "Jow Gar."

Lau Gar (Lau Clan) is a southern style purportedly derived from a form of boxing from Kuei Ling Temple in Kwong Sai Province. Lau Gar is "classically southern," relying on short range attacks from low stances, and employing individual techniques from the Shaolin animal styles. Some Hung Gar stylists have incorporated Lau Gar into their curriculum. The style is also well known for its ch'in na.

Liu-Ho Ch'uan (Six Combinations Fist) is a northern style, possibly created during the Sung dynasty at Hua Shan in Shansi.[127] Many believe that one of the extant murals at the Honan Temple depicts Liu-Ho boxing.

Liu Ho Pa Fa (Six Combinations through Eight Methods) is a style based on combining elements from Hsing-I, Pa Kua, and T'ai Chi Ch'uan. For this reason, it is somewhat more complex than any of those three styles. The synthesis of this style, also known as "Water Boxing," is likely fairly recent, but some proponents claim that it's just as old as the three classic "internal" styles. Making exaggerated claims of a style's age is nearly as popular as claiming that the style was developed by Shaolin. (Many so-called "Shaolin" styles are not Temple-derived at all. They are no "better" or "worse" than Temple styles, merely different.)

Long Fist (Chang Ch'uan) is a product of debatable origins. Some claim it was Shaolin, but most assert it was invented by the first Chinese emperor of the Sung dynasty, T'ai Tzu, and then largely practiced as a folk martial art in many areas near the Honan Temple. Today's Long Fist might be the result of hybridizing Choy Li Fut and White Crane with earlier northern arts. Regardless of its origins, this style has few kicks and uses long-range punches, including a vast arsenal of uppercuts. Long Fist, Modern Wushu, and some recently synthesized gung fu styles are currently practiced in the vicinity of the Honan Temple.

Lost Track (Mi-Tsung I, or Yen Ch'ing Ch'uan) relies on the principle of one's opponent losing track of what is going on. The style is similar to Long Fist, has three core forms, and uses a trademark palm where the thumb and forefinger curl towards each other. The style is also called the "Labyrinthine Art," and features swift turning and befuddling attacks. The style was popularized by Huo Yuan-chia, the founder of Shanghai's Ching Woo Association.

Monkey (Tai Sing, or Hou Ch'uan) is noted for comical facial expressions and noises, rolling and tumbling, and sneaky, usually open-handed attacks. Footwork is complex, and kicks are generally low and powerful, aimed at vital spots such as knees and groin. There are many monkey-inspired styles, including: Hou Er Ch'uan (Young Monkey), Taodo Hou Ch'uan (Harmony of Monkey Fist), Bai Hou (White Monkey), Sun Wu Kung Men (Monkey King Style), and Ta Sheng Men (Great Sage Style). Sun Wu Kung Men is closer to Wushu than a martial art; it is purely theatrical and used in Chinese opera. Taodo Hou Ch'uan has three key forms: *Iron Monkey*, *Crafty Monkey*, and *Drunken Monkey* (which blends techniques from Drunken Style and Lost Track). Ta Sheng Men, Great Sage style, is a widespread version. Today, Ta Sheng Pek Kwar, or Great Sage Axe Hand, is probably the most common variant and has five core forms:

1. *Lost Monkey*: appears lost, circles opponent;
2. *Drunken Monkey*: deception by feints and high-low combinations;
3. *Tall Monkey*: long arm movements and long, low sweeps;
4. *Stone Monkey*: powerful, most direct form;
5. *Wooden Monkey*: sneakiest, uses many feints.

Moving Shadow is a variant on the Drunken style, but here a practitioner is either working to stay behind the opponent or "shadow" his moves. For example, if an aggressor throws a left straight punch, the defender throws the same left straight punch while also twisting to avoid the oncoming attack. Fascinating to watch, devilish to master.

Pa Kua Chang (Baguazhang) is a style whose forms are performed while walking a circle, making angle of attack very difficult for an opponent to follow. This is one of the "internal" Wutang styles, and the movements are based on interpretations of the trigram pattern of the I-Ching. There are strong connections between Pa Kua, Snake, and Dragon. See the glossary for more information.

Phoenix-Eye Fist (Chu Gar, or Chuka) is a style descended from a Shaolin nun who taught what she knew to two sisters by the name of Chu, years after leaving the Fukien Temple.[128] The Chinese characters for "Chu Gar" (sometimes written "Jow Gar") are the same whether the words refer to this Phoenix Fist style or to the Southern Praying Mantis variant (discussed in the chapter on centerline styles), but they are two very distinct styles. Phoenix Eye Fist emphasizes the hand technique of the same name, and appears to have an eclectic heritage. A *Six-and-a-half-point* (or *Six-point*) *Pole Form* appears in a variety of styles, including Northern Praying Mantis, Wing Chun,[129] and Phoenix-Eye Fist.[130] The Phoenix-Eye Fist version shares basic techniques with other versions, and is considerably shorter than the Northern Praying Mantis form. There is some evidence that this style may have been influenced by Southern Praying Mantis, Wing Chun, White Crane, and perhaps White Eyebrow. Another Phoenix Eye style credited to Kew Soong and usually referred to as "Fong Ngan" (or "Fong Gai," or "Fong Nyan"—all mean "Phoenix Eye") is also floating around.

Poison Hand is a largely dead, forbidden system. A protective coating was applied to the user's hand, then poison was added as an outer layer. A person even mildly cut by a practitioner of the poison hand in combat would suffer toxin effects within seconds. The poison hand artist, protected by the waxy undercoating, would simply wash the poison off after combat and suffer no ill effects. "Poison Hand" is also used by some to refer to dim mak. Poison Hand may sound like something from a bad movie. It isn't.

T'ai Chi Ch'uan, which translates as "Supreme Ultimate Fist," was developed as an internal art for elite soldiers. The movements are practiced slowly at first, but contain many subtle and effective martial applications. Today, few instructors seem willing to admit to (or are aware of) the style's martial nature. Many family systems have come from the original. See the glossary for more information.

Tao Gar is a northern art similar to Choy Li Fut and Eagle Claw that very probably influenced the development of Chinese Kempo and definitely influenced Korea's Hwa Rang Do. There is also an arguably Tibetan art with the same name that employs some ch'i exercises.

Though there are over 1,000 styles and subsystems recorded for the Chinese martial arts, a far smaller number count as being truly distinct styles. A slight majority of these seem to developed from the classical animals—crane, leopard, tiger, snake, praying mantis, dragon, eagle, monkey, and horse—and the rest from historical or mythical figures and unusual sources.

Chapter Nine

The Circular Styles

The Tao stretches away into the far distance,
like a circle, only to return again.

Lao Tzu

It is not possible to present a discussion of Shaolin's moving meditations, or gung fu, without putting them into proper context. From its earliest days at Honan and before Shaolin became a distinct new sect, meditation was very strongly centered upon observing other living creatures and understanding the links among all life. The earliest exercises taught by Tamo to his new monks were derived from traditional Hatha Yoga postures, themselves taken from nature. These included cobra, bird, deer, and bear postures. Stretching and marrow-washing exercises were very mindful of anatomical and physiological processes, and Tamo made a detailed knowledge of anatomy and kinesiology essential to each monk.

A cornerstone of Shaolin philosophy was the study of nature, so we might see it as it really is. In order to achieve the Buddhist goal of seeing past illusion, it is often easier to start with a subject somewhat removed from us. Darwin's friend Herbert Spencer gave the world the descriptive phrase "nature red in tooth and claw," pointing out that the "wild" world is not necessarily more idyllic than the human world. By actually observing nature we see the beautiful butterfly pollinating the flowers, then become prey for a swooping bird; the fearsome bear and tiger gently and carefully tending their offspring; clever monkeys stealing from each other. We also see the tiny praying mantis ward off a much larger adversary by using elaborate bluff; the combination of cleanliness, grace, and deadliness in the secretive cobra; and the cleverness of a mother bird feigning a broken wing in order to redirect a predator away from her nest.

Kill or be killed, eat or be eaten, slither silently but carry a formidable arsenal. These are lessons that we learn from nature, lessons that are so important to both seeing ourselves as part of the living mosaic and in perfecting skills for self-defense. In studying other creatures, the monks learned that animals are indeed sentient, at least to some degree. The snake knows when its prey is within striking distance and when it is too far to be reached. Apes and dogs know the hierarchy of their groups, know which comrades may be readily approached and which require submission.

It was not the intent of nature study to emulate the animals in gung fu practice, because the practitioner would remain a human. Rather, it was intended that principles and movements could be imitated to the advantage of the human martial artist. Memories of first-hand observations were used in guided meditations, special mental exercises aimed at bringing the higher mental faculties together to analyze and synthesize new concepts from existing ones. The results of these meditations would then be practiced and tested, with the successful results eventually becoming part of an existing martial arts style or, more rarely, forming the basis of a completely new style. Many disciples and masters would practice their techniques only in their minds if it were inappropriate to do so physically. Many claim that this mental practice is as valuable as actual physical drills.

Forms are not forms. They are constructed in the manner of an illusion
by your own mind.

Tamo

Crane

Dealing systematically with the various systems, and excluding the Choy Li Fut style because it is not part of the strictly and characteristically Shaolin school, we first touch upon the Crane systems. For convenience's sake, we may recognize three major systems, or schools, of Crane:

Tibetan White Crane: traditional, from Tibet, and very stylized.

Shaolin White Crane: derived from Tibetan White Crane. (Also called "Shaolin White Crane" is Fukien White Crane, which was derived from the core Shaolin White Crane style.)

Fukien Shaolin White Crane: a non-Temple variant of Shaolin White Crane emphasizing a closer range than the older Tibetan-influenced white Crane. There are many branches of this style, many of which share more than a few traits with Wing Chun, Southern Praying Mantis, and other southern Chinese styles

Black Crane: the traditional hand sets of Shaolin Crane including ch'in na. Predates White Crane in China. Style allows penetration to elbow distance but does not engage in in-fighting. It begat ch'in na and uses "southern" footwork with "northern" hand work.

The crane is a large wading bird with long legs, neck, and bill. Their posture and movements have made cranes favorite subjects of Asian artists for centuries. Belying their graceful and artistic poise is the agility and speed displayed by these birds. They slowly stalk submerged prey — generally frogs and fishes — which they swiftly impale with their strong bills. They look lanky and fragile, but are actually formidable fighters. Several Chinese martial arts are based on the crane's movements, but the style most well known is actually Tibetan in origin.

There are few, if any, techniques unique to Crane; it is the combination and use of techniques that sets the style apart from others. Even the signature single-legged *white crane stance* (made familiar by the film *The Karate Kid*) has its parallel in other styles where it is often called the *hanging horse stance*. "The [crane-like] movements [are] used to develop control, character and spirit. Movements [in] the one-legged stance [are] performed with a considerable amount of meditation."[131]

From Crane, a martial artist learns how to move with grace and precision. The self-control involved in merging complex footwork while executing a limited number of striking techniques requires great mental control and physical dexterity. Because this style strikes at soft vulnerable targets, it also develops the eyesight and targeting acuity of the practitioner. The "trick" to mastering this style is to fluidly merge the high single-leg stances with the low sweeps, all the while defending against attacks to the legs. Crane stances leave a practitioner quite vulnerable to attacks to the knees. This style takes considerable effort to master.

Crane, generally, is a long-range style, rarely allowing an opponent to get closer than arm's length away. The Black Crane system deviates on this distance, getting elbow distance away, but still contains no in-fighting. As a rule, the principle weapons of a Crane stylist consist of the 1) *crane's beak* strike, formed by touching each finger tip to the thumb tip, and striking in a fast whipping motion at soft vital targets, 2) *crane's wing* or *finger fan*, using the finger tips in a swiping motion aimed at an opponent's eyes or throat 3) the *vertical* (or *sun*) *fist*, with the thumb up, to harder targets, 4) outer forearm strikes, 5) elbow strikes, described further below, and 6) *crane's neck* strikes, using the bent top of the wrist. Kicks are usually high, and include both *inner* and *outer crescents*, *front snap*, *side snap*, and *flying front*. Both *forward* and *reverse sweeps* are executed from very low stances. Shaolin White Crane delivers fist techniques along straight lines and small circles, while Tibetan systems use larger circular motions. We shall now cover the two major Shaolin Crane systems in more depth.

Crane Neck and *Crane Beak*

Crane Beak

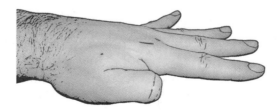

Crane Wing

White Crane

Shaolin White Crane is a southern style with Tibetan origins. According to legend, a Tibetan monk named Ordator (1430 - 1498) was looking for a quiet spot to meditate near a pond and stumbled onto a battle between an ape and a crane. Asiatic apes are both strong and vicious, so it seemed as if the ape would tear the crane apart. However, the bird continually stymied the ape, flapping its wings and deftly darting in and out with its beak before finally driving the injured ape away. The graceful movements of the bird were noted by the monk who copied the striking techniques and legwork into his gung fu style. The principle weapons of the system are its long-range kicks and the *crane's beak*.

One day, two armed robbers attacked the monk who, without thinking, defeated them both with his crane movements. When he meditated on his actions, he realized that he had mimicked the movements of the crane he had watched, in preference to his more traditional training. He then set about to study and preserve this knowledge, which today is called the "Tibetan White Crane" style (the style was originally called "Lion's Roar"), and the founding date for the version of Tibetan White Crane similar to that which persists to the present is placed at 1470. In the 1600s, the Tibetan monk Dorawkitan codified the version of Tibetan White Crane we recognize today. Prior to Tibetan White Crane's introduction to Shaolin, Black Crane was the Crane style taught in the Shaolin Temple. Shaolin White Crane supplanted Black Crane in 1837 (this is the formal date, yet the evolution of Shaolin White Crane from Tibetan and Black Crane sources actually took many years).

Black Crane is an uncharacteristic northern system because the footwork and close-in fighting are trademarks of southern gung fu (that is, low stances, low kicks, and close-range techniques). The choice of the name "Black" Crane comes from the Taoist principle of opposites, or yin/yang. When White Crane became a well known system in the South, the pre-existing northern Crane style took the complementary name: "Black Crane." By the same token, White Crane is southern and takes its footwork, long-range striking, and tall stances from the Tibetan martial artists.

Major characteristics of Shaolin White Crane include wide-armed, wing-like movements, high kicks, and the *crane's beak*, a hand weapon made by joining the fingertips firmly. The original Tibetan martial system we call White Crane is rather impractical for modern use, requiring many years of practice before it can be well employed. Fortunately, it has undergone various modifications throughout the centuries, and it is today one of the major, revered schools. It retains its strong long-range applications, but has modified many techniques so that they are suitable in urban environs.

White Crane is a bit like ballet; if properly performed, it looks graceful and simple. In fact, also like ballet, good White Crane is very physically demanding, and is perhaps the most difficult style to truly master. The range of motion may go from a high long-range punch to a very low spinning *backward sweep* which blends seamlessly into an aerial spinning *back kick*. As one practitioner put it after some five years of study, "This style is not for wimps!"

There is much more to the graceful-looking movements than aesthetics. Crane moves feed each other, so that the momentum of one move is transferred to initiate the next. A Crane practitioner who is not fluid and graceful is not only doing the set incorrectly, she is also doing it with no power. It is paramount that the Crane stylist learns to control and manipulate her own ch'i in order to make the techniques work.

Much of Shaolin White Crane evolved from around 1837 as martial techniques were exchanged between Tibetan and Shaolin monks. *Lama Sing P'ai Ch'ing Ch'uan* is a White Crane form, supposedly one that Tibetan Lama Sing showed to the Chinese Ch'ing dynasty emperor and empress, resulting in the imperial guard being the sole recipient of the art for many years. (The Manchu Ch'ing held Tibetan lamas in very high regard.) Many Pak Hok, Hop Gar, and Lama Pai schools trace their lineage to Lama Sing. Prior to Lama Sing's entrance into China, the imperial guard used Shaolin's Black Crane. The exotic and long-range movements practiced by Tibetan monks also appealed to military commanders, who quickly adopted the style for use by the most prestigious of the Chinese imperial guards - as well as the imperial infantry.

Yang offers considerable, yet differing, information about the roots of White Crane.[132] The discrepancies are likely due to the fact that there are numerous branches of the White Crane style. Most of the White Crane practiced in the world today is derived from the Flying Crane, Sleeping Crane, Eating Crane, and Screaming Crane branches of a Fukien White Crane style created by a Fukien Temple Shaolin monk and his daughter. This evolution of Fukien White Crane, created outside the temples, was widely taught, and proliferated in Taiwan, southeast China, and Malaysia. These Crane styles share some aspects with the Shaolin White Crane style perpetuated and studied within the Order, although Fukien Shaolin White Crane is more of a short hand, classically southern style whereas Shaolin White Crane more strongly reflects its Tibetan roots.

In addition to its empty-hand forms, Shaolin's White Crane gung fu also boasts a full set of, and arguably one of the most beautiful of all, weapons forms. Long knife (a weapon with a long, thick, single-edged blade) and sword (the saber, known as the "tao") sets are intricate, graceful, and deadly. Some White Crane traditions heavily influenced by T'ai Chi Ch'uan include sets using a a long, slender, double-edged sword known as "chien" in Mandarin and "gim" in Cantonese. Crane stylists may also master the segmented (chain) whip, trident, and spear. Some branches of Chinese White Crane also incorporate the short, paired butterfly knives into their curricula.

White Crane stylists were the traditional physicians of the Shaolin Order. They received the most in-depth training in medicine and healing, and were the monks who performed the most complex medical and surgical treatments. The tradition of learning Chinese medicine as a part of the integral White Crane curriculum exists through the present: there are very few senior White Crane practitioners who are not also qualified acupuncturists or Chinese physicians. The University of California at Berkeley even used to offer a White Crane degree program that included Chinese medicine.

The style encompasses six primary forms, yet ranges from hard, external physical development, to soft, internal ch'i movements. Examination of the style shows it to be an excellent natural progression for a student of a single style.

Forms of Shaolin White Crane

Beginners to Shaolin White Crane are started on the *Fei Hok Sao Kuen*, or *Flying Crane Hand* form. It is almost purely a conditioning exercise, stressing long, deep *horse stances* and punches thrown from 90 degrees to the body. The form is fairly long, having 175 separate moves, each to be mastered slowly, and with great precision.

A new practitioner may also begin with the *Lou Sing Sao*, or *Shooting Stars Hand* form, which emphasizes balance on one leg and rapid manual coordination. The use of kicks is somewhat restricted here, compared to *Flying Crane Hand*, but the development of balance in *Shooting Stars Hand* highly complements the leg training of *Flying Crane Hand*. Mastery of this series of techniques is not taxing, but learning the stance shifts and single-leg balance of this key form may take years.

The ranking of White Crane, when taught as a separate entity, is unique to the style. By the time a novice completes either of the above sets, he or she moves in rank from a black sash, which represents blindness, to a red sash, symbolizing sunrise. The student now begins to develop the accurate use of long-range kicks and evasive footwork. The *Five Form* set delineates the method of positioning the body to draw an attack, and then shifting the stance to allow a counter from unexpected quarters. In essence, this sidestepping is preparing the student for multiple opponents and the beginning of ch'i development. At this point, the student advances to disciple level and may wear a yellow sash, representing brilliance.

The *Cotton Needle* set, a soft form, is common to several martial schools sharing Crane ancestry, including Shaolin and possibly Hung Gar (in that it may have influenced the development of the *Iron Wire* set). It is designed to exercise all of the internal organs and enhance the flow of ch'i energy. So powerful and strenuous is this form that it is considered to be therapeutically superior to T'ai Chi Ch'uan. The work in this form is based on ch'i breathing, pushing breath into each strike or parry, and then inhaling sharply to replenish. Students who master this set will be able to walk along a 2-inch thin pole (much like walking a tightrope) and do formwork on tree stumps and other narrow and challenging surfaces. For a student to master this level may take several years, and success grants the blue sash of firmament.

Lau Hon Sao, or *Buddha Guardian Hand*, is another external set, but one utilizing all the maneuvers of the style, and thus requiring an adept, conditioned practitioner. Parts of the form may be taught at the beginner level, but rarely is it mastered until this point. As an adjunct to learning this form, students often incorporate the long knife into their practice. The mental control one has learned from the *Cotton Needle* set is required before learning the sword work that accompanies the *Lau Hon Sao*. The teaching philosophy of this approach is that one must master self-control before learning a weapon, and the weapon is a way to ensure that the student maintains control at all times. Even a momentary distraction could cause serious injury to the sword-wielder!

The *Lau Hon Sao* form is followed by *Dow Raw Sau*, the *Knife Foot and Hand* form, the most complex and important internal set. This form is learned in three stages, each taking considerable effort: the basic, combat-speed method; the slow, meditating method; and the super-speeded conditioning method. In contrast to most White Crane sets, which use *crane's beak*, swinging *hammer fists*, and *finger thrusts* as primary weapons, this set predominantly employs *knife hand* techniques. Even the standard bottom of foot thrusting and *crescent kicks* are replaced by edge of foot *side kicks*. At completion, one is truly a Crane master and wears a silver sash.

Shaolin White Crane Forms and Rank Progression, from Most Advanced Down to Most Basic	
Form	**Sash Color**
Knife Foot and Hand	Silver
Buddha Guardian Hand	Blue
Cotton Needle	Yellow
Five Form	Red
Shooting Stars Hand	Black
Flying Crane Hand	Gray

We are told that these forms remain essentially unchanged since conceived by Dorawkitan. Elements of some are seen in many other styles, and are perhaps even enhanced by the more varied methods. *Flying Crane Hand* appears in part in the Shaolin Black Crane style, as well as in ch'in na and Eagle Claw. *Knife Foot and Hand* is seen in Hong Tiger, Northern Praying Mantis and Monkey, while *Buddha Guardian* is seen in Pa Kua and Lohan Hart Ch'uan.

Traditional White Crane is highly dependent upon long-range strikes. To develop the timing and technique required to achieve that end, the forms are sequenced so that primary training develops the muscles, while coordinating the hand and eye. Once that concept is established, the training can increase in complexity, thus teaching coordination of stance and foot attack. A student at this stage has usually completed one year of study, and can be considered as fairly capable in self-defense.

The next phase develops the arsenal in terms of variety of weapons available and the choice of targets. It is here that a Crane stylist begins to decrease the striking targets to a few vital spots, as he is technically able to position himself for a thorough assault. This close link between Crane's martial techniques and pinpoint striking is obviously enhanced by the study of acupuncture. This precision hitting of vital spots—some not obvious as weak spots—may go a long way towards explaining the link between White Crane and Chinese medicine.

Finally, the highest level comes in being able to completely avoid an opponent's assault, and having the option of either evading the assailant until he is too exhausted to continue or deliver a fast, effective terminating strike. That a Crane stylist is effective is beyond question. Integrated with broader combat skills, the style can be actively employed in teaching any novice the basic discipline and coordination that can enhance further martial study.

Applications of White Crane

The white crane is one of several birds related to storks found throughout southern Asia, the most common being the Asiatic saurus crane (*Grus antigone*). All are tall, long-necked, long-legged birds that are quite frail in appearance. The beak is long, pointed and strong and is used as a defensive weapon. However, the morphology of these birds is not such that a stand-and-fight strategy would be successful against most potential predators, so evasive behavior evolved that removes the bird's body from the line of direct assault. Wings actually parry incoming force, or act as weapons when opened quickly, while the long talons also are effective for defense. The long neck and legs make almost all attacks long-range. Ultimately, the crane tries to intimidate an opponent long enough for the bird to get airborne and escape.

The gung fu practitioner following this school uses two basic hand techniques, the *crane's beak*, formed by contacting the thumb with all four fingers to make pinpoint strikes, and the *crane's wing*, a finger rake. The *sun fist* is also employed, by beginners more often than by masters. As the defender physically evades an assault, the torso turns with force that accelerates the force of a strike, making even minor contacts painful to the antagonist. Furthermore, evasive footwork forces the opponent to work harder to target in on the gung fu practitioner, who in turn has the opportunity to tire his opponent before launching a definitive counterattack.

A partially turned *sun fist* becomes a *hammer fist*, another long-range weapon common to Crane. It is delivered like a war hammer blow, propelled by tremendous centripetal force at the end of outstretched arms. Upon striking the opponent, the Crane stylist allows the reaction to bend his elbow and set up a smaller circle second strike. This strike and second strike combination is unusual and gives Crane stylists a tactical advantage over many other boxing styles.

Then, too, the open palm is a major weapon. In the beginning, a student uses the palm in a standard striking manner, sometimes using the *palm heel*, otherwise the *star of palm*, as the striking surface. More advanced practitioners, though, convert the palm strike into a *warding hand*, or *pushing hand*, taking the opponent off balance by lifting his center of gravity and shoving him backwards. This latter application is identical to the *warding palm* techniques of T'ai Chi Ch'uan. Yang, in his nice reference work on White Crane, also compares Crane and T'ai Chi Ch'uan.[133]

Crane motions rely heavily on using large circular motions to initiate a block or strike, then converting to a smaller circle, often at right angles to the first, to make a second blow. The notable exception is the *crane's beak*, which is short, linear, and made as a quick peck. Grapplers watching a White Crane stylist throwing punches sometimes remark that shifting the hips into each punch puts the Crane stylist off balance and makes him vulnerable to being thrown. However, when this hypothesis is tested, the well-centered stance of the Crane stylist is discovered: the hip shifting is a balanced shifting, not a leaning or redistribution of weight that would open the stylist to being thrown.

Crane's wing parries use the whole arm in graceful upward or downward sweeps to move not only an arm or leg strike, but the body of the opponent as well. Properly executed, these parries shift the opponent off balance, forcing him to open a vulnerable target. Frequently, they are executed with enough centripetal force to double as palm or backhand strikes while simultaneously parrying.

From an interception with the arms may come locks and throws (ch'in na), pushing or warding back (which uproot the opponent and hurl him forcefully backwards) or a direct counterstrike. Ch'in na used by a White Crane stylist is often designed to procure a living "shield" during multiple assaults, or to throw one or more people into other assailants. Even here, though, the Crane stylist is constantly hopping around, never taking a solid stance or restricting his own maneuverability.

Footwork in White Crane is legendary, targets being anything from head to groin. Bottom of the foot kicks are effective, as are crushing stomps, generated at close range and with great speed. Other kicks are designed to dislocate or unbalance opponents. Part of White Crane philosophy teaches control over an adversary, and to maim only as a last resort. Even in footwork, evasion is the primary goal, to allow the opponent(s) to tire, perhaps withdraw, or at worst, open up for a minimal, decisive counter. Notably, White Crane uses two very low kicks that are equally properly called sweeps. The *forward sweep* uses the shin as the striking surface, particularly against softer targets such as calf muscles, while the *reverse sweep* uses the calf against an opponent's leg. The ability of a master Crane stylist to move from a high kick to a low sweep and then back to a flying kick has resulted in many Chinese of days gone by to think of White Crane as a magician's style!

White Crane gung fu originated and spread through largely inhospitable regions of Tibet and China. Preparatory training, though rigorous, was not particularly difficult for a person accustomed to harsh conditions. Instead, they served to limber and tone muscles to provide greater mobility in the heavy clothing of the region. However, like the namesake bird, the practitioner was vulnerable to attack in a greater manner, perhaps, than other Asians. A severe cut could cause hypothermia and attendant shock, so being rendered "merely" unconscious could also cause freezing, making even a minor engagement quite serious.

Evasion is necessary to avoid stress created by slippery terrain (ice) and large adversaries. In thin air, an aggressor is likely to tire relatively quickly, and so conflicts could be altogether avoided by a skilled evasion artist. The low sweeps characteristic of this style may take an opponent to the ground where he will be unable to rise quickly (again, bulky clothing tended to hamper movement, and opponents were often winded).

Practice of forms stresses long, loose movements that maximize speed and ch'i flow as an end product. The result is threefold: total evasion of any incoming force, control of opponent with little or no harm inflicted, and ability to maim or (rarely) kill with great speed if necessary. Each form is initially practiced slowly, so that the nuances of each movement are patterned into the brain and each muscle employed. Next, the forms are done with exaggerated breathing and force, so that the body learns each strike, parry, and recoil motion to a subliminal level. Gradually the form is practiced faster and faster until, finally, it moves with the grace and precision of the great oriental bird.

Black Crane

Black Crane is the original Shaolin Crane style, created well before the introduction of Tibetan martial arts. Though it resembles a "typical" southern style, emphasizing hand techniques and solid stances, it was created in the north and codified as a style at Honan Temple. Refined movements from Black Crane called ch'in na (capture holds) were taught to civil police during the 1600s; these techniques are also practiced today by police in both China and Taiwan. Near the end of the Ming dynasty (1368-1644), Ch'en Yuan-ping traveled to Japan to teach ch'in na, thus introducing basics that would become jujitsu. In 1911, Herbert Giles remarked, "…it was undoubtedly from [Shaolin] that the Japanese acquired a knowledge of the modern *jiu-jitsu*, which is simply the equivalent of the old Chinese term meaning 'gentle art.'"[134] Giles was no great authority on Shaolin, but his comments reflect the common belief in late Ch'ing China that jujitsu was indeed rooted in Shaolin. The movements of Black Crane are still practiced outside Shaolin today, where they are simply called "ch'in na".

Black Crane ch'in na teaches locks and throws from basic physiological principles instead of making up hundreds of unique names for every unique combination of movements. Many short drills and two person exercises are used to teach these concepts to the Black Crane student. Much of the ch'in na included in White Crane styles today originally came from Black Crane. Black Crane has all but disappeared as a lay tradition simply because the style was supplanted by White Crane so long ago.

Over time, Shaolin modified Black Crane by adding techniques from White Crane (60%) and then organizing the style into 20 forms. In 1968, these forms had been reduced to eight and have now been condensed to a mere four. These are an introductory drill (the first form), a balance exercise (*Crane Leaving the Marsh*) and the combined techniques of Black Crane (the *Synthetic Fist* set and *Defending the Four Angles*). There are essentially six stances found in Black Crane: *black crane #1*, *black crane #2*, *low black crane*, *poised black crane*, *stork* and *hanging horse*. The first two are merely numbered for convenience. *Black crane #2* can be one-legged or not, while the last three are all one leg positions. *Hanging horse* is found in the second form and is seen in Hung Gar.

Black Crane Forms and Rank Progression, from Most Advanced Down to Most Basic	
Form	**Sash Color**
Defending the Four Angles	Black
Synthetic Fist	Black
Crane Leaving the Marsh	White (3rd Grade)
Basic Movement	White (1st Grade)

Black Crane #1 Stance

Hanging Horse Stance

Tiger

Tiger is a vicious method of fighting utilizing powerful kicks and clawing motions. Like the tiger, the practitioner fights fiercely by rending, tearing and breaking any limb or open space of skin that an opponent leaves unguarded. Tiger is highly defensive in nature, waiting until being backed into a corner, then unleashing an unstoppable assault. Its principle hand weapon is the *tiger claw*, also useful for unarmed defense against weapons. By clasping the weapon between the hands or enmeshing it in the crushing grip of the hand, the enemy's advantage is lost. Tiger movements develop the bones, tendons and muscles. The execution of these movements is the physical opposite of those of Dragon, the yang to the more fluid yin, since Tiger puts emphasis on strength and dynamic tension.[135] Movements snap with great physical power, and are generally more reminiscent of Karate moves than of gung fu techniques. In fact, many Okinawan, and subsequently Japanese, systems of Karate have been influenced by various Tiger practitioners. Still, Tiger is not linear, but subtly circular in its motions. The movements are similar to the piston action of the rods on the wheels of a steam locomotive, making small, fast circles that give a cursory observer the impression that they are moving back and forth linearly.

Tiger teaches the sophisticated use of physical power, making the most of available resources. Unlike the constantly shifting Crane, Tiger uses firm stance work that gives the artist a strong anchor on the ground. The tenacity of a tiger is also learned, for this creature can strike from almost any position, whether advancing or retreating, standing or falling. Tiger has always been the most popular of styles, probably because of its obvious martial applications and the fierce reputation of the animal. In any case, this popularity has allowed the style and its offshoots to survive and proliferate well into modern times.

Though there is great variety of techniques in the various Tiger systems, only five stances are regularly employed. These are the *X, hill climbing, cross, back,* and *cat stances.* What Tiger sacrifices in fancy footwork it more than makes up for in hand, elbow, and grappling techniques. The main hand weapons include *straight, leopard,* and *back fists;* the *tiger claw,* and the *knife hand.* Tiger uses all elbow techniques. Depending on the particular system employed, kicks are generally either snap or crescent types, but Southern Tiger and Hung Gar employ both types.

There is also no denying that Tiger techniques are not subtle! Punches are for pulverizing, claws are for tearing, and grappling moves are for dislocating joints. Tiger strikes are the ones aimed at breaking bones, so if you wish to spend a lot of practice time breaking boards and other hard objects, this is the style to learn. (Practitioners of other styles can certainly develop breaking skills, but their techniques are more often aimed at making lighter hits against smaller, vulnerable pressure points.) While non-martial observers may understandably describe a White Crane or Dragon form as "dancing," there is little likelihood of seeing a Tiger set and making a similar error. In practicing Shaolin's Tiger forms, every strike is performed as if breaking an opponent's bones. There is no subtlety in the moves, and no hint that any particular strike could easily double as a throw. Among Shaolin sets, those of Tiger style are the most vocal, with many ch'i cries and hollers to distract an opponent.

Tiger Systems

Tiger is an incredibly diverse style, with many dozens of systems that originated throughout China. Additional Tiger influence is seen in styles from Burma, Malaysia, Thailand, and the Philippines, and no doubt many techniques found their way from Shaolin sources to these other countries. Within Shaolin, though, are the following systems:

Southern Tiger: When most people think of Tiger moves, it is Southern Tiger they generally envision. There are five basic stances and a wealth of hand techniques that include strikes, blocks, clawing moves, and grappling. There are also numerous elbow, low kicking, and throwing techniques. Along with its close offshoot, Fu Jow, Southern Tiger uses clawing and raking techniques more than any other Tiger style. There are few aerial or acrobatic moves, so it is not a technically difficult method to learn. However, the diversity of techniques and the variety of applications for each makes Southern Tiger a style that takes considerable time and practice to master at even modest levels of proficiency.

Tiger Claw (Fu Jow, or Fu Jow Pai): Similar to Southern Tiger is Tiger Claw, which is descended from Hark Fu Moon, which is the Chinese language designation for (southern, not Shantung) Black Tiger.[136] There is greater emphasis on punches and clawing techniques than on kicking or throws. This is a very physically demanding style, with low solid stances that place considerable stress on the thigh muscles. There is an active core of practitioners that has spread Fu Jow to many countries. Fu Jow Pai has used the following ranking system in recent years:

Fu Jow Pai Rankings	
Rank Title	**Sash**
yat-kup	beginner, gray sash
ye-kup	add gold stripe to sash
sum-kup	add green stripe
yat-choun	black sash with gold stripe
ye-choun	four years, add gold stripe
sum-choun	six years, add gold stripe
ng-choun	ten years, add green stripe
but-choun	twenty years, add red stripe
gow-choun	twenty-five years, add white stripe
sup-choun	thirty years, add black stripe

Shantung Black Tiger: This is the easternmost Tiger system, formed near the Korean peninsula. The footwork is more typically "northern" than in any other Tiger style, and the hand movements longer and more fist-oriented than in other systems. By almost any standard of analysis, the Shantung system is a hard, linear martial art.[137] Shantung Black Tiger was reinvented in the Honan Temple before being released in its modern form, and is the most yang style in the Shaolin repertoire. It was the only Temple style to never have a female master. It places more emphasis on footwork than the southern forms and bears some resemblance to the Southern Eagle Claw system. In addition to emphasizing *hammer* and *backfist* strikes, Black Tiger also has a very large repertoire of grabbing and joint controlling techniques in its arsenal.

Tiger-Crane (Hung Gar, or Fu-Hok Pai): Hung Gar is another well-represented art in many countries. As the name suggests, this system incorporates elements of Southern Tiger and White Crane, producing an unusual and very effective hybrid art. This hybrid is very demanding in terms of stance and footwork; stances are often very low and shift quickly. Hand techniques favor long-range punches and both high and low close-range kicks.[138] The style is among the most physically demanding of all gung fu; it is also (by far) the most widely dispersed of the Shaolin Tiger styles. Aspects of Tiger-Crane are manifest in Okinawan Goju-ryu Karate. Three important forms are the *Gung Gee Fook Fu Kuen* (*Taming the Tiger Form*), the *Fu Hok Seung Ying Kuen* (*Tiger and Crane Double Form*), and the *Tiet Sin Kuen* (*Iron Thread Form*). These three forms were published for the public by Lam Sai Wing, a noted early Hung Gar practitioner.

White Eyebrow (Pak Mei): This system is a controversial one as regards its origins and resulting offshoots. There are two Shaolin origin stories, one crediting the style to the Taoist teachings of Lao Tzu, the other to the renegade priest named White Eyebrow. This system is quite distinct from much of its Tiger origins, and is covered in the chapter on centerline styles.

White Tiger (Pak Fu): This ancient system blends techniques and meditation practices from Tibet with early classical Shaolin Tiger. It exists today as a "closed door" system taught only to senior practitioners of Tiger or White Crane. There is also an established non-Shaolin school. This system has more flow than Hung Gar and is faster than Tiger. It is Chinese in origin, founded by a monk who consorted with White Eyebrow. One studies this style after mastering one's own system or, if a Tiger stylist, after learning all below it. The third form consists entirely of aerial kicks, one covering 360º in the air. We believe that White Tiger's saber set is the most advanced form devised for that weapon. The remaining material in the style provides a lead to Ruby Dragon techniques.

Leopard: Another large cat system, Leopard is notable for its constant moving stances, the *leopard's paw fist*, and the tendency to prefer lower targets such as the solar plexus, abdomen, and groin. Leopard combines elements of Mantis and Tiger: it waits for an opening, strikes largely at secondary vital points, but once in motion continues a barrage of strikes until the opponent is neutralized. Leopard differs from Tiger in its greater use of lower stances, strikes to lower targets, and its primary aim to render an opponent unconscious instead of maimed or dead. Shaolin's Leopard has been largely incorporated into Tiger and, to a lesser extent, Snake. Non-Temple versions of Leopard proliferate in many places.

Shaolin Monkey (White Ape, or Bai Yuan): Monkeys form an especially important part of Chinese mythology, and an ancient story entitled simply "Monkey" may be the oldest known novel in the world. Shaolin's Monkey style is really based on the actions of the large native apes (which are tailless; monkeys have tails). There are similarities between the Temple's style and the much later and radically different Monkey styles. In White Ape, the practitioner uses complex footwork, irregular patterning (neither linear nor circular, but bits of both), and considerable ground fighting. Hand techniques are strongly derived from Leopard and Tiger; they are used as strikes and grabs, respectively.

Monkey styles share many features with Drunken systems, particularly misdirection and whipping "soft" strikes. They aim to mislead an opponent into dismissing the practitioner as mentally deficient (or intoxicated), and then respond with finger and hand or foot techniques that whip the opponent with great force. Recall that F=ma (force equals mass times acceleration), or more appropriately $E = \frac{1}{2} mv^2$ (where energy equals one half mass times the square of velocity), so these "soft" techniques actually are quite powerful because of the velocity at which they are delivered.

In the Tiger styles, we first encounter the concepts of "time and system," meaning we have a choice about which system is best suited for a particular situation. Because of the diversity within Tiger, we have systems for most occasions; it is simply a matter of experience that determines when a particular system is best used.

Monkey (not to be confused with non-Shaolin Monkey styles) and Leopard are especially useful at night, when the blinding hand and foot movements are nearly invisible. These styles employ movements that are faster than the eye can compensate for when light is absent. Leopard is also good on slippery or wet surfaces, because it uses low and well-anchored stances. Tiger is useful during bright daylight, as well as on hills, but is difficult on wet ground because it favors higher and twisting stance work than Leopard or Monkey. White Eyebrow is excellent in hot weather, when frustration is easily created in an opponent. White Eyebrow's speed and economy of motion are plenty bewildering without aggravating environmental conditions added to the mix.

As for defense against weapons, all systems cover that aspect, but the strong points are found in Tiger and Hong Tiger. In Tiger, momentum allows painless, swift reactions to weapon attacks while Hong Tiger trains the body to absorb shocking blows. Hong Tiger was founded primarily as a defensive art against armed soldiers (and so is excluded from the primary listing of Tiger systems above).

One other consideration about Tiger and its subsystems is that the opponent is more likely to be maimed, permanently, than with most other systems. The sheer use of power in Tiger blows typically causes broken bones, dislocated joints, blood clotting, and can even cause so much damage as to require amputation.

Tiger Forms

Because Shaolin's Tiger style has enveloped so many other styles and systems, the breadth of a Tiger master's education is phenomenal. Listed (opposite page) are the major forms studied by Tiger practitioners.

The forms of the core Southern Tiger style are the primary emphasis for students pursuing Tiger. *The Five Points of the Star* is the key form, and contains a wealth of technique, in addition to tactical training. The entire form is repeated off the opposite side of the body in the *Golden Tiger* form. *Tiger versus Crane* is another foundation set. *Rain* contains no footwork and a substantial amount of ch'in na. Just as *Tiger versus Crane* is a "cross-over" form teaching the Tiger stylist aspects of Crane, *Tiger and Old Man* provides a student of Tiger an entry into Dragon. Much can be said about these and other Tiger forms that will have to wait for another volume.

Dragon Rides the Wind is a technique prominently featured in The Five Points of the Star, the key form of Southern Tiger

Major Tiger Forms, from Most Advanced Down to Most Basic	
Form	**Source Style or System**
Golden Tiger	Southern Tiger
Tiger Bares its Claws	Southern Tiger
Leopard Bares its Claws	Leopard
Eagle 1-3	Southern Eagle
Tiger's Revenge	Southern Tiger
Monkey with Ball of String	Shaolin Monkey
Monkey in Grass	Shaolin Monkey
Monkey 1-10	Shaolin Monkey
Spear	Southern Tiger
Panther	Leopard
Longbow and Arrow	Southern Tiger
Seven Pushes	Southern Tiger
Tiger and Old Man	Southern Tiger
Hong Tiger 1-8	Hong Tiger
Sh'u Tiger 1-3	Sh'u Tiger
Snow Leopard	Leopard
Leopard at Dawn	Leopard
Rain	Southern Tiger
Tiger versus Crane	Southern Tiger
The Five Points of the Star	Southern Tiger

The Sh'u Tiger forms are weapons forms, and are studied along with the Hong Tiger forms, which emphasize disarmament. Sh'u and Hong Tiger are military subsystems that made their way into the Shaolin curriculum. Monkey, Southern Eagle, and Leopard are also very important aspects of Tiger. These styles were grouped under Tiger some time ago by the Shaolin Order, as they share very similar tactics. The inclusion of these styles also makes Tiger accessible to practitioners of different temperaments and body types. A Shaolin master od Monkey gung fu would technically be considered as a Tiger master, respecting the ancient custom of five animal styles.

Snake

There is precious little written material available about the Snake styles, though they provide foundation sets in traditional Shaolin, family styles, and are incorporated in a host of peripheral styles such as Pa Kua and T'ai Chi Ch'uan. It is possibly because of the near-universal inclusion of Snake techniques in Chinese and extralimital styles that little specific work has been presented on the style. Much as Dragon style, however, Snake has always been a "closed door" style only taught within the Temple, and so a scarcity of Snake masters may be more responsible for the lack of published material. Snake is probably second only to Tiger in appearing overtly martial to the untrained observer.

Snakes are conspicuous predators that have always intrigued humans, likely even prior to our ancestors becoming bipedal. Large snakes often constrict prey, preventing the rib cage from expanding to allow inhaling and causing death via asphyxiation (true, constrictors such as pythons may "crush" their prey, but only if the prey animal is strong enough to break its own bones while trying to inhale). Many small and colorful snakes are deadly venomous, and to early humans the mysterious death caused after a small bite was probably seen as nothing short of magic. Such creatures, then, combined elements worth including in a martial arts style.

Snake styles probably developed as some of the first codified martial arts creations. The emphasis on hitting weak points along the ch'i *meridians* suggests that such meridians and primal acupuncture had already been worked out (it has been suggested by some practitioners of acupuncture that the meridian routes were mapped based [to some degree] on common sites for mosquito bites; many bites induce discomfort in distant parts of the body—interesting idea). The two universal aspects of Snake techniques are pinpoint open-hand strikes and twisting arm postures to disguise line of attack. Such movements are most often seen in Wing Chun forms, particularly the third, or *Bil Jee*, set, in which most of the hand techniques are Snake-derived. The *finger thrusts* are aimed at soft and vulnerable targets including the eyes, throat, temples, and solar plexus, and at debilitating acupuncture points. Contrary to what one may see in the movies, Snake practitioners generally do not practice thrusting their fingers through boards and bricks.

Most Snake practitioners use an upright, mobile stance, appearing less *horse stance*-like than most other styles. The intent is to employ rapid advance/sidestepping footwork; Snake stylists don't trade blows, or "tough-out" attacks. Using fast, alternating jabs, the practitioner drills at an opponent, sidesteps counterattacks, and drives home his attack. There are some stylistic variations, such as one Fukien-based system that employs low sweeps (and is thus an exception to the general rule of sweeps being confined to northern styles), and the systems that follow the Python route involve considerable grappling, mainly by securing a hold around the opponent's neck. On those occasions when the practitioner wants to use a strong and thrusting strike, the *leopard fist* is employed. Northern Snake stylists will use a *leopard fist* as a temple strike in preference to a *thrusting finger* strike.

A Shaolin practitioner is taught to use these techniques as a last resort, for there is little subtlety in the action of pressure point strikes. But as a consequence of this limitation, Shaolin also teaches Snake style as a quick response system—it is not about enduring and trading blows, but positioning for one quick and decisive strike to end a fight.

Snake Forms

The number and variety of forms linked to the Snake style is staggering: there is practically no style that lacks one or more Snake-based sets. Within traditional Shaolin, though, about eight to ten unarmed sets are usually taught. We will discuss a few of the forms which might be taught to a student pursuing Snake studies. (In Shaolin, there are around 40 Snake forms - one needn't study all of them to learn the style.)

Most basic in movements is *White Snake Leaves its Burrow*. Unlike most other Shaolin sets, this particular form has beginning moves that serve as a stretch and warm-up. The moves of this White Snake form are initially slow and deliberate, making the student learn the very precise way in which Snake techniques must be performed.

Leopard Fist is a long Python form that bears little resemblance to other Snake sets. It stresses strong low stances, hard thrusting punches, and forearm blocks. The purpose of this form is to teach a variety of principles, including strength punching, rapid shifting to a variety of stances and attacks, and the endurance that is needed in a long combat situation. The physical demands of the *Leopard Fist* make it a cornerstone of Snake's body conditioning regimen.

Snake Strikes Multiple Opponents is a Viper attack set, one of the very few such sets in Shaolin gung fu. Using a flurry of *thrusting finger* and *knife hand* strikes interspersed with low kicks, this form uses the philosophy of "the best defense is a good offense," taking combat to several attackers simultaneously. Though the moves are simple—and not deceptively so— the timing and body posturing may take several years to master.

Snake stances are typically either very low, or very high

Major Snake Forms, from Most Advanced Down to Most Basic
Shooting Fingers
Snake Becomes a Dragon
Crane and Snake Fight Over a Frog
Hidden Viper Comes Out
Python Attacks the Ape
Snake Strikes Multiple Opponents
Leopard Fist
White Snake Leaves its Burrow

Python Attacks the Ape is the closest thing Snake offers that can even remotely be called grappling. Though several sets exist with this name, the Shaolin Python version uses sliding parries to evade attacks by knife-wielding opponents, leading to neck and head grabs that allow the Snake stylist to break the opponent's neck. Students are taught that the techniques learned here are absolutely last resort techniques. A true master, however, has the ability to modify the grabs so the opponent merely passes out, but this is a very difficult level to learn.

In *Hidden Viper Comes Out*, the student learns how to use Snake techniques in the most inconspicuous ways. Using light and well-aimed technique against pressure points, the resulting strikes can produce responses from temporary paralysis, to unconsciousness, to immediate death, to death following several hours. In learning this Viper set, the practitioner is taught details of the *delayed death touch*, known as *"dim mak,"* particularly the use of the *viper's bite.*

Crane and Snake Fight Over a Frog is a very complicatedViper form that uses perhaps the widest range of Snake techniques. Among its special characteristics is the rare use of flying kicks, and a rapid combination of *finger thrusts* and punches. It also incorporates several White Crane moves, so that the resulting hand and elbow techniques closely resemble Wing Chun. The tendency to combine elements of different styles is widespread in gung fu. Examples include Wing Chun's Crane-Snake, Hung Gar's Tiger-Crane, Dragon's Dragon-Snake, and others.

Snake Becomes a Dragon is an advanced Viper set that uses Snake striking techniques, but uses Dragon style stances. Instead of evading the incoming attacks, the practitioner of this form "digs in" and becomes the focal point of the attack. In its ability to move attacks around the defender, this set has several aspects that resemble Aikido.

Shooting Fingers, known to Snake people as *Chum #3*, is similar to the form of the same name in Wing Chun, except this Viper form includes substantial stepping footwork.

Snake Applications

Snake conveys lessons in striking pinpoint vital spots repeatedly, and doing so with a rhythm that confuses the opponent. It also teaches suppleness to move past an opponent's defenses so a strike is almost always successfully delivered. Its stance work is simple, its hand and foot techniques few in number. Snake does not aim to trade blows or jockey for position. Instead, it is based on the concept of "wait, one strike, fight is over." Consequently, all its techniques are potentially lethal, making it the easiest style to learn. It takes far more effort to evade or control an adversary than to injure one. Deadly strikes do not require as much precision to hurt an opponent (i.e. it takes more skill and care to *not* hurt an opponent), hence they are easier to learn and deliver.

Snake's adherence to unassuming stances and rapid attacks make the style deceptively simple-looking. Snake stylists are taught to spring from rest posture to full attack; there are no preparatory stances or "threatening" gestures. If attacked, the Snake stylist bobs and weaves, looking much like anyone else, until an opening presents itself. The strikes then fly quickly, in succession, hitting the same opening over and over. Should the attacker block one of these Snake-strikes, the Snake changes targets and continues its barrage. This machine gun approach to multiple rapid strikes is also characteristic of a much more recent innovation, Southern Praying Mantis. In Snake, kicks are low, snappy, and aimed at the shins, knee, or top of foot.

Snake is an interface between the high styles and low styles. It is the easiest style to learn and also one of the most deadly. It is classified as transitional because it has the movements of a spiritual style and the physical applications of a low style. The spiritual movements are all flowing and continuous, akin to the movements of a cloud. The stabbing hand motions to the face, throat and genitals are typical applications of such movements. Ch'i is present in the practitioner as his body mimics a snake in its coiling, undulating motions; for only through ch'i can the proper flow be achieved to allow the technique to work. It is an earthly animal by nature, yet still somewhat spiritual due to its mysterious character. The snake has thus been appointed as the guardian of the dragons. (Snakes play an important role in many eastern mythologies. In China, certain ancient snakes metamorphose into dragons, and nagas frequently recur in accounts of the Buddha's life and in Buddhist legends.)

The Snake movements, expressing a constant interplay of Taoist yin and yang, are used to develop endurance, mental flexibility, and the ability to confound the opponent. "Breathing [is] done slowly, deeply, softly and harmoniously. Movements [are] flowing and rippling with emphasis on the fingers."[139] Beginning Snake students are taught forms and techniques that are largely taken from Leopard and Choy Li Fut, with the intention of teaching the student important stance work and using a multiple set of striking techniques from the same limb in quick succession. Eventually, the narrower and more upright Snake stance is introduced along with the more characteristic moves of the style. One source aptly classifies five essential Snake tactics as follows:

Hitting—using quickness and surprise.
Winding—maintaining closeness.
Ambushing—attacking from a hidden position.
Escaping—getting free when outclassed.
Leaping—evading attack by jumping up or to sides.[140]

Snake Sub-Systems

Southern Snake is really a tripartite style, including Viper, Python, and White Snake. Cobra is discussed here for completeness, but isn't necessarily studied, and all of these sub-systems employ dim mak skills.

Viper: This is the "standard" Snake approach, with a small variety of hand strikes, elbow techniques, and low, snappy kicks. The stance is a *high horse*, with occasional shifts to the long and low "snake creeps down" posture (*snake stance*). It is taught as an almost entirely offensive martial art, and is used only as a last resort. This system employs the first two fingers as striking weapons that target vital points on the arms, throat, and groin of the attacker. The grasp-and-pinch techniques of the *viper's bite* are aimed at sealing acupuncture points to cause paralysis, unconsciousness, or death. Viper is the most generic, and probably most recent, Snake system.

Python: As the name implies, this aspect of Snake uses grappling techniques to choke an opponent. Python is the most external of Snake sub-systems, usually employing a closed fist.

White Snake: White Snake is the most ancient of Snake systems, and includes Snake's saber work. Before the development of Viper, White Snake constituted the core of Shaolin Snake. Much of White Snake is Dragon-like in appearance.

Cobra: This unusual northern system, which appears to be a typical southern style, is all but extinct today. Only a few bits and pieces of the system survive. Its movements resemble a cobra rising from the grass with spread hood. The typical stance is a variation on the *bow and arrow stance*, and all hand techniques are open and use *finger thrusts* or, less commonly, *palm strikes*. Kicks are low and straight, but the style does use one high *crescent kick*. The strikes are strictly defensive in nature, tend to target vital striking points, and are followed by hanging on and taking pains that the opponent will die. Beginners are taught a variety of wide, arcing parries. Cobra was designed for speed, simplicity, and combating armed foes.

A Cobra ready stance

Delayed Death Touch (Dim Mak): Legendary beyond words is the martial art of *dim mak*. The principle behind *dim mak* technique is simply an extension of acupuncture, using pressure point strikes to cause ch'i flow errors along certain meridians. It is said that a master of the art can strike a person in such a way as to cause death to occur from minutes to days after the appropriate strike or strikes have been delivered. Though the early origins of this art are lost to history, we hold to prevailing Shaolin lore that it was devised as a Cobra style application of acupuncture. It was once believed that to temporarily induce death and then revive a patient, certain serious disorders could be overcome. Note that we frequently hear of drowning or freezing victims who are resuscitated several minutes after clinical death has occurred. We also clear up many computer problems such as locked-up keyboards by doing a system reboot. In truth, early *dim mak* may have begun as a medical technique to "reboot" a seriously ill patient. As with so many other discoveries, a martial application was discovered as well, taking *dim mak* on a notorious path through Asian history.

Snake practitioners do not specialize in one particular subsystem—rather, all Shaolin Snake stylists will study all Snake subsystems. You will never encounter a Shaolin Python stylist, for instance, only Shaolin Snake stylists. Today, Snake is a style seldom heard of and rarely seen, and its presence in a school's curriculum is a good litmus test for discovering whether that school has genuine Shaolin roots.

Northern Praying Mantis

It is generally agreed that the founder of the Northern Praying Mantis school (T'ang Lang Ch'uan) was the boxer Wang Lang, who developed the method of combat around 1600. (Although, according to at least one source, Wang lived during the 10th or 11th century.[141] By now, you've realized that dates aren't very reliable or standardized when it comes to Chinese martial arts history!) Wang, who was probably a Ming patriot,[142] left his native Shantung province to improve his gung fu at the Honan Temple. It was during this stay that Wang was disappointed with his level of skill, and by chance came upon a praying mantis in battle with a much larger cicada. (Keep in mind that the Chinese mantis, *Tenodera aridifolia sinensis*, is about twice the size of the American/European species *Mantis religiosa*.[143]) The mantis overcame the adversary, and Wang took the insect back to the Temple to study its movements. These he systematized with his previous knowledge, incorporating the erratic footwork of the Monkey style,[144] and thus created the basic Northern Praying Mantis style.

Mantis Systems

The diversification from Wang's original style becomes more complex and confusing as each splinter group claims a more direct lineage than the next. Wang Lang's students—four according to some pai sources who count Yin-yang, Seven Stars, Plum Blossom, and Bare as the original four variants;[145] only three according to other pai sources[146]—each went out to find a representative mantis and alter the style to suit their needs. Another source makes no historical claims, but traces four major schools: Seven Stars, Six Combinations, T'ai, and Wah Lum.[147] (The popular Wah Lum style is actually a fairly recent version of Mantis.) Our Shaolin oral tradition holds that there were seven primary students, although we admit that hard data on these details are not available. Of the original students, one named his style after a mantis with seven spots on the thorax (according to some sources), and his school became the Seven Stars Praying Mantis, and similarly with the other six students. They founded the earliest systems, including Southern, Tall Buddha, T'ai Mantis (also known as "T'ai Chi"), Seven Stars, Plum Blossom, Bare and Yin-yang. Later developments include Orchid Blossom, Northern, Tibetan, and Mongolian as well as a Mantis-Snake hybrid. The subtle distinctions regarding the more prominent Mantis variants, in no particular order, can be described as follows:

Seven Stars (Chi Hsing or Tsi T'sing): Footwork follows a pattern resembling the seven classical stars in Chinese astrology, i.e., being intricate in nature. While all branches stress emitting power from the waist, this school is largely soft-style, evading direct power confrontations. Some lineages point out that the style was not named for a mantis with seven stars on its back, but rather for the characteristic footwork.

Plum Blossom (Mei Hua): Stresses *plum flower fist* strategies, such as three or five staccato punches in sequence; using a fist in preference to open hands; and is considered by many to be an introductory style,[148] not going on to truly advanced techniques. Plum Blossom is a fairly "hard" style.[149]

Six Combinations (Liu He): Combines three yin and three yang principles to evade or absorb an attack softly and attack in a hard manner.

Spotless or Bare (Kwong P'an): The branch northern stylists refer to as "southern," the wrists are kept bent and hands open in order to generate great whipping power over short distances. Relies more upon hand work than other northern styles. (This style differs slightly from the Northern Mantis style that is actually called "Southern." But *neither* Bare Northern Mantis nor Southern Northern Mantis is the Southern Praying Mantis style discussed later in the text!)

Secret Door: The most prevalent family style of Mantis, Secret Door uses low stances and frequent elbow strikes. Transitions are far more complex than other styles, used as feints to get into the preferred close-range striking position. One of Secret Door's specialties is defenses against other Mantis styles.

Jade Ring: Named for its peculiar footwork.

Dragging Hand: Uses grappling and grabbing techniques, not unlike Aikido. Back of wrist strikes are common, and the style prefers breaking to striking (Mantis's answer to ch'in na).

Eight Step: Emphasis here is on sticking hands, and leading an opponent to a point of vulnerability. Little actual evasion is employed, as practitioners are taught the superiority of leading the assailants.

Hua Lin, or T'am/T'an T'ui: This style, Seeking Leg Praying Mantis from the Hua Lin Temple, aims to check the opponent's move into a favorable attack position. Kicks are uncharacteristically low and fast, delivered with snap, and rarely above the knees. Practitioners of this branch are taught the use of feet over and above handwork. Hua Lin is best known in Shaolin as a system of Northern Praying Mantis which utilizes T'am T'ui training methods, with many kicks, sweeps, and rolls.

Sometimes the style is called "Hua Lin T'am T'ui" or "T'am T'ui," which is a quite popular name and refers to other styles as well. Elements of the largely Muslim-originated T'am T'ui style found their way into Long Fist, (Northern) Eagle Claw, and Mantis. This kind of stylistic crossover is very common in Chinese gung fu systems.

T'ai Mantis (T'ai Chi T'ang Lang): T'ai Mantis is the Shaolin school of Northern Praying Mantis, corresponding to the southern Choy Li Fut style in having a variety of high and low stances, strong fist and open hand strikes, and often acrobatic kicks. This system is famous for wild flying kicks, acrobatic stunts, and ground fighting. It is similar in methods to White Crane, but the differences are obvious when observed. Strikes are delivered with great internal power, using a penetrating strike rather than sub-surface impact. Parries are favored over blocks, and power generates from the ground to the waist to technique. T'ai Mantis specializes in the staff, three-section staff, and chain whip.

To this school belongs probably the greatest arsenal of elbow techniques known. Breaking, locking, and throwing by using the elbows is so highly developed that these stylists rarely need other tactics. Beginners, however, prefer the flashy footwork of the system. Shorter women are able to employ T'ai Mantis tactics to excellent advantage, as the style's low center of gravity is very well suited to a woman's lower center. Noted T'ai Mantis Grandmaster Chiu Chuk Kai is largely responsible for spreading the style in the 20th century.

A T'ai Mantis ready stance

Among the founders of the various Mantis styles, the T'ai Mantis founder was expelled from the Honan Temple and spent some time in exile in a small Buddhist temple that had been removed from the Shaolin Order. (We no longer know exactly why this occurred, only that it did.) His style achieved prominence because of its simplicity and linear movement. In time, both the monk and his system of combat were reunited with the Honan Temple, and the T'ai Mantis style became one of the core elements of the five-formed fist of Shaolin. Historically, Mantis has been reserved exclusively for the fut doo, the monks who remained in the Temple.

Mi-Tsung Lohan (My Jong Law Horn): Although Lost Track Buddha Guardian style was influenced by the Lost Track style, My Jong Law Horn is in fact a synthesis of many styles which were taught at the Ching Woo Association. Attempts to classify this system place it as either a White Crane or Northern Praying Mantis derivative. Because the style was popular in Hong Kong, the White Crane elements became very pronounced. However, we consider it to be a branch of Northern Mantis due to the heavy influence of Seeking Leg Praying Mantis and other Northern Mantis systems. This classification is somewhat arbitrary, though.

Shen Chi: Uncommon northern style of Mantis.

Wah Lum: Named after the Wah Lum Temple, this is another Northern Mantis variant largely shaped by T'am T'ui influences. Movement in the style is exceptionally springy.

Yin-yang: A variation of Seven Stars, in which grappling plays a lesser role. It was named after an insect with a marking that resembled the yin/yang device.

Stylistic variations, as noted above, are actually quite minor, and a practitioner from one branch will usually have very similar training to one from another branch. The hand motions, elbow strikes, and nimble footwork are common to each. As so often happens in creating "new" styles, one branch may use a *seven stars stance* while delivering a particular punch while another may use a *bow and arrow stance* or *cat stance* instead; one may favor the closed fist, another the open hand. The forms themselves are quite uniform, following very closely a single pattern of movement and targets, though using variations in stances or type of strike employed.

Confusions sometimes arise from the fact that the yin-yang is also known as the "T'ai Chi," or "Supreme Ultimate," symbol. So, Yin-yang Mantis might also be referred to as "T'ai Chi Mantis," but T'ai Chi Mantis (discussed above) and Yin-yang Mantis are distinct subsystems, so we'll employ the "Yin-yang" name for that style. (It is also true that some lineages refer to T'ai Mantis as "Yin-yang Mantis," leading to further complications.) Adding to the frustration of the martial taxonomist is one branch of Plum Blossom Mantis, which refers to itself as "T'ai Chi

Mantis."[150] There are probably other "Supreme Ultimate" Mantis styles as yet unknown to us!

The evolution of numerous schools stemming from Northern T'ang Lang is due, in part, to the multi-faceted training undertaken by expert boxers. It has always been rare for a Chinese gung fu practitioner to study a single style. Normally, one is introduced to the popular style being taught by a relative or a town instructor, and with time the man may go on to study other styles from other teachers as they become available. Before settling into a given style, this exponent may have been involved in ten systems of combat, and was often involved in actual application, before mastering the chosen branch. Thus, one sect of Mantis may use a solidly-planted front *toe kick* taken from a Spring Leg style form, while another master may teach his students to use a flying *crescent kick* taken from his northern Shaolin training. Personal bias of the individual founder was often as important as practicality in making such distinctions.

In its purest form, Northern Praying Mantis as taught in the Shaolin Monastery at Honan included all of the material that would eventually be fragmented into the non-Temple "family" styles, and included a ch'i set as well. Because the parent style of the Northern Praying Mantis was invented to overcome the conventional non-Temple styles, it was the pinnacle taught to the most advanced adepts in the Temple. Although T'ai Mantis is the official Mantis system of the Shaolin Order, we try to practice the Mantis style in a holistic manner—studying relevant stylistic variations and even non-Temple Mantis styles. The special place accorded Mantis only served to increase respect for the radical new style, and for that reason Mantis masters are in far greater demand than supply.

The existence of so many family sects of Mantis must, then, be a cause of consternation, for how did the most revered combat method of the Temple manage to escape to the populace at large? During the period concerned, the latter 17th century, the Honan Temple became a center for insurgents fighting the newly established Manchu hierarchy. Patriotic boxers from all parts of China took "refuge" under the Shaolin roofs, more to learn to combat the new regime than to undertake the ways of the monks. Some priests, and other highly skilled boxers and military men, trained rebel forces to overthrow the Ch'ing, and in so doing disseminated many of the external styles, including T'ang Lang Ch'uan. Wang Lang, along with some other rebels and Shaolin, escaped an imperial attack upon the Honan Temple.[151] They ended up in Shantung Province, where the Mantis style proliferated and evolved further.

Praying Mantis ended up being widely disseminated both in Honan and Shantung Provinces. Reentering civilian society, soldiers who had survived kept their Mantis skills a closely guarded secret, only passing on their knowledge to close members of the family (usually the sons). The exact extent of the consequent dilution can be seen if one compares the identical form being performed by a Shaolin Mantis stylist and a family practitioner. There is no good or bad involved, because each had different uses; they are merely different.

Northern Praying Mantis teachings that left the Temple and became common throughout northern China were a combination of Seven Stars, T'ai Mantis and some White Ape that was taught in Honan. Internal sets and ch'i development were carefully guarded secrets by the priests, and these methods required too much time and subtlety to be of use to insurgent soldiers. Because of this, many of the Mantis variants have very little internal training. Some Mantis stylists, however, list the Wutang internal styles as important influences upon their lineages.[152] (Later notes from our internal records indicate that the version of Northern Praying Mantis which "seeped" out of the Honan Temple was a hybrid of Black Crane, White Ape [Shaolin's Monkey], Eagle Claw and various Mantis styles from the North). This stylistic blending is not an original approach, but it is a popular one; Shaolin's T'ai Mantis crystallized into its modern form around 1880.

Mantis Forms

Northern Praying Mantis forms are, like those of the Snake style, relatively straightforward, made of simple moves and a limited number of stances. Unlike Snake, however, the vast majority of Mantis techniques have multiple applications, such that a *straight punch* can actually be an elbow break, wrist grab release, arm release, lateral strike, or even a simple *straight punch*. The variety of stances employed is limited to *bow and arrow, hill climbing, back, seven stars, kneeling, hanging horse, scissors, cat,* and *low horse stances.*

Mantis stylists often employ Scissors and Seven Stars Stances during transitions

Possibly the most familiar and widely taught of all Northern Praying Mantis sets is the *Bouncing Step* (*Bung Bo Kuen*). *Bung Bo Kuen* has even been incorporated into numerous non-Mantis styles (Northern Eagle, for instance[153]). Despite its simplicity, there are at least three major variations of the form in existence. One has a high spinning aerial *back kick*, another has high front *snap kicks* and *finger thrusts*, and the third has no high kicks and uses only closed fists. The set does teach most of the basic Mantis techniques, with later forms differing mainly in their length and complicated footwork.

Other well-known classic sets include the *Punch and Jab* (*Spear Hand*), which teaches short range, snappy hand strikes, and the *Small Circular Fist* (*Syau Wan Ch'uan*), which has a wonderful variety of directional transition moves and joint breaking strikes. (Some sources even list *Small Circular Fist* as being a style with only a single form, sharing the same name. Whatever the form's origin, it has been incorporated into Shaolin's Mantis.) The forms for Northern Praying Mantis are fortunately finite in number (although it may seem otherwise at times), and may be listed in rough order of complexity (see below).[154] These are the core forms in the Shaolin syllabus - there are *many* more Mantis forms, including weapon forms. Bear in mind that complexity entails physical ability at one level, and use of inner power at another. A physically simple set may in fact be far more advanced than it appears.

Major Northern Praying Mantis Forms, from Most Advanced Down to Most Basic
Interception Form (a recent composite set)
Seven Stars Fist
Six Harmonies Fist
Very Important Fist
Plum Blossom Hand
Plum Blossom Falling Fist
Plum Blossom Fist
White Gibbon Steals the Peach
White Gibbon Comes Out of the Cave
Small Circular Fist
Lohan Skill (a ch'i development set)
Punch and Jab
Eighteen Ancestors
Avoiding Hardness
Four Way Running, Hitting Step
Bouncing Step

Mantis Applications

It is most likely because there were so many branches of Northern Mantis, and the style was both simple and effective, that it has survived as one of the most widely taught and familiar of Shaolin styles to this day. Common to all northern styles is the use of the *mantis claw*, the hand being held to resemble a mantid's talon, for striking, blocking and parrying. As a general rule, the mantis "claw" is symbolic in Northern Praying Mantis, where one grabs with the claw hand but does not hook or stab (while Southern Praying Mantis hooks but does not hang on—see section on centerline styles). Advanced practitioners learn to lock onto the opponent by employing sticking or leading techniques, but never maintain a strong grip. In this way, the practitioner may take a "free ride" into a strike as the opponent withdraws, or the *mantis claw* may release the opponent and allow him to yank back and off-balance. Mantis further employs breaking of joints, particularly at the elbow. Ironically, most breaking techniques are themselves elbow strikes, but the *star of palm* is also utilized.

The Mantis style is both efficient and well organized. Mantis has eight lethal and eight non-lethal attack points. These are struck with finger, fist, or elbow strikes. Kicks are used to distract or wear down an opponent. The style has 36 throws, many of which involve the use of elbows as leverage points or as adjuncts to sweeps. Northern Praying Mantis does not use lateral blocks with the forearm. Northern Mantis prominently features the *hill climbing* and the *seven stars stances*. The latter uses the toes-raised front foot to check the opponent's lead foot. Low and high leg sweeps are used on occasion. Other characteristic techniques include *p'eng pu* (throwing opponent off balance), *lan t'she* (redirect, restrain, or reduce opponent's force), and *pa tsou* (8 elbow offenses). These classic elbow strikes are as follows: 1) upward forward thrust, 2) upward reverse thrust, 3) forward horizontal thrust, 4) hooking sideways horizontal thrust, 5) downward thrust, 6) diagonal upward thrust, 7) diagonal side thrust, and 8) reverse side thrust.

From a tactical perspective, Mantis students were traditionally taught to become the mantis: to sit and wait until the time is right to strike instead of going out to the attack. While Snake strikes from constantly moving hands, Praying Mantis holds its weapons in check until an opening is presented. Then, shooting like a harpoon, the strike lashes out with great force. Mantis practitioners must therefore master techniques of speed while practicing patience. Thus, the Mantis practitioner behaves much like the insect in its natural setting: the mantis waits for its prey to venture near, and is capable of striking out with its forelegs faster than a fly can flap its wings to escape. Targets are often joints and secondary vital spots, places that cause great pain but not necessarily permanent injury or death. The simplicity of Mantis is its difficult part and if you "muscle" a technique, you "goofed" it. Beginning Mantis students often put more effort into a technique than is necessary for the technique to work.

Non-Chinese Mantis Systems

The efficacy and mystique of the praying mantis was an inspiration well beyond the influence of Shaolin or even Chinese martial arts. The insect itself is a formidable fighter, capable of overpowering prey larger than itself. With its long, hooked forearms lined with an impressive and piercing set of spines, the insect seems designed specifically to inspire a martial art (though, in a strange twist, Europeans saw the animal as being in prayer, not on guard, yet another example of how differently East and West view their worlds). To this day, Asian peoples engage in gambling on the results of fights between mantises they keep in small bamboo cages.

Three major non-Chinese versions of Mantis fighting are known within Shaolin. Yin-yang, Tibetan and Mongolian are obscure styles of Mantis. Yin-yang was not a Temple style and thus lacked an internal base. Its founder later ventured to Malaysia and began the Orchid Blossom system. Tibetan Mantis stems from elements of Northern Praying Mantis and Tibetan White Crane.

Mongolian Mantis is very swift, variable, and heavily imbued with grappling shunned by the other schools. Unlike other Mantis schools, the observer is rarely going to see mantis-like movements, or even a distinct pattern of movements that help differentiate this style from others. Its primary concern is not whether your strike was perfect but rather whether it was effective. The style is from Outer Mongolia, an offshoot developed when various crusades were assembled to take over Mongolia. It was derived from schools already extant and was developed by the Mongolians. There are six sword sets and three *quando* sets in addition to the unarmed forms, reflecting the style's goal of dismounting a cavalry soldier prior to grappling with him on the ground.

The popularity of the Mantis style should be clear from the proliferation of prominent non-Chinese branches. Praying Mantis is an incredibly *evolved* style, taking some of the best techniques from other styles and incorporating them into the curriculum. The highly developed specialization of the Mantis stylist seems somehow...appropriate, given the style's namesake.

Dragon

No creature, real or imaginary, holds a place of greater veneration or mystery in Asia than the dragon. Dragons are powerful near-deity creatures that are a composite of different known earthly animals. All could fly but, unlike their western counterparts, Asian dragons lack wings. Some had tiny legs with only two claws, while the imperial dragon had five claws and a round golden mane. The use and display of dragon symbols was tightly controlled by the government and, excepting some monastic orders, was limited to highly placed families. Anyone other than a member of the royal family seen with a representation of a five-clawed dragon could be put to death. Dragons have always been taken seriously in China.

Long before Saint George encountered his legendary beast, the dragon played an influential and beneficial role in Chinese culture. An amalgam of several creatures, including monitor lizards, pythons and the Chinese alligator, the polymorphic dragon was a water spirit, responsible for bringing the rains and thus insuring the survival of crops. The dragon was a symbolic guardian to the gods, and was the source of true wisdom. This latter feature most likely resulted from the observation that their living reptilian counterparts (usually at rest) seem to be in a near constant state of contemplation.

The dragon represented two of the ancient elements, Earth and Water, endowing the creature with illusion and power. A yang symbol, the Taoists saw the dragon as a personification of the Tao itself—"the dragon reveals himself only to vanish." (Ironically, although the dragon is a yang symbol, Shaolin teaches Dragon as a primarily internal style. Finally, it is the harmonious blend of yin and yang which make Dragon such a formidable style.) Shaolin Buddhists saw him as a vision of enlightened truth, to be felt, but never to be held. Certain very old men were called dragons, these being well versed in the life-supporting skills of herbal medicine, agriculture, and gung fu. In early China, these skills were surely a matter of life or death, and those so educated were held in high esteem. This partly exlpains why Shaolin uses Dragon titles for masters.

Some dragons are on a par with deities while others are guardians to deities, philosophers, and emperors. It is fairly accurate to say that in China there is a dragon for any purpose, or there can be if one so desires. The dragons of Shaolin symbolism bear five claws, the same as the imperial dragon. This came about for two reasons. First, the original Honan Temple was to bear the "seal of approval" of its founding emperor, so he allowed the Order to use a five-clawed dragon. Any other use of this creature, by any person in China, was a crime punishable by death. By the same token, anyone who displayed a five-clawed dragon did so with imperial permission and, by implication, protection. Later emperors, though, feared the Shaolin, and used their continued use of the imperial dragon as grounds to issue arrest and death warrants against its members.

By the end of the first millennium, after the martial arts were a well-established part of Shaolin practice, the dragon took on extra symbolic significance because its five claws represented the Order's five-formed fist of gung fu. Over time the Order's monks began to alter the appearance of their dragon, retaining the five claws but making a variety of "streamlining" changes to the anatomy. Over a period of some 300 years, this mythical creature underwent an interesting evolution.

Many phrases describe the attributes of the Dragon styles: going with the flow, riding the wind, merging into the Tao, and so on. The common theme is that Dragon merges with an opponent so thoroughly that only one entity exists, a combined attacker-defender. Dragon leads and responds to incoming energy mindlessly because the proponent is in a meditative state that allows swift reflex action to redirect an adversary to defeat himself. Many Dragon techniques are simple to learn and execute, but mastery of the style is the most difficult achievement in Shaolin martial arts.

The fact that dragons are mythological creatures might lead one to think that determining their properties would be difficult. Unlike cranes, tigers, snakes, leopards and praying mantises, dragons represent the only mythical creature in Shaolin's stylistic pantheon. But the properties of dragons, coming from several Asian sources, are fairly well established, and amply reflected in the different Dragon gung fu systems.

Dragon Properties and Corresponding Systems

Chinese dragon lore holds that dragons are bringers of rains, providers of fertility, and defenders of the deities. They are above all human pettiness and therefore defend only righteous causes and persons. Their ranking among themselves is determined by their color with, of course, a very Confucian hierarchy. Because the dragons were seen as pure, the possession of jade (believed to be dried dragon sperm) was practiced as a way to entice dragon protection and ward off evil. As a yang symbol as well, jade was kept to promote virility.[155] To this day, high quality jade is among the most valuable and costly of precious stones.

The Dragon systems are divided up into categories for six dragon gods. Each of these six dragon deities has other dragons as its guardians, corresponding very roughly to the theory of the *Five Elements*. In a practical sense, each Dragon system has elements of other Dragon systems to cover its defects. The Dragon of the Air has the Fire Dragon and Water Dragon as its guardians. Fire, Air, and Water constitute the system of White Dragon. The Dragon of Earth has Water and Air as its guardians. Earth, Water, and Air make up the systems of Black Dragon and Green Dragon. The Dragon of Fire has Spirit and Earth as its guardians. These three dragon entities—Fire, Spirit, and Earth—jointly symbolize the systems of Green Dragon, Blue Dragon and Red Dragon. The Dragon of Water conquers all below and has as its guardians the Air Dragon and Earth Dragon. Together they encompass the systems of Ruby Dragon and Sapphire Dragon. The Dragon of Spirit is the motivating force for the other dragons, for the spirit is in all things. The Spirit Dragon is supreme and all below it guard it (that is, the Dragon of Spirit has a symbolic role in all Dragon styles). Spirit, along with its guardians, comprises the systems of Sapphire Dragon, Emerald Dragon and Silver Dragon. The Dragon of Heaven controls the Spirit and thus all. It has patrons from all major dragons. The Dragon of Heaven corresponds to the systems of Emerald Dragon and Silver Dragon. The Jeet Li is the supreme ultimate dragon. This title is bestowed upon the Gold Dragon for achieving perfection of all below it. As a rank given to Dragon masters of the highest level, the Jeet Li is not listed in the following chart, which diagrams the various dragon gods and their interrelationships.

Dragon God Domains, Guardians, and Style Associations

Domain/Title	Guardian Dragons	Corresponding Styles
Dragon of Air	Dragons of Fire and Water	White
Dragon of Earth	Dragons of Water and Air	Black and Green
Dragon of Fire	Dragons of Spirit and Earth	Green, Blue, and Red
Dragon of Water	Dragons of Air and Earth	Ruby and Sapphire
Dragon of Spirit	Dragons of Fire, Water, Earth, and Air	Sapphire, Emerald, and Silver
Dragon of Heaven	Dragons of Fire, Water, Earth, Air, and Spirit	Emerald and Silver

A related taxonomy of dragons can be seen below. Emotional dragons (low to high) are black through red. Ethereal dragons (ruby and above) are celestial and more powerful. Some of the more common symbolic meanings associated with these dragons are listed here:

White: terrestrial association, southern
Black: terrestrial association, northern
Green: water, western
Blue: air, eastern
Red: fire, heat, energy, southern
Ruby: the earth's core heat or solar power
Sapphire: all gaseous matter
Emerald: oceans, massive water
Silver: mind, thought, intelligence
Gold: matter, hence all-encompassing
(White and silver were late additions.)

White Dragon and Black Dragon are complementary and when combined form the old system of Orange Dragon. The old Yellow and Orange Dragon systems are now extinct as such, their remaining techniques having been incorporated into Green Dragon and Blue Dragon. Neither Green nor Blue is distinctive. Red Dragon resembles Ruby but does not yet require total reliance on ch'i.

Ruby Dragon is the beginning of a new field, the epitome of all below it. It teaches functional use of a single-leg stance, circular use of Tiger tactics, advancement of the pinpoint techniques of Crane, and is the first Dragon to work completely without the use of strength. At the level of Ruby Dragon, the transition is made from the low dragons to the high dragons.

Sapphire, Emerald and Silver are all as different as Judo, western boxing and T'ai Chi Ch'uan. Sapphire Dragon makes use of powerful combat leg maneuvers even though it is a southern style. It exercises the lower back and nervous system tissue near the bone. It is similar to Tiger in its exercise of sinew except that it penetrates more deeply and promotes greater suppleness and nervous system response.

Emerald Dragon teaches flying kicks for balance and demands mastery of all hand techniques, including Mantis. To achieve expertise at this level, the practitioner has to learn all the Dragon sets in slow, T'ai Chi Ch'uan-style motion and apply each technique in soft ch'i-based form. But each set must also be demonstrated with roaring Tiger-like strength and speed, such that the same form, indeed the same move, will appear as different as night and day. Every self-defense movement will have low-level simple deflection, as well as high-level lethal strike, applications.

For Silver Dragon, the martial artist transcends all the previous styles, eschewing traditional forms for a natural and instinctive freedom of form that expresses the best use of his or her own body in combat. As no two people are identical, no two people will respond to an attack in precisely the same way. The Silver Dragon level of expertise thus takes the encyclopedic knowledge of combat, applications, and your own body's strong and weak points to evolve a truly unique fighting style. By having a style without style, there is no way an opponent can analyze your movements to find a predictable or familiar opening. In reaching this liberation, Silver Dragon closely parallels the method of approaching combat developed by what the late Bruce Lee termed "Jeet Kune Do," or "the way of the intercepting fist."[156] Like Jeet Kune Do, Silver Dragon is expressly not a style, but is rather a name for a method of self-learning and self-evaluation that allows a martial artist to capitalize on his or her strengths while also learning where his or her weaknesses lie. In knowing one's weaknesses, a practitioner may elect to improve weak techniques, abandon techniques that just do not work for him, or find ways to compensate for openings that such weaknesses might offer to an opponent.

Sage Points the Way may look flamboyant, but is in fact a simple technique requiring very little physical strength

The high dragons (ruby through gold) are the dragons that are used to rank the masters of the Temple. Thus, if a monk held the title of "Ruby Dragon," he held that rank, otherwise known as 6th degree. This title may refer even to a practitioner who knows very little of the Dragon style. Additionally, each Dragon system has its own ranks and a cumulative rank is awarded for all Dragon studied. For example, a disciple might learn several Dragon sets from different styles (or "colors"), but hold a single rank for overall Dragon proficiency.

There are a few aspects of Dragon study within the Shaolin Order that are especially notable. First, Dragon is a required area of study for high ranking Shaolin. Along with this, Dragon is not studied in much depth until practitioners are at least of the disciple level. Second, the Shaolin monk typically masters a non-Dragon style before pursuing Dragon. This is because Dragon is meant to inform other styles. What we mean here by "inform" is that study of the Dragon systems deepens the practitioner's understanding of ch'i and body mechanics in ways that will allow him to continue practicing gung fu up to and beyond 100 years of age (if he should live so long) in the monk's style of choice. Finally, the colored Dragon sub-systems are a Shaolin trademark—to our knowledge, lay persons were not taught Dragon in this fashion.

Origins of the Dragon Styles

The original stretching and twisting movements associated with Dragon (Lung Ch'uan) were part of Boddhidarma's exercises, taught to monks in the Shaolin Temple of Honan. Dragonish movements were part of the Temple's physical curriculum around 680. In the early days, cerebral training dominated combat training. Some of the physical maneuvers were developed by watching large lizards. The true emergence of the modern martial discipline of Dragon can be traced to about 1565, but the origin is uncertain. Two legends are noteworthy. One states that the Shaolin priestess Ng (or Wu) Mui created the style by using moves of deception and melding with an opponent. The other credits a monk, Mui Fa San Yang with contemplating his gung fu training and daydreaming about countermoves, when he became inspired by the twisting movements of the dragon. His style was later called "Yow Kung Moon" ("School of Flexible Work"), and was advanced by the monk Tit Yang Sum Si.[157] Both these stories place the origin at Honan Shaolin Temple.

Since then, Dragon gung fu has evolved into two distinct styles, Southern (1565) and Northern (1680). Over the years, units of instruction have been taken (incompletely) from each style and molded into family "Dragon" styles. Likewise, some of these non-Temple variants have found their way back into Shaolin's Dragon systems. As a result, the number of forms in the Dragon styles has grown quite large. A new synthesis to organize the Shaolin styles and systematize a combined approach was begun in 1972, and will be discussed further in a subsequent volume. Of historical note, the style considered "Southern" was the earlier form brought south to Fukien from Honan, while Northern Dragon originated in the North after the burning of the Honan Temple in the mid-17th century—this explains why there are two different origin stories for the Dragon style. The two major styles of Shaolin Dragon gung fu can be described as follows:

Northern Dragon: Created around 1680, the style is characterized by its use of the *back leaning stance* (*yu ma*), the style's signature on-guard posture. There are thirteen traditional fist forms plus four newer sets, and significant emphasis is given to traditional weapons training. Northern and Southern Dragon are very different in terms of posture and footwork; hand techniques are similar in each. This is because much of the posture and footwork of Northern Dragon was taken from other animal styles, while the hand techniques were mostly taken from the older, root Dragon style that went south. Regardless of differences, the two styles easily share enough features to be called "Dragon." Northern Dragon, like Southern, also has colors, but their meaning is completely different. In Southern Dragon, the different colored dragons actually represent very distinct systems within the overall style. In Northern Dragon, colors represent branches, or lineages—yet there is more stylistic continuity amongst the colors. A key form capturing the essence of Northern Dragon is the *Hanging Horse Form* of White Dragon.

Civilian practitioners of a style descended from Northern Dragon call their style "Yow Kung Moon." We do not know whether Yow Kung Moon's "internal" forms represent a single branch of Northern Dragon, such as White Dragon, or Red Dragon (for instance); a piece of a branch; or whether they incorporate aspects of multiple lineages. Some Yow Kung Moon stylists may be surprised to discover that, although their style came out of Southern Shaolin to the public, this venerable style was a proverbial phoenix that rose out of the ashes of (one of the many burnings of) the *northern* Temple at Song Shan. Yow Kung Moon grandmaster Ha Hon Hung, who learned a version of the style from Shaolin monk Tit Yang, initiated widespread practice of the style in the early 20th century.

Southern Dragon: Founded around 1570 by Wu (or Ng) Mui (1515-1604). The noted lay master of Southern Dragon, Lam Yiu Kwai (1877?-1964), is largely responsible for spreading the style and giving rise to many of today's schools. (Lam's Dragon was influenced by Hakka and Taoist arts, and so differs somewhat from Shaolin Dragon.) Once in the South, "Southern" Dragon continued to evolve, incorporating many southern influences, which explains why the style does not look "northern" even though it originated at the Honan Temple. Probably the most foundational difference between Southern Dragon and Northern Dragon rests in the footwork, although there are many other discrepancies as well. Most of our discussion in this particular text concerns Southern Dragon.

Dragon Applications and Forms

Ed Parker points out that "…Dragon movements were devised to develop alertness and concentration. These movements were executed without the application of strength, but with emphasis on breathing in the lower abdomen along with the coordination of mind, body and spirit. Movements were long, flowing and continuous."[158] The remark about executing a technique "without the application of strength" is a nod to Dragon's reliance upon ch'i. The basis of the Dragon systems is ch'i, the inner power of Taoism. Where a Tiger stylist would break a rock by sheer force and physical technique, a Dragon stylist would shatter it by ch'i projection. At the level of Ruby Dragon, a Dragon stylist's reliance upon ch'i becomes total.

Lower Dragons use fists, claws and wide sweeps. As you progress, the moves are tighter and less sweeping. The saber is typically the weapon studied by Dragon practitioners. If a student has developed solid skills in Tiger and Crane, Dragon will be relatively easy to learn.

Although Dragon movements have been incorporated into many modern gung fu styles,[159] the classical style is quite distinguishable from the other components of the five-formed fist. Four stances are utilized, these being *bow and arrow stance, standing stance/adduction stance (kim ma), pressing stance (pik ma)* and the *back leaning stance (yu ma).* Each stance in turn is used at different heights to respond best to an opponent. For example, the relatively familiar *dropping dragon stance* is merely a very low *adduction stance.* Transition from one stance to another is typically fluid, the feet almost constantly in contact with the ground. Such movements, properly executed, make the practitioner appear serpentine.

Kicks are of two types: low, linear *thrust kicks*, generating power blows at low target areas, or wide *crescent kicks* used to bridge a gap and generate momentum for more powerful follow-up techniques. These latter kicks may be quite high or even aerial in delivery, but are executed only as a surprise counteroffensive.

Combat position for a Dragon stylist involves sloping the shoulders in to restrict access to the upper thoracic region, while keeping the elbows in near the centerline, as in Wing Chun. Defense rests primarily in restricting accessibility to targets, and by employing twisting or adduction maneuvers to avoid incoming assault. Should an opponent strike at the solar plexus, the Dragon stylist would adduce, or draw back his lower trunk, thus moving the intended target out of range while simultaneously moving the shoulders forward, thus increasing the power of a retaliatory fist strike. Though hand techniques are quite diverse in this style, even the basic, middle knuckle extended *dragon fist* would be a powerful attack from an extended stance.

Dragon is essentially an internal, ch'i cultivating method, but initial training is far more similar to a hard, external style than a delicate, reptilian approach. In learning the moves, the student will strike hard, block hard, and stomp into each position, with the idea of learning the proper place to be once each movement is complete. Eventually, the method of transmitting power is retained, and the physically strengthened body is able to make transitions in the proper, fluid manner. In turn, this reptilian smoothness helps disguise the attack, making it extremely difficult for an adversary to effectively counter.

Once a purely physical semblance to flow has been mastered, the disciple incorporates the deep hissing sounds to train ch'i flow. Inhaling is silent, but exhalation is deliberate, tense and controlled. Inhaling lightens the body for aerial maneuvers, while exhaling drives power into each technique. Blocking is dispensed with, and parries or simple strikes substituted. At this point, novice and advanced student show very little in common.

On the highest level, an opponent is allowed to tire himself out, evasion becoming the Dragon's key defense. Ch'i control is highly developed, and the degree to which the body must be moved to redirect or avoid impact is under greater control.

Dragon is designed to complement your opponent's moves and blend with them. Moreover, Dragon should blend so well that you can't tell when technique starts or stops. It is not the same as Aikido, although it looks similar. In fact, we strongly suspect Aikido's founder, Morihei Ueshiba, was profoundly inspired by observing a Southern Dragon style. Dragon uses less motion than Aikido, and Dragon throws differ from Aikido in that the former seldom retains a grip. By *not* retaining a grip on your opponent, you do not present a fulcrum for the application of counters. But the manner in which Ueshiba could "disappear" is quite characteristic of Dragon. Some stylists argue that Ueshiba was influenced by Pa Kua. This is possible—Pa Kua shares much in common with Dragon, more so than any other Wutang art. Yet Ueshiba's tactics are more reminiscent of Dragon (where the stylist frequently feints and follows with a throw) than of Pa Kua (where the stylist normally strikes and follows with a throw).

The major forms of the Southern Dragon style are presented in the table below. In each form, one is taught to "ride the wind," a phrase which, in large part, means follow rather than lead. Provide no opening without first letting your opponent open. Unlike Crane, which also relies heavily upon evasion as a tactic, the Dragon evades primarily by rotation of upper or lower torso with little or no stance movement. The Crane stylist, alternately, hops frequently to reposition the entire body. Both styles employ pinpoint strikes to vulnerable meridian targets, but Dragon also heavily uses Tiger-like punches and clawing techniques, Snake-like stance shifts, and Leopard-like hit and run strikes to weaken a physically superior combatant. Dragon also regularly employs low sweeping techniques, but these are not unique; most senior stylists of any gung fu system use these on a weakened adversary.

Major Dragon Forms, from Most Advanced Down to Most Basic	
Form	**System**
Seven Ways of Plum Flower Fist	Emerald
Plum Flower Fist	Green
Five Horses Returning to Stable Palm	Sapphire
Turn to Hook and Hit	Ruby
Cross Standing Five-Form	Sapphire
Standing Five-Form	White
Confused Ape Runs Away	Ruby
Venomous Snake Moves Tongue	Emerald
Touch Bridge	White
Bridge Smashing	White
Eagle Claw	Ruby
Press and Hit from Four Sides	Red
Single Sword and Mount	Red
Rescue Master from Single Side	Sapphire
Fierce Tiger Leaping Over Wall	Black
Passing Bridge Three Times	Blue
Sixteen Holes	White
Four-Way Fist	Black
Sweeping Hands	Red
Hammer Fist	Green

There are many other Dragon forms (about 60 total in Shaolin Southern Dragon), eve more taking family styles into account. The *Box Form* of Blue Dragon (which is a portion of *Rescue Master from Single Side*) is taught to one entering Dragon to determine the student's future course of instruction. The form is shown without explanation and the student is left to figure out various applications. Advanced Dragon forms are all ancient, thus are taught first to see if the student is capable. If a student could learn the *Box Form* thoroughly, further Dragon study was permissible. The level of excellence displayed when performing this set determined whether the student would major in Dragon or some other style. It is a gauge form with many styles subliminally represented. The *Box Form* may also be practiced with butterfly knives. *Touch Bridge* is also of note, as the form initiates sticky hands training for the Dragon stylist. *Touch Bridge* is considered to be the key form of Lam Yiu Kwai's Dragon school. If we *had* to pick one form as a "key" form in Shaolin's Southern Dragon, it would be *Bridge Smashing*. (Note: Many of the names of Shaolin Dragon forms appear in Lam Yiu Kwai's Dragon syllabus as well, yet most are completely different forms.)

Chapter Ten

The Centerline Styles

The shortest distance between two points is a straight line.

Chinese martial arts tend to borrow techniques and principles rather liberally from one another, despite so many of the arts being taught in a secretive manner. Still, the essence of Sil Lum arts is based on the principles of stances, gates, attacks, and defenses. Stances are the backbone of gung fu, providing strong and flexible platforms from which to move. Stances are the footwork of movement, and styles favor high or low postures based on intricacies of local terrain, variety of foot attacks, and personal preferences of a training master. Attacks are any delivery of force intended to control or injure an opponent, and include joint manipulations, throws, hand strikes, kicks, and sweeps. Defenses are movements to evade or deflect incoming attacks, and include posture shifts, parries, counter strikes, and blocks.

Gates, however, are the pivotal point around which stances, attacks, and defenses are based. They provide the strategic position for a martial artist's tactics. Gates generally describe the preferred, or general, angle of engagement employed by a martial artist in a combat situation. Styles that fight by using sweeping, circular movements, generally moving from the outside of an opponent's defenses to the inside, are termed "ch'i styles," and include Dragon, Snake, T'ai Chi Ch'uan, and Pa Kua. Alternately, a stylist may use circular defensive movements coupled with linear attacks to areas outside the defensive gate (the area between an opponent's arms). Such linear styles include Tiger, White Crane, and Northern Praying Mantis. The third school of gates keeps the hands or elbows on the defender's centerline, and traps or circles an incoming attack so that a direct counter-attack to the opponent's centerline is possible. The centerline styles are Wing Chun, White Eyebrow, and Southern Praying Mantis (although centerline elements are notably present in Northern Praying Mantis and Snake as well).

The centerline is most simply described as an imaginary shaft that runs through your body, starting at the crown of your skull, running down your spine, and down to the ground as an imaginary tail. If you see the centerline as a pole, then it is the axis around which your balance moves. Force that reaches your centerline unbalances you, dissipates force from your attacks, and disorients your coordination in defense. It is therefore of primary importance to defend your centerline at all times.

These styles were all created (or heavily modified into their present-day forms, as with White Eyebrow) at about the same time, but at different temples. Centerline styles are either southern or refined largely in the south (as with White Eyebrow). As a consequence, the simplicity of hand techniques is supreme. There are many techniques, but none that are complex or would impress an audience thrilled by movie-style martial arts. Kicks are low, and stances are predominantly upright *horse stances*. These are the styles of masters, given to tactical superiority through good strategy; they are not the acrobatic, wild-barrage styles preferred by many young people. Centerline styles lack flash, but pack incredible punch. They are truly arts for practitioners who do not wish to fight.

Fighting Towards the Centerline: White Eyebrow

White Eyebrow was a senior monk at Honan Temple who was expert in Tiger and Leopard styles. He also knew Northern Eagle Claw and other non-Shaolin styles. As a senior monk, he was able to develop a martial style of his own, unfortunately one that broke the Buddhist ethic of non-violence by concentrating on striking only death-touch pressure points. According to our tradition, White Eyebrow was tempted by (tangible and perhaps intangible rewards offered by) a general who, under orders from the emperor, was sent to destroy Shaolin. The Manchu feared the martial monks, and this fear was partially justified, as many disciples and younger masters left the Order to engage in battles against imperial troops. The cruelties inflicted on the common people by imperial decree were more than many monks could stand to observe without becoming involved. White Eyebrow was the most senior monk to betray his vows; additionally, he betrayed the Order. With his help, the army destroyed the Temple, and many monks and students were killed. For this reason, his name is considered a profanity to our monks, and his style was long forbidden to be taught (save among the masters). In fact, we never discard anything useful, and White Eyebrow's innovations were indeed important. For many years, White Eyebrow was only referred to indirectly, or as the "The Forbidden Style." Though a forbidden style, we are compelled to include it in this text because of its intrinsic value as a martial art and because White Eyebrow is part of Shaolin history—though a truly dark part.

White Eyebrow, or Pak Mei, is a style with the aggressive clawing hand techniques of Tiger, and the simple footwork characteristic of the centerline styles. Favored weapons include the *finger fan strike* to the eyes or throat, *phoenix fist* to the solar plexus, and *crab claw* strikes to the softer sides of the lower abdomen. In Sil Lum tradition, only the most senior practitioners of the Southern Tiger and (now largely defunct) Leopard styles were allowed to learn this forbidden art, and it is considered a privilege to be allowed access to this "closed-door" teaching.

White Eyebrow has the most complicated footwork of the centerline styles, being the only such style that traditionally employs low, sweeping take-downs, or kicks above the groin. Nevertheless, the stance work is very similar to the other centerline styles, and involves mainly the *high horse stance*. This natural stance allows a practitioner to quickly adapt to a threat and defend from a position of strength.

213

White Eyebrow deviates from other centerline styles in two significant ways. First, though the other styles will occasionally grab an opponent to gain momentary control or redirect an attack, only White Eyebrow will hold on long enough to effect true "grappling" techniques. In contrast, Wing Chun and Southern Mantis typically grab only long enough to straighten joints for breaking or pain-inducing counterstrikes. Second, White Eyebrow uses body pivoting as a technique to generate strike/parry torque-power. The pivoting helps deflect any intended attack point from fully absorbing a delivered strike (thus dissipating incoming force) while providing centripetal force that can be redirected into a counter-attack. It is worthwhile to point out that Pak Mei was developed shortly after the Dragon style. Later, both styles were refined in the South. Although very different styles, there are a few striking similarities between them, such as the use of an *adduction stance* and use of the waist in generating power.

There is a thriving civilian Pak Mei tradition in southern China, largely due to the teaching efforts of Chang Lai-chuen (1880-1964). Chang studied White Eyebrow through a Taoist lineage distinct from Shaolin, and by his own admission incorporated forms and exercises from a variety of other arts into his curriculum.[160] The original forms of White Eyebrow are relatively few in number. The key form is *Nine Step Push*, or *Gau Bo Tui*. Chang was responsible for teaching Pak Mei to a large number of people.

After the Honan Shaolin were routed in the 17th century, Pak Mei was put in charge of the Honan Temple, were he trained military officers in his art. Some of these officers practiced and treasured what they had learned, and passed it on to their relatives when they retired from military service. This gave rise to some Pak Mei branches in northern China. Shaolin White Eyebrow is very soft compared to other lineages.

The next two styles are decidedly different in appearance, but share two important similarities. On the mundane level, both styles employ rapid machine gun-like, repeated hitting of the same target, literally smashing through an opponent's defenses and weakening an opening for as long as possible. More important, though, is the essential employment of "sticky hands" techniques. Sticky hands exercises teach a martial artist to intercept an opponent's attack, and then ride the hand (or foot) to keep contact. This contact may add velocity to your counterattack, or allow you to feel a change in the opponent's movement at the same instant it is initiated, giving you more time to redirect and use the incoming force against the enemy.

Sticky hands practice is well-illustrated in many books, notably those about Wing Chun, but actually learning the techniques requires regular practice with a partner. The point is to learn to respond reflexively to a change in your opponent's movements, without being fooled by your eyes. While sticky hands is not ESP, it is a subtle practice that requires you to sense the movement of your partner even before you are *consciously* aware of that movement. Many martial artists show off their sticky hands skills while wearing blindfolds; in fact, it is almost impossible to develop good sticky hands skills if you *do not* regularly practice while blindfolded.

Fighting Outside-Inwards: Wing Chun

Wing Chun was developed during the late 1770s at the Kwangtung and Fukien Temples. Sil Lum senior female monk Ng Mui (not the same Ng Mui who, centuries earlier, developed the first Dragon style) *and colleagues* decided to pool their skills to develop a "key" style that would incorporate the best and simplest methods of gung fu into a new style. Borrowing liberally from White Crane and Snake, the composite style was refined into a series of techniques that fitted into three short forms. The style was subsequently taught to a young woman named Wing Chun ("Blessed Springtime"), who became sufficiently adept that the creator named her style for her first pupil. The subsequent unrest that put China into a state of regional wars allowed Ng Mui and Wing Chun to disseminate their style, first around southern China, and later to the northern Temple at Honan. This is because the two women became wanderers who taught various aspects of gung fu to earn a living. The core of Wing Chun, though, was reserved for Shaolin monks taught later by Ng Mui, and relatives of Wing Chun (once she married and settled down). Wing Chun's efficacy and ease of learning made it popular with both monks and the non-Temple martial artist, to such an extent that the style is one of the best known and widely practiced today.

Wing Chun is arguably the most famous single style within the Shaolin system. It was made known to the West by Bruce Lee and James Lee in the late 1960s in what was the most influential introduction of Chinese gung fu outside China (one might equate Bruce Lee's bringing of gung fu to American television in 1964 with the arrival of the Beatles in America two years earlier). Despite Lee's rapid evolution of a personal style away from traditional Wing Chun,[161] his association with that style was a major factor in its continued success over the years. More recently, the style has received new publicity following the death of long time grandmaster Yip Man as at least three of his senior disciples have waged an acrimonious conflict over who would inherit the supreme mantle for the style.

Despite the ongoing politics of the "upper echelons" of the style, Wing Chun remains an efficient, popular form of martial art. Novices mistake the small amount of material in the style (three unarmed kuen) for ineffectiveness, but seasoned martial artists appreciate the streamlined and highly simplified combat material offered. A variety of stories circulate regarding the origin of the style. All agree that the style was developed by (or with the input of) the Shaolin Order. The most popular stories tell of priestess Ng Mui, a senior gung-fu practitioner who was interested in combining the best techniques from the broad array of traditional Shaolin gung fu into a simple, master style. There is quite a bit of controversy about this origination story for Wing Chun. Other accounts of Wing Chun's origins include the posit that the style came from Shaolin, but omit the Yim Wing Chun story. These accounts explain that the Wing Chun style was developed exclusively to combat the Manchu, and that the name "Wing Chun" had symbolic meaning for the revolutionaries.[162] Some sources also assert that Ng Mui's very existence is doubtful—the evidence being that (a) the Shaolin were all celibate and (b) that women were not allowed into the Order.[163] While we have no internal evidence of the existence of Yim Wing Chun and realize her story may be a pleasant fantasy, both (a) and (b) are simply incorrect, as is the assumption that Ng Mui is a fictional character. On these matters, we rely upon firsthand reports. Of course there are numerous, legitimate Wing Chun lineages that did not flow directly from Ng Mui to laypersons, but Ng Mui was instrumental in Wing Chun's development. Wing Chun incorporates numerous elements from Snake, White Crane, Dragon, and Tiger (the former two mainly in the offensive techniques, the latter two in defensive maneuvers).

The three unarmed forms of Wing Chun begin with the style's key form: *Sil Lum Tao* (or *Siu Nim Dao*). The name means *"Little Imagination,"* and refers to the need for the practitioner to use his or her imagination in the practice and application of techniques. Most moves are repeated three times, the primary attack is a *sun fist* (thumb facing upward on impact), and a variety of arm parries/blocks are employed. There is no footwork. This form is well illustrated in a variety of publications (in fact, this may be the most widely published gung fu form in the world), though each technique has several applications, most of which remain unpublished.

The little imagination needed to make each technique work is merely the first step in mastering the set, for a myriad of applications can be found for the relatively few moves. Despite the simple and non-combative appearance of the form, there are ready throws, joint breaks, finger thrusts, and open hand strikes in the *Sil Lum Tao*. ("*Sil Lum Tao*" *here* means "*Little Imagination*". To avoid confusion: "Sil Lum Tao" may also be translated as "Shaolin Way" when the Chinese is transliterated into English.)

The second form is *Chum Kil* (or *Chum Kiu*), or *Bridge-Seeking*. *Chum Kil* adds a few new moves to a skeleton of techniques from *Sil Lum Tao*, but adds more sticky-hands and bridge techniques. Bridge techniques are extended arm moves that intercept and redirect incoming attacks without using the brute power required in blocking. These techniques take advantage of the physics of swinging objects, in that there is very little force generated by an object the closer one moves towards the point of origin of the attack (e.g., it is much easier to stop a kick by intercepting it above the knee than below). Correct use of bridge arms lets a Wing Chun practitioner safely defend against attackers using clubs and other swinging weapons. The simple looking footwork hides a real variety of body shifting around the centerline, giving the fighter greatly increased power over the *Sil Lum Tao* attacks. Additionally, this form introduces the three basic kicks, all aimed at the knees or lower, of Wing Chun.

The last form is called *Bil Jee* (or *Biu Gee*), or *Thrusting Fingers*. This is primarily an offensive form, using finger thrusts/spear hands in a variety of ways. There is more footwork, including a sweep, low kicks, and stance shifts. Once this form is learned, the student should immediately see ways to modify and improve all previous techniques from the first two forms. There are several versions of this form being taught, with each instructor claiming that his is the authentic version. In reality, Wing Chun has evolved under many different practitioners since its inception in the 1770s, and each version is "authentic" in its own way.

Wing Chun also has long pole (sometimes called the "dragon pole") and butterfly knife forms that build upon the principles of the unarmed sets. The long pole form is unusual in that it is a long range set,[164] while all the other sets in the style are close-in sets.

When Ng Mui devised this style, she planned that its effectiveness would be structurally suitable for a much weaker defender to overcome a physically superior adversary. It was perhaps her acid test to teach Wing Chun, a young woman with no prior physical training of any kind, to see if the theoretical constructs of the new style would actually be effective. Wing Chun, by all accounts, was a teen-ager little more than 100 pounds in weight. To allow such a person an advantage in trading blows, the new style must allow the defender to pivot outside the incoming attack, and deliver a counter strike from outside the opponent's gates to his centerline.

The obvious success of this approach may be appraised by the style's long and popular practice in much of the world. This popularity was increased with the television introduction of Wing Chun (plus many Southern Praying Mantis techniques) by the highly skilled Bruce Lee on the *Green Hornet* series, and the concurrent release of an English-language book describing the basics and the first form by James Lee, assisted by Bruce Lee. (There is a picture of Bruce Lee—no relation to James—working with a wooden dummy at the back of the book). Yip Man had several excellent and senior students around the world who are now taking the style in different directions. In addition to Yip's branch of Wing Chun, there are many other lineages and excellent schools. And of course, we wouldn't have included this section on Wing Chun were there not a Shaolin branch of the style. The difference between branches of Wing Chun is analogous to that found between Northern Praying Mantis sects, or perhaps a bit less so.

Wing Chun techniques are developed in a progression. The student begins with defenses employing forearm and slapping blocks, and attacks delivered with a tight *sun punch*, and progresses to a more subtle use of forearm and slapping parries, evasions, and attacks of low kicks and palm and elbow strikes. Even new students are taught the essential defense/attack principles of inner- and outer-gate punching, in which an incoming assault is simultaneously being deflected by one's own outgoing attack. This economy of "defend and counter" is a common element of all centerline styles, but is introduced earlier in the training program of a Wing Chun stylist.

Fighting Inside-Outwards:
Southern Praying Mantis

If any style truly emphasizes the direct use of attack as defense, it must be the Southern Praying Mantis, or Kwong Sai Jook Lum ("Kwong Sai Bamboo Forest," the full Chinese name would be "Kwong Sai Jook Lum T'ang Lang"). The few moves that initiate as parries (or, rarely, blocks) are deceptive in that they are actually subtle strikes against pressure points in the wrists or elbows that, in turn, generate reflexive force to drive a second, more obvious strike at the opponent. As with the other centerline styles, both the number of moves and forms is limited, but what the style lacks in variety and flamboyance, it more than compensates for in efficiency.

If Northern Praying Mantis is the epitome of popularized, widely dispersed gung fu, then the true southern counterpart must be the most secretive. The Southern Praying Mantis style developed around 1830 at the Bamboo Forest Temple in Kwongsai Province. A monk named Sam Dat was trying to improve his techniques for opening an attacker's defenses, and was inspired by the movements of the predatory insect. He meditated upon the movements of the insect, and devised a style formally known as Bamboo Forest Praying Mantis. This is one account of the roots of the style. According to oral history within the Shaolin Order (and prominent Jook Lum stylists such as Lum Wing-fay [also known as "Lam Sang"]), Sam Dat developed Southern Mantis with the aid of Shaolin monks and Ming insurgents. Whatever the truth, he developed his style with his disciples at the Jook Lum Temple, and the resulting system became available only to senior, and most-trusted, disciples and masters. Sam Dat, who later became abbot of the Bamboo Forest Temple, developed Southern Mantis as a style around 1830-1835, but the style's inception dates from the 1770s in the way of early influences. Little else is known surrounding the origins, but the style evidences elements of lamaistic training and close adherence to yin/yang philosophy. Practitioners are skilled in *dim mak* (death-touch techniques, using non-apparent attack modes) and healing arts.

Two schools later developed from the root style, these being the Hakka styles of Chu and Chou Southern Praying Mantis, and both share so much in common that they are essentially just different names for the same method (although evolved in a slightly different direction when compared to the root style).[165] The Hakka people, without a province or locality of their own, were considered to be outsiders by the other indigenous peoples of Kwongsai Province, and needed a system of gung fu for personal defense in the often-hostile social environment. Hence, the Hakka made the very effective art of Southern Praying Mantis their own.

Sometime in the mid 1800s, the style was officially embraced by the Shaolin Temple at Fukien. There was often a period of many years between a style's first incarnation and a style's becoming developed enough to be included in the Shaolin curriculum. In this case, Southern Praying Mantis was initially developed as a style and then practiced by both Shaolin and non-Shaolin exponents for many years before the council of masters at Fukien made the assessment that the style should become a permanent aspect of our curriculum.

The secrecy surrounding Southern Praying Mantis is replete with myths and legends, largely initiated and propagated by the practitioners themselves. This also means that there are several different oral histories about the origins of the style, and these histories are often somewhat (or very!) contradictory. Becoming a student is extremely demanding and involves nothing less than being adopted by the master and pledging one's life to him. Even family ties are second to attitude and mental readiness in choosing the disciples.

Unlike the northern schools, Southern Mantis rarely emphasizes one type of technique; the *mantis claw* is employed, but so are numerous other trapping and controlling maneuvers. The typical closed fist of other styles is absent from the southern sect, which instead favors the *mantis fist*, a modification of the *leopard fist*, but concentrating all of the striking force through a single finger. Stances are low to moderate, but firmly anchored to the ground. There is tremendous use of the knees, elbows and low, powerful kicks. There are few feints or distraction strikes; everything is designed for 100 percent power output, and is thus potentially lethal.

We believe at least some of the reason for the continued development of Southern Mantis was a direct result of efforts to ward off political oppression during the mid-19th century, an idea that is further reinforced by the "secret society" nature of early Southern Mantis founders and practitioners. Southern Praying Mantis employs fighting philosophies common to Wing Chun and White Eyebrow, and there is stylistic evidence to support the notion that some exchange of information has occurred between these schools.

The two Hakka branches, the Chou and the Chu, are largely distinguished by one's preference for using fist and mantis-finger strikes, and the other's preference for using finger-fan and clawing techniques.[166] Such branch differences are actually the result of early practitioners' preferences, and in no way constitute a major barrier to Southern Mantis "unity" of style. In truth, people who require fine use of their hands in their work (artists, surgeons, typists) may favor using *palm strikes* and *finger fans* over the more demanding fist or single-finger strikes.

At least one source posits that Chu Gar is the original Southern Praying Mantis.[167] It certainly may be true that Chu Gar Mantis was the first Southern Mantis variant to reach a civilian audience, but our history maintains that Chu was a later offshoot from the Temple-developed style. The evolution of Chu Gar away from the Jook Lum model might be explained by the fact that the Hakka art traces its lineage back to Shaolin monks Wong Tao-yun and Chu Fook-too (also known as "Chow Ah-nan"), and not any Jook Lum practitioner. Shaolin monks are allowed to teach civilians at their discretion, but often alter what they teach to make it distinct from the Temple style. So we conjecture that Chu Gar was a modification of the Southern Praying Mantis root style, influenced by the particular backgrounds of monks Wong and Chu. This does not mean that the Hakka branch lacks "purity" or efficacy—only that it is different. With respect to Chu versus Chou, the Chu variant came first and the differences between the two styles are quite minimal ("Chu" and "Chou/Chow" [and "Jow"] are really just different spellings/pronunciations of the same name).

The Shaolin branch of Southern Praying Mantis shares most of its forms with the Jook Lum lineage (although often with different emphasis), and practitioners begin with the following 5 forms: *Basic form*, *Introductory form*, *Intermediate form*, *Advanced form*, and *Three Step Arrow*. The first four forms listed here are basic training forms (most Jook Lum schools do not include these preliminary forms), and *Three Step Arrow* is a "second stage" training form. The *Basic Form* is taught in two versions. The first version taught is a long range form (by southern standards), while the second version is short range. It emphasizes the elbows, and is practiced very slowly to sense ch'i flow. The Hakka branches of Southern Praying Mantis (Chu/Chou) also have a version of the *Introductory Form* (which they perform off both sides, making the form twice as long) and the *Three Step Arrow*.

Three punch combinations delivered with blinding speed at the same target are a standard attack in Southern Praying Mantis. Northern and Southern Mantis are *not* closely related in execution. With respect to weapons, Southern Praying Mantis prefers the use of mantis knives (twin daggers), broadsword, staff, and butterfly knives.

Part 3:
Integrating the Practices of Shaolin

We step into and we do not step into the same rivers.
We are and we are not.

Heraclitus

If any disciple heaped together the seven treasures forming an elevation as high as Mount Sumeru and as many Mount Sumerus as there are in the three thousand great universes, and bestowed them in charity, his merit would be less than what would accrue to the disciple that simply observed and studied this teaching and in kindness explained it to others.

Shakyamuni Buddha, referring to the teachings of the Diamond Sutra

Chapter Eleven

Foundations of the Shaolin Path

If one is hungry, both char siu bow and pizza will satisfy.
But if one is hungry for pizza, one **must go** to where pizza is served.

Shaolin Priest and Grandmaster Ben Ch'i Lo

There are more martial arts schools around the world now, in the early 21st century, than there at perhaps any other time in history. Many of these schools describe themselves as Shaolin, yet there are only a handful of kwoons that can legitimately make that claim. For the student in search of a true Shaolin environment, knowledge of precisely what Shaolin is becomes paramount. There may even be unethical instructors who will read this text and then alter their programs to continue *capitalizing* on the word "Shaolin". Maliszewski notes in his recent martial survey: "Many experienced practitioners exhibit behavioral features, personality traits, and a general level of psychological maturity indistinguishable from a neophyte in the art."[168] Again, there is a difference between the many schools teaching Shaolin *gung fu only*, and the few schools teaching Shaolin *Buddhism* (we're mainly discussing the latter here). Of course, any martial school which emphasizes Buddhist ideals would probably be an excellent place to train. In *any* kind of school, it will be the student's burden to see if the school is practicing what it preaches or has erected a clever façade.

Shaolin activities center upon a variety of major goals, the sum of which is the Shaolin path (Sil Lum Tao). Each goal has distinct exercises and drills, their actions aimed at making the student a fully rounded person capable of making a positive contribution to society. To those who are familiar with Buddhists' overarching aim to be free of the rounds of rebirth and to awaken, this involvement in society might seem contradictory. After all, aren't Buddhists supposed to eschew this world and focus only on the great universal one-ness?

The answer is a qualified "Yes," but the qualification involves two aspects of our Shaolin sect of Buddhism. First, Ch'an is founded on the premise that enlightenment is possible in an instant (sometime in *this* lifetime) if the eightfold path and proper meditation practices are followed. This is in stark contrast to the views espoused by many Buddhist sects, where it is believed that enlightenment must follow after innumerable lifetimes of slow and careful practice and spiritual learning. In Shaolin's firm devotion to the coincident development of mind, body, and spirit, the imminence of attaining a sudden enlightenment is considered possible. Second, Shaolin believes that accumulated wisdom, especially that which leads towards enlightenment, is to be shared by the wise. Shaolin venerates the bodhisattvas above all others. A bodhisattva is a person who has attained the enlightened state in this world, but postpones the escape from the karmic wheel of rebirth and life so that she may stay behind as a teacher. Helping other souls find their way towards enlightenment is seen as the highest level of benevolence, because the bodhisattva puts off escape from earthly suffering with the intent of benefiting others. Thus, by studying for the traditional thirteen years as a Shaolin student, followed by the time in wandering, a Shaolin monk becomes a servant of the world at large. In this way, Shaolin training emphasizes the bodhisattva ideal.

A Shaolin master is, first and foremost, a Buddhist teacher. Shaolin beliefs hold that one teaches in two ways, by word and by example. In teaching through words, a teacher shows a student how to do something by demonstration or description. Even if a master is incapable of performing a particular technique, he or she can still convey how to do the technique to a student. Thus, practical ability is put a notch below teaching ability, because only in this way can we largely guarantee that all aspects of Shaolin survive. For example, a one-legged master would not be able to demonstrate a low leg sweep, but could still convey through words and drawings how to execute the technique. Most, but not all, martial teaching falls into this category of direct instruction.

Secondly, a master must always teach by example. Shaolin detests hypocrisy in all its forms. Students are expected to learn as much about being Shaolin through observing the behavior of their masters as they do through formal training. In Shaolin, students are asked to "Do as I do," and not, as we often see in the world, "Do as I say, but not as I do." Teaching by example plays a profound role in imparting the meaning of Shaolin Ch'an. The role model responsibility of a Shaolin master is considerable.

The major goals of Shaolin training and, in fact, the entire Shaolin lifestyle, were given equal weight in the temples. These goals are integrity, scholarship, gung fu, meditation, and detachment. As you can see, gung fu represents only one part of this curriculum, though each goal has numerous aspects that blend into the others. This section of the book will provide basic information on each of these ideals.

Integrity

We must become the change we want to see in the world.

Gandhi

There are people who can be trusted, who have and respect manners, and who are dependable and loyal. When these characteristics are present, they represent integrity. While it is true that Shaolin instructors have accepted, as students, people of little integrity, the normal formal process of admission to Temple training requires a candidate to display an already well developed sense of deportment and ethics. Readers who have watched the original 1972 pilot for the TV series *Kung Fu* may recall the scene where our young hero is sitting outside the Temple, suffering rain and sun, waiting quietly while other boys play and fight. Eventually, only he and a very few other patient boys were admitted inside the Temple. This view of the initial screening process was one of the more authentic depictions in the series of how Shaolin worked. Why was integrity so highly prized? Simply because the masters knew well that knowledge, once imparted, cannot be withdrawn. While you could take a sword away from a renegade, you could not repossess the martial skills, nor keep the swordsman from acquiring a new weapon. In short, Shaolin recognized that life spans are finite and that the fewer values masters had to teach, the more time would be available for materials that a student would not learn elsewhere.

Paul Eng's discussion of the "Eight Places not to Hit" nicely highlights both the role of integrity in gung fu generally, and provides some insight into why compassion might be prized above justice:

Through generations and generations all masters have warned us not to use the **eight places not to hit**. The master realizes that at the moment he tells his students, they may not understand the philosophy behind this. We as students, respect our masters because of the way they have affected our lives. We can thank them a million times or offer them expensive gifts, but to the masters this may not matter. What is more important is to obey their words. It is not difficult to understand that it is wrong to haphazardly apply the **eight places not to hit**. As the saying goes, **a good sword never leaves its scabbard**. Yet, through history many great martial artists have led violent lives. These were often good, honorable men trying to uphold justice. However, they chose the life of the sword and quite often suffered great tragedy in [their] lives. It is the solemn wish of any master to have his students live happy and fulfilled lives. To disregard their words would be to stray from this path; to the master nothing could be more painful.[169]

Eng's comments touch upon issues of respect, gratitude, loyalty, obedience, and caring. These all contribute to Shaolin's holistic notion of integrity.

Integrity requires a keen mind that is capable of learning, evaluating, and making informed decisions. Kindness is not taught merely as a manner, but because of the informed knowledge that we will all get along better only if we treat each other with kindness and courtesy—ultimately, because suffering is universal. In turn, manners (and ranks for that matter) are not seen as subservience or as ways to establish a "pecking order" in which some people are more elevated than others. Rather, manners provide a framework in which courteous acts may function. Through manners we are given guidelines about when and how to be properly kind (without becoming maudlin or false).

Custom dictates ritual, and in Shaolin we have several rituals that convey our integrity. When we bow, it is not the bow of inferior position practiced in medieval Europe, but the Chinese equivalent of a handshake. It is an act that acknowledges the presence of the other person while also saying through body language that we have the manners to make such an acknowledgement. The custom of bowing before and after classes derives from acknowledging the teacher (and she her students) and as a mental "start" command, signaling the start and end of a particularly defined time.

Integrity begins with "I", both literally and metaphorically. *Our* bodies and clothes must be clean when we are with others. *Our* language should be smooth, appropriate, and allow others time to reflect and reply. *We* must know when a colleague wishes companionship and when he wishes time alone. All of this integrity is simply an extension of the "golden rule" of treating others as *we* wish to be treated ourselves (unless told otherwise). This aspect of integrity is based on true respect: respect for others as living things, respect for individual needs, and respect for courtesy and kindness if we are all to get along.

Integrity also entails traits of loyalty and dedication. If you commit to Shaolin training, you must focus on Shaolin training and not become too diffuse trying to learn other skills. This emphatically does not mean you should only study gung fu but ignore algebra or work! Rather, it means that each piece of your practice should be concentrated so you get the most from it. For example, there are many people who claim black belts in three or four different styles of martial arts. But what have they really learned? Rarely do these individuals achieve the level of proficiency (or rank) in any one style to be an effective teacher or superior practitioner. Shaolin does allow for incorporation of learning other styles but at determined times. Do not let enthusiasm dilute true achievement. Do what you *are* doing to the best of your abilities. The rest will follow when and if it should.

One way a student can determine if a teacher is genuinely Shaolin is to see how much integrity the teacher displays, and how closely he or she lives the ideals described below.

Scholarship

When you have even a single thought of looking for a shortcut in Zen,
you have already stuck your head in a bowl of glue.

Zen Master Dahui

Shaolin teaches the value of learning as a life-long pursuit. The mind that feels complete is the mind that soon becomes stagnant and dated. The integration of training the body, mind, and spirit requires nothing less than fine scholarship in a variety of disciplines. In this regard, Shaolin's teaching approach is similar to the Greek Olympian ideal of scholar-warriors, who were sound in body and mind. (Their belief stemmed from the idea that only inferior generals [not to mention the enemy!] wanted a city's armies to have stupid soldiers.) An old Shaolin saying goes: "Weak mind, weak fist; strong mind, no need for fist." Perhaps this saying developed after a group of masters and disciples reformed to start a new temple and its curriculum.

While it was certainly an acceptable and even expected goal of Shaolin training that graduates should become priests or priestesses, it was never expected that one practiced with the goal of becoming a professional martial artist or fighter. It is sad that people today wish to study Shaolin techniques so they can open a martial arts studio that will offer precious little of what Shaolin has to offer. Returning to the subject of integrity, a teacher or school claiming to be Shaolin that only offers gung fu and limited meditation practice is truly not Shaolin. Such a school lacks true scholarship as described by having a comprehensive and complete curriculum; although, such a school may be an excellent place to learn a martial art.

The large number of wandering monks, scholars, government officials, and even members of the intellectual elite who visited the Shaolin temples brought a huge influx of both books and human resources. Over time the temples became similar to the universities of Europe, where a great diversity of scholarship was conducted. To become a Shaolin monk, one was in essence entering a program of serious academic, as well as physical and spiritual, training. A Shaolin priest or priestess in today's world would be a college graduate schooled in subjects apart from Asian philosophy or martial arts. He would be perhaps an artist, engineer, physician, or writer, as well as a trained martial artist and Buddhist meditator. The real obstacle in becoming a master of Shaolin is not mastery of gung fu, but the requirement that one master several disciplines in the physical, mental, and spiritual domains.

This revelation could be bad news for bullies, tough guys, and other people interested in Shaolin because they want to become "tough." Without a well trained and disciplined mind, there is no way for a student to become Shaolin. In acquiring learning and being exposed to new ideas and new experiences, a true Shaolin is not only an eager scholar, but a person imbued with a lifelong love of learning. For many centuries, Shaolin masters have agreed that no one should be entrusted with so much power and martial skill without having at least equal measures of intellect and compassion. For this reason, we do not believe that the highest level of Shaolin's transformative practices should ever be made "public knowledge," a suggestion that seems to appear every so often.[170]

> Books can...become merely a means to escape from reality;
> they can provide an excuse for not really making an effort
> to examine things in detail for oneself.
>
> *Chögyam Trungpa*

Gung Fu

> The purpose of a fish trap is to catch fish, and when the fish are caught,
> the trap is forgotten.
>
> *Chuang Tzu*

Martial arts practice is but a tool in traditional Shaolin practice. The goals of gung fu—literally "skilled practice"—are to train and discipline the body and mind, to develop the confidence that comes from physical success, and to discover how to defeat the fears and limitations we harbor in our minds. A 1950s science fiction movie, *Forbidden Planet*, featured a terrible monster that was generated from the mind of a scientist. This "monster from the id," based on the psychological term for the subconscious, is a representation of not only our fears, but also the incredible power they can have over us and others. It was only by acknowledging that the monster was a projection of his own mind that the scientist was ultimately able to defeat it—and in the process it also killed him. In proper gung fu, we work first to strengthen our bodies, and second to conquer and control the monsters in our ids, and to do so long before they cause anyone harm. The martial artist who goes off looking for fights is one who has been defeated by his own id monster.

No matter what style you study, there are certain basics that transcend the Shaolin curriculum. Each is an exercise that tests and, hopefully, strengthens the student along different levels of achievement. Each drill (unless otherwise noted) should initially be practiced slowly and with great precision. Precision teaches us to move each tiny muscle in exactly the right way and at exactly the right time. It also teaches us to ingrain the finest details of each action so that we maximize the use of that technique. Finally, the learning of exquisite precision is mental training, gradually putting the mind in greater control of the body. From this learning one will eventually be able to control more and more bodily functions, including some degree of control over heart rate, perception of pain, and even the retardation of bleeding when wounded. We now present a series of basic exercises—not forms, but exercises that are to be mastered by all practitioners of authentic Shaolin gung fu.

Basic Training Exercises

Horse Stance Training: The most basic exercise, and one traditionally used to help evaluate the integrity of a new student, is the *deep horse stance (ma bo)*. Almost every Asiatic martial art has some variation of the *horse stance* in its repertoire, so it is at least familiar to most students. In Shaolin, basic *horse stance* is taught as a test of commitment and physical stamina. At the intermediate level, disciples do *horse stance* training in conjunction with static meditation.

To assume the *horse stance*, begin with your feet in a V-position, heels touching, the V forming a 90-degree angle. Now twist your feet from the balls of the feet, moving the heels as far apart as possible. Plant the heels and move the toes in opposite directions as far as they go. Now move the heels again, until your feet are wide apart and parallel to each other. Your feet should be a bit farther than shoulder width apart. Next comes the hard part. Slowly squat down as if you are going to sit in a low chair, but *do not move either foot*. Your thighs should be parallel with the floor, your behind at the same height as your knees. You are now (however briefly) in a *deep horse stance*. If you are a complete novice, try holding the stance for just one full minute, and try to hold it for 5-10 seconds longer each day. Practicing often, you should aim for maintaining the stance, solid and without sifting or squirming, for about ten minutes.

During the first month it is alright to have some distraction as your muscles adjust (yes, the lactic acid buildup will cause considerable soreness at first which you can treat by stretching first and taking warm baths or showers after practice). Listen to music, or watch a video, but hold your stance. After the first month, though, you want your mind to take increasingly more charge over controlling your discomfort. Even if it hurts, hold your *horse stance*. When your mind is fully in control and you do not break the practice, you are ready for the second basic exercise.

Shifting Horse Stance Training: The second exercise offers a bit of relief for tense muscles, but is still quite demanding and needs to be done long enough for the muscles to be under full control of the mind. You begin by assuming a *deep horse stance*, and chamber your fists on your waist. Keep your body facing forward throughout this exercise, but slowly shift to your left. You are moving into a forward-facing *bow and arrow stance*: your left leg will be very bent, so your behind is almost in contact with your left heel, while your right leg is straight. Both feet should be parallel and facing forward. Hold the position for 30 seconds, then slowly shift back into the *deep horse stance*. Then slowly shift to the right, in a mirror of the first shift. Practice this sequence daily for two weeks, then move on to the next phase.

Start as above, but as you shift left, turn your torso so it also faces the left, but keep your head looking forward. As you turn your torso, slowly launch a right fist straight out at midbody level. Remember, you are moving several body parts simultaneously: drop the left knee, turn torso, and punch as one motion. Slowly retract the fist as you shift right into a *deep horse stance*. Repeat movements to the right. You should try to do this drill for 5-10 minutes each day as your preliminary warm-up exercise, even after you move to intermediate and advanced levels.

By the end of the second month, begin increasing speed, so that your punches are driven by the torso shifts and are hitting with power. By the end of month three, try doing this drill at least twice a week with a punching bag to hit.

Punching Africa: This exercise has a longer traditional name, "alternately swatting flies and plucking stars from the heavens," but a particular manner in which the exercise was taught in the early 1970s gives us the shorter name. A poster depicting the Earth from space hung on a wall, and the main feature was the continent of Africa. A student would use the map as a target punching drill. It is an exercise with three goals. First, to teach the student to respond without thinking. Second, to learn to rapidly vary the level of an attack, and third, to learn to punch at a variety of targets with blinding speed.

Find a poster, or make a target picture on a piece of wood or posterboard. You want areas that can clearly be distinguished as high, medium, and low. (The Africa poster offered Egypt, Zaire, and South Africa as clear targets.) You will need a partner with fairly good reflexes—at least vocally.

Begin by taking a *deep horse stance* facing the poster with target markings. Slowly practice punching with alternate hands at a high, medium, and low target along your body's centerline. After a few minutes of warm-up, have your friend call targets and heights for each punch. For example:

"Left, right, left; high, high, low," translates into your punching with the left fist at the high target, then a right fist at high target, followed by a left fist at the low target. Spend the first weeks going at a moderate speed, without worrying about power. Strive to get the targeting and sequencing correct and only gradually increase your speed. By the end of the third month your speed should still take a second place to power, making each strike as forceful—yet fully balanced—as you can.

If, after six months, you can do well with both speed and power, begin the exercise as a kicking drill. On alternate days use either *front snap kicks* or *side kicks*. It may help to lower your poster so the lowest edge of the poster is on the floor. Shaolin rarely uses high kicks—movies notwithstanding—so put your effort into wonderful kicks at shin, knee, and bladder levels.

Plum Flower Fist Exercise: This is an essential exercise for developing strong punches without also developing huge or calloused knuckles. This is also a potentially dangerous exercise because it must be done gradually so as not to break your fingers. On the surface this seems a simple exercise, for one "merely" punches water. But as physicists can explain, water does not compress well, so hitting it must be done properly or the result will be like punching concrete. This exercise should not be initiated until you have been doing other gung fu practices for at least three years.

You will need a large round basin that can hold at least twenty gallons of water. Fill the basin with water, and assume a *deep horse stance* so that the basin is directly in front of you. Move slowly and practice punching at the dead center of the basin. Your arm should not penetrate deeper than the lower third of your forearm. For the first week, practice only slow punches, making sure that you do not penetrate either too deep or too shallow, and be especially careful to hit the water with your knuckles—not fingers—first.

Once you start punching water seriously, you should aim again at the dead center of the basin, and withdraw your punch as quickly as you can. Your mental goals are to 1) hit the water in such a way that the resulting splash resembles a symmetrical flower (hence, "plum flower") and 2) to do so in such a way that your hand and forearm barely become wet.

Intermediate Training Exercises

Silk Handkerchief Exercise: Finally, an exercise that frees you from being in a required *horse stance*! Find a silk handkerchief and tie strings to two ends. Suspend the handkerchief from a ceiling so a limp square of material hangs at about the height of your heart. For this drill you will employ *straight, sun,* and *leopard fist* strikes. Your aim is to strike the silk fast, so your incoming air cushion keeps the handkerchief from touching you, and then withdrawing your strike quickly. If properly done, the vacuum of your withdrawing fist should draw the handkerchief after your fist. This is much easier said than done, so it may take a year or more to do this correctly. A martial artist who learns this technique will punch with incredible speed and force, and withdraw fast enough to avoid being blocked or grabbed by the opponent.

Flying Crane Exercise: Traditionally, this exercise was performed on tree stumps, but cinder blocks will work well, too. Lay out a series of five blocks in a random pattern, each block about 4 feet from the next. Stand on a block and assume the *white crane* or *hanging horse stance*. For the sake of our example, begin with your right foot raised. Jump high, kicking with the right foot, and landing on another block with the right foot, so now the left leg is raised. Continue to jump, kick, and land with alternating feet. As you get better with this drill, move the blocks a few inches further apart, until after two to three years they are some 5 ½ feet apart. This exercise can be dangerous if you misstep and fall. Be very careful at first, and if need be, move the blocks closer together until your balance and coordination improve.

Rim Walking Exercise: This exercise requires a special setup, in the form of a circular rim about six feet in diameter and at least two feet above ground. A concrete culvert will do very well, so long as the edge is no more than three inches wide. Your initial balance exercise is simply to learn to walk around on this narrow edge. As you gain balance, begin doing forms work along the rim, starting with simple and kick-free sets. With time you should employ kicks and even a few jumping kicks. Do not expect to learn this exercise quickly; in fact, it should not even be started until you have about 3-5 years of solid gung fu training behind you.

Snake Hand Exercise: This is a very fast exercise, aimed at giving your hand techniques blinding speed and thrusting power. Begin by raising a forearm perpendicular to the floor, in front of your body. Bend the wrist so it is horizontal to the floor, palm facing down (so your posture is somewhat of an Egyptian stereotype). Place a pen or pencil across the knuckles of your hand, so the pen is lying across all four knuckles.

To practice the exercise, you must jerk your hand straight back towards you so the pen stays in its relative place, then thrust the hand forward to catch it before the pen drops more than a few inches. This is easier said than done, and initially you will probably just drop the pen a lot. As you start to grab it successfully, you will also have misses and bat the pen away from you. For this reason, we suggest you practice from a distance of about a yard in front of a wall, so you won't have to keep chasing the pen as it flies away from you.

Advanced Training Exercises

There are reasons why some gung fu is considered "closed door" material—instruction only passed from master to disciple. Among these reasons are a need to insure the character of the disciple, complexity or absurd simplicity of a technique, and the role of direct transmission of material as a way to reinforce lineage. For these reasons, advanced gung fu exercises are not presented here. The serious student is advised instead to seek and study under a competent sifu.

A Basic Gung Fu Workout

When American astronaut Neil Armstrong first put a human footprint on the moon, he relayed the message to earth: "That's one small step for man, one giant leap for mankind." On a much more humble scale, the first step into gung fu practice is a small step for you as an individual, but if you step into a rounded Shaolin curriculum you have made a giant leap. Just as Neil Armstrong had to train long and hard before rocketing into space, so too must a Shaolin aspirant endure an arduous training program to gain real skill.

It is important to establish some sort of regular schedule when you begin training, with distinct times for physical workout, meditation, and study. The physical workout was traditionally done in the morning. But the frenetic pace of contemporary life, coupled with the times at which schools are open and lessons given, makes the evening gung fu session predominant, at least among beginners. Meditation time is initially either a morning or evening event, until the student progresses to the stage where he or she sees meditation in all of life's actions. Study time, which involves reading, writing, taking classes or having serious conversations about something other than gung fu or meditation, can be done at any convenient time. Establishing a regular pattern of activity is almost universally required for students given that our society already compartmentalizes so much of our day, not to mention the dictates of our biological clocks. In time, of course, the times and places of practice may be varied, but initially the practice of making regular times for each activity is itself a part of mental training.

Gung fu is a skilled exercise, meaning that it requires serious mental discipline and physical activity. In Shaolin practice, there are no warm-up calisthenics or preparatory exercises apart from the martial practices themselves. A basic workout generally starts with *horse stance* sitting for several minutes, followed by slow and careful shifting. For example, if you start with a *deep horse*, then you might shift to a right *bow and arrow*, then twist into a *scissors stance* and unwind back into a *horse*. The point is to both memorize correct movement and foot placement for each stance and exercise the legs in preparation for other drills that will follow.

An extension of the stance work should follow, with each shift of the stance accompanied by one or two hand techniques, such as a parry followed by a punch. Each shift should use different combinations, even when you return to a stance already employed. Learn variety along with precision and you will make the most of this drill. Maintain proper posture at all times, with the spine and head straight, feet flat and at proper angles, knees bent to the proper degree, and balance centered. Parries should be fluid and short, while blocks should be delivered as if they were going to be strikes (indeed, in many cases a strong block *becomes* a strike).

Horse stance work and simple *horse* plus hand techniques should occupy some 30-40 minutes during your workout. After you have been practicing for some months—and this is where the call from a qualified sifu is important—your second phase *horse* work should include kicks as well as hand techniques. When doing kicks, your initial aim should be to execute each part of the move slowly and hold it. For example, if you are practicing *side kicks*, break it down into a) chambering, by lifting the knee to the proper height and bend the lower leg back, b) aim the knee at the desired target, c) slowly extend your lower leg, keeping the kicking edge of the foot in precise position, d) re-chamber the leg, and e) resume your stance with both feet on the floor. An excellent graphic example can be seen in the 1973 movie *Enter the Dragon*, where hero Bruce Lee keeps his *side kick* extended while having a short conversation with antagonist Bob Wall.

As your leg muscles loosen and get warmer, you should increase the speed and force of each kick, preferably by hitting a target. A small ball suspended from the ceiling is useful for target hitting and accuracy, while a heavy bag is preferred when you need to practice increasing strength in your techniques. Every body is different, so you might need to warm-up by doing *snap kick* techniques while your training partner might do better by starting with *crescent kicks*. Most people, though, do not do sweep drills until after they have truly loosened up with kicks.

After doing 40 minutes of warm-ups, you will typically start doing formwork. Forms are taught as basic drills, as moving encyclopedias, and as a way to practice complex sequences in preparation for combat. Basic drill forms are used to teach new moves in a sequence so that they are easy to remember and learned in combinations. Encyclopedic forms are longer sequences that incorporate either a wide variety of techniques, different applications of already learned techniques, or a combination of both. Contrary to legend, combat forms do not teach a student how to fight. They are practiced "as if" the student was in combat, moving quickly, punching and kicking with force, and incorporating the nuances of stance shifting and balance. Why, then, are they called "combat" forms? Because learning to execute techniques quickly and with power and precision is necessary in combat, and this is how a student moves from the gentle "flailing" of basic forms to the power-packed sequences needed in a real fight situation. But remember that no matter how powerful your moves, no matter how well you do combat forms, you cannot learn something as unpredictable and unpatterned as combat by practicing predictable and patterned moves. American general George Patton once commented that all battle plans become obsolete as soon as the enemy is engaged. His wisdom reflected the fact that people are given too many choices in almost all situations, and the specific response after the first technique is launched is rarely predictable. From moment to moment, technique to technique, combat is too alive, too much an entity of its own, for any of the participants to predict specific moves and responses.

How, then does a person learn combat? Bruce Lee noted: just as you cannot learn to swim without going into the water, you cannot learn to fight without sparring. Sparring is where you test your techniques and methodological understanding against another thinking martial artist. From sparring you learn which techniques work well for you, which need more practice, and which you should discard for lack of effectiveness.

Try to do sparring and form work on different workout days. When sparring, try to engage a variety of opponents with different levels of knowledge. An energetic and belligerent drunk with no martial training may be as dangerous an opponent as a sober black belt, because of both his enhanced resistance to pain (from the alcohol) and his unpredictability. Do not assume an untrained opponent is not dangerous; in fact, a wise person never underestimates his or her opponent.

To spar in a manner appropriate to Shaolin, if you are sparring with any power you will want full body protection, including head, groin, and joint pads. This is because Shaolin has no "illegal" techniques, and all strikes are allowed. Shaolin strike joints, eyes, groin, and knees, which also explains why Shaolin stylists are at a disadvantage in tournaments and sport events. While many people enjoy competition and sporting events, it is sometimes difficult to learn both effective combat *and* sports techniques. There have been occasions of martial artists of black belt level who were mugged or beaten because they were so used to aiming only at sport "legal" targets (which are difficult to hit at all, let alone in combat), or pulled their techniques (because true full contact is rarely allowed in sports events). Again, we make these comments not to denigrate sports, competition, or other martial arts, but to point out a potential limitation of authentic Shaolin training on your martial arts activities.

The act of seated meditation is offered in many martial arts schools from a host of philosophical backgrounds. There are many classes where students are led through about five minutes of seated meditation both before and after workouts. It is important to understand that such an interlude offers little more than a mental "change of channels" with no importance as meaningful meditation. Remember that meditation—the Ch'an and Zen of the arts—is the major goal of the Buddhist based arts and is not, therefore, relegated to a mere five-minute session as an afterthought to a workout. In fact, as noted above, meditation practice is traditionally done at the opposite end of the day from the physical workout, and rarely lasts less than thirty minutes even by beginners.

Meditation

Whatever harm a foe may do to a foe, or a hater to another hater,
a wrongly-directed mind may do one harm far exceeding these.

Shakyamuni Buddha

When most people think of meditation, they picture someone sitting cross-legged, head bowed, and trying to think about nothing. There is some truth in this image, but it is far from complete. Successful meditation, which is the literal meaning of the word "Ch'an," is the penultimate goal of all Shaolin practice. It is a Shaolin belief that all effort, all action, should represent a form of meditation. For this reason, we sometimes make a distinction between quiet or static meditation, and moving or dynamic meditation.

Before discussing specific meditative techniques, we wish to explain what meditation is actually a tool *for*, what it is intended to accomplish. Our normal life experiences serve to convince us that we are not a part of this or that, and that people can be divided into "us and them." Meditation is an effort to bring the mind home, so the practitioner is centered and sees all reality and activity as a unified whole. One way in which this can be accomplished is by becoming one with every activity or action in which you engage. For example, washing dishes by hand is a very potent meditative practice. The dishes, water, and visible completion all merge into a single reality. Properly done, the time spent washing dishes becomes the single activity in your universe. It *becomes* the universe.

Where novices go astray is in assuming that "this" is meditation time and "that" is time for something else. To a Shaolin, all time is for meditation, every activity part of the universal one-ness. "I am myself, and my action, and the result of my actions." When you understand this intuitively through personal experience, then any distinctions about meditation should fade. The central lesson to effective meditation is to be where you are; if that seems difficult, call your attention back with a personal mantra such as "be here *now*."

Simple meditation is about finding tranquility, from a position of being centered. From that point, the mind can simultaneously open outward and envelope the totality of reality, and it can dive inward to the very essence of our personal nature. At the point when you no longer distinguish between meditation time and other time, you will have arrived at the correct state of mind. This is sometimes called "one mind" and although it is not the end of Ch'an development, it is an important stage. Following are some elementary meditative practices.

Basic Meditation: You should sit on a pillow in the cross-legged position (or a lotus or half-lotus if you can manage it). Keep your back straight, head tilted slightly forward, and let your shoulders rest. Put your hands on your knees with the palms facing down. Close your eyes and just relax for a few minutes. Imagine your body becoming more and more loose, your breath more and more gentle.

Now you begin the exercise portion. Basic meditation is about getting the conscious mind turned off so that mental relaxation can follow. Do not change the strength of your breathing, but start to breath while counting slowly to yourself: a four count to inhale, a four count to exhale, and a four count with empty lungs. There is no holding of breath when the lungs are full. Let all thoughts go away, and focus only on counting your breathing cycle. Breathe in through your nostrils, and let air fill your belly and then lungs. Exhale through your mouth, emptying the lungs first and belly last.

The hypnotic nature of this exercise will eventually lead to your being able to relax every muscle, and your mind. Start by doing this exercise for about twenty minutes each day, and increase your time slowly up to one hour. Morning meditation works best for most people, because after sleeping the body is rested. Some people prefer evening meditation, and others like afternoons. Once you pick a time, try to stay with that time. This will become your basic meditation ritual.

Golden Deity Meditation: This meditation, shared with our order by our Tibetan comrades, is used when you need additional mental strength to accomplish a goal. Begin by doing the basic meditation exercise, but once your breathing is established, make a mental image of a golden statue of a god or goddess. As you inhale, imagine blue light coming in through your nostrils and filling the interior of the statue. As you exhale, picture the blue light moving dark sooty smoke out of the statue's mouth. The blue light represents ch'i under your control, while the soot is garbage that bogs and inhibits your mind and ch'i flow. As more blue light fills the statue, there should be less and less soot being exhaled.

Once the statue's interior is clear of soot, picture the blue light slowly transforming the deity statue into a pose that represents the action needed to accomplish the task at hand. Continue this exercise for as long as needed, but be advised that you must keep your back straight and head slightly bent throughout the whole meditation. You must also maintain focus on the inhalation of blue light and the posture (but not movement) of the statue.

Iron Needles Meditation: Unlike the previous meditations, this exercise is dynamic and the practitioner has more than just breathing upon which to focus. The goal of this meditation is to open clogged ch'i channels, improve energy circulation, and use inner power to enhance physical strength and health.

Begin by opening to a wide *horse stance* and simultaneously chambering your fists at your waist. Keep your spine straight and head facing directly forward. Relax and begin breathing as you did in your basic meditation. Do this for a few minutes until your breathing is controlled and you are at least somewhat in control of the aches from the *horse stance*.

Next, open your hands and form two *iron needle* positions: palms open, index fingers extended, other fingers folded, and thumbs at right angles to the fingers. When your hands are at your waist, they are held palm up. Now inhale and, as you slowly exhale, extend both *iron needles* forward. When fully extended, your palms will face forward, index fingers facing upwards, and hands straight out in front of each shoulder.

Maintain your four-count breathing: four counts inhaling, four counts exhaling, and four counts with empty lungs. As you do so, imaging a blue arc of light between your two index fingers. If your stance becomes uncomfortable, breathe harder and imagine the blue arc becoming thicker and stronger. Your goal is to use breathing and imagination to overcome physical pain and discomfort. Start doing this for five minutes every second day. After a month, increase to ten minutes; after four months, increase to 15 minutes. Slowly increase your exercise until you can hold this stance for about an hour.

Keep in mind that meditation is a working practice and should not be engaged in with a firm end goal in mind. Shaolin sentiments regarding meditation are similar to those of Master Dogen, who asserted that one does not meditate to reach enlightenment, meditation *is* enlightenment.[171] Meditating is dealing with purpose itself; it is about becoming one with reality. Even though we already are one with reality, meditation helps remove any doubt.[172] Allow us to also administer a final word of warning regarding meditation: meditation is but *one* aspect of the path. "Bondage samadhi" was a term used by ancient Ch'an masters to describe those who came to crave and covet meditation. Shakyamuni Buddha himself achieved the fourth and highest level of meditation under his ascetic teacher Udraka, but found that he returned to bondage. Realizing that he was headed the wrong way, he eventually abandoned asceticism and discovered the middle way.

Do not rely on following the degree of understanding that you have discovered,
but simply think, "This is not enough."
One should search throughout his whole life how best to follow the Way.
And he should study, setting his mind to work without putting things off.
Within this is the Way.

Yamamoto Tsunetomo

Detachment

When an archer is shooting for nothing
He has all his skill.
If he shoots for a brass buckle
He is already nervous.
If he shoots for a prize of gold
He goes blind...

Chuang Tzu

Detachment has been given a great deal of bad press. In some schools of Buddhism, detachment is practiced as a complete severing of all ties to the world. This means the practitioner forms no relationships, has no property, and belongs in no place. In consciously detaching from the world in all its aspects, the practitioner believes that attainment of nirvana will be easier to cultivate. This is often referred to in Buddhist traditions as "undertaking the homeless life", the importance and value of which partly explains the revival of the forest-monastic tradition in Thailand. Members of other religions and philosophies also practice this interpretation. This strict interpretation, though, is not part of Shaolin teachings.

Detachment is not about having *no* connections, but about having no sense of ownership or possession. Things are not ours if we cannot take them past this particular lifetime. Things are here for us to use, to help us perfect ourselves, to make the world around us better. When our time comes to leave our lives, the things will remain behind. Perhaps the Australian Aborigines state the doctrine best when they explain that land cannot belong to people because people belong to the land.

People should not interpret this to mean that Shaolin monks do not love or care for anything, or that we walk away from everything. Quite the opposite is true: we do not possess that which we love, but allow it to be loved as long as it's appropriate. We care so much for our world and other life forms that we train to become bodhisattvas. Neither do we just quit a task when it becomes difficult—so do not abandon school work (for instance) because it is unpleasant—but rather tackle it again and again until we either master our task or determine that it is truly not worth pursuing.

What does it mean to be detached? It means walking away when we must, from a person, place, or thing. We may hold part of something in our heart, but not in a covetous way. We may want to be here or there, but not as an overriding desire that neutralizes anything else we might do. It means being free to love and be loved, yet able to walk away intact if that love expires. It means not becoming so self-involved in a goal that it becomes a debilitating desire.

The meaning of detachment becomes especially important when

considering the nature of compassion and its centrality in the Shaolin ethos. True Buddhist compassion is not what the ancient masters called "compassion with a loving view."[173] Often, students of the way come to believe (mistakenly) that sentient beings actually exist in some ultimate, fixed sense; and due to various reifications, those students feel pity, sympathy, and other loving attachments to suffering beings. And so compassion is produced—but *this* kind of compassion is only a recipe for further suffering. Chögyam Trungpa explains that, sometimes, when you try to help someone:

> …you want him to be different, you would like to mould him according to your idea, you would like him to follow your way. That is still Compassion with Ego, Compassion with an object, Compassion finally with results which will benefit you as well—and that is not quite true Compassion.[174]

Shaolin compassion is an attitude produced by Ch'an *seeing* or *grasping*, especially awakening to the universality of all life and the truth that all sentient beings are already buddhas. (Language doesn't really do an adequate job of description here!) Detachment is critical to true compassion. A Buddhist attitude of detached compassion is not predicated upon any particular outcome; in a sense, it is directed at relieving suffering—but with the important caveat that we do not covet or thirst for the relief of that suffering. There is no egocentric grasping; no caveat such as "if you love me, I will love you." The one who can practice this "universal love" for all beings without attachment is truly a bodhisattva.

Detachment does not only apply to cultivating compassion, of course. One aspect of the eightfold path is right resolve, and one part of right resolve is the resolve to renunciate. A true renunciate is a person who can walk the path eating rich and appetizing foods *or* a steady diet of bread and water—without suffering. A renunciate can sleep in a feather-bed, *or* in the dirt. A renunciate can practice celibacy, *or* not. Detachment is an essential to renunciation, and both are vital aspects of the Buddha's teaching. Part of Shaolin's unusual approach to detachment (and especially renunciation) is that students are encouraged to forge a middle way. Most sects focus upon specific kinds of deprivation to help spiritual seekers develop these qualities. There is excellent evidence that this is an effective method, and we apply this technique in certain instances. Yet in Shaolin, we also have excellent evidence that our broader method works. This is why our vows are now so individualized and less rigid.

Bodhisattvas do not look upon blessing and merit
as a private possession, but as
the common possession of all animate beings.

Shakyamuni Buddha

Chapter Twelve

Ch'i and Inner Power

That which is seen is not all that there is.
That which is named as "all" is not the true "all."

Lao Tzu

The concept of inner power as an unseen but controllable life force has long been intellectually suspect in western cultures. People believed to have such extra power were customarily branded as witches—a general term for allegedly evil people who were not part of the ruling church order—and condemned to death. Similar ideas existed in much of Asia, unless the practitioner was also a "holy one" associated with a religious order or on a recognized and approved spiritual path. In time, people who had learned to cultivate their prana, ch'i, or ki were highly regarded.

Persecution against such peoples today is largely confined to remote areas, such as the New Guinea highlands, where native spiritual beliefs have been strongly coupled with Christian missionary teachings. As recently as November of 2000, seventeen "witches" were executed in Papua New Guinea. These activities aren't completely confined to remote and primitive societies, though. In April of 2003, residents in a Mexican town stoned and machete-hacked a man to death for "witchcraft." They then partially burned his body. He was what many locals considered a traditional "white magician." In China, past and present, many openly religious or spiritual figures have simply "disappeared." These examples, clearly, also demonstrate an extreme of religious intolerance. The time of persecution unto death is sadly not at an end.

Few cultures, though they may castigate individuals who don't fit into the accepted religious scheme of the majority, deny the existence of some "inner power" that is the spark of life. This ethereal energy is present in living things and absent from dead ones, yet its physical nature is still inexplicable in proper scientific terms. Yang classifies four basic kinds of Ch'i Kung: Scholarly (for healthfulness), Medical (for healing), Martial (for fighting), and Religious (for enlightenment).[175] Yang recognizes that these divisions are somewhat rough, as one kind of Ch'i Kung training can serve multiple purposes. This is certainly true in the case of our training regimen, which, although closely aligned with his description of Religious Ch'i Kung, overlaps into other areas.

In Shaolin arts, one must accept the concept of inner power, or ch'i, as real or advancement is not possible. Some practitioners rationalize the concept in their own minds as a manifestation of simple physical dynamics of matter and energy: force equals mass times acceleration (F=ma). This formula demystifies the great breaking feats by explaining how even a flimsy human hand, traveling with sufficient velocity, can break five inches of pine or crush through a 150-pound block of ice. But such simple explanations do not account for many variables inherent in the properties of different materials. For example, while wood may compress under force, water does not, and these differences greatly affect the ability of a tool to break them.

To a Shaolin student, ch'i is real, though perhaps inexplicable in rational terms. Humans cannot yet define or imagine the realities of many phenomena: a universe without a beginning or ending, the nature of life, the vastness of geological time. Nevertheless, we accept these ideas as real and go on with our lives. So it must be in developing control of ch'i. We all have it, but we can do so much more if we acknowledge its presence and work to exercise our control of this force. Shaolin teaching does not consider ch'i training to involve mysticism or the supernatural. Rather, we accept the reality of this universal life force and exercise it as we would our minds and muscles. For many students, believing in the reality of ch'i may come only after a fair degree of mastery has been obtained. No matter—acceptance of this force, rather than explanation, is more important to its cultivation. The various pieces fall into place when appropriate.

Development of ch'i is part of the core curriculum for Shaolin, for inner power control is essential in mental, martial, and medical practices. Chinese physicians use a variety of techniques to determine where and how ch'i energy is flowing in the patient. A blockage can be the cause of an illness or disability, so once the energy flow is determined, the doctor applies treatment to restore normal flow. Acupuncture uses the exact same principle, the metal needles helping conduct energy from one meridian—the channel along which ch'i flows—point to the next. By the same token, a person armed with such knowledge may concentrate defensive strikes to such meridian points, causing immediate paralysis, unconsciousness, or death in the opponent. The Chinese sometimes refer to these pressure point strikes as "poison fingers," which are common to the Viper system of Snake gung fu, and known in Japan as Tuite, or Atemi.

Closely related to medical applications is the martial application known as "the *delayed death touch*," or *dim mak*. By altering ch'i flow to certain organs in a precise way, a martial artist may set up a slowly acting process that can cause death in an opponent days, weeks, or months after a strike. The initial strike or strikes may be delivered fairly lightly, so the victim doesn't even know he has been attacked. *Dim mak* was more likely to be used by assassins than priests, of course, but knowledge of the techniques was essential in order to effect a cure, if possible. Knowledge of *dim mak* was also essential to defend against it, for otherwise a practitioner might not realize the severity of the attack.

The highest level of physical ch'i application is known as the ***vibrating palm*** technique. *Vibrating palm* is distinct from what is often called *"iron palm," "tieh sha chang,"* or *"iron sand hand"* by some practitioners,[176] which is a hard Ch'i Kung training technique resulting in a powerful striking weapon *sometimes* at the expense of interrupted ch'i circulation, destroyed hand nerves, and sterility[177]. True Shaolin training methods never involve self-mutilation (recent demonstrations by "Shaolin monks" in China involving suspending weights from the testicles and various other sensationalist antics are not the legacy of the historical Shaolin Order at all). Many training techniques causing permanent harm to the practitioner are erroneously labeled "Shaolin," yet these methods violate the eightfold path, and should not be viewed as authentic Shaolin techniques. In *vibrating palm*, the practitioner places an open palm against an object, such as a pine board or slab of concrete, and allows his ch'i to resonate in harmony with the board's structure until it shatters. To those who have witnessed or performed the *vibrating palm*, it represents a real conundrum for accepting the formula F=ma!

The training of inner power involves considerable (often tedious) physical, mental, and dietetic training over many years. Ch'i is universally present (like muscle), and it takes a combined practice to promote discipline, mental and physical training, and diet. It also may take years to develop a significant increase in ch'i control abilities.

The practice of ch'i cultivation (or, more precisely, control over ch'i use) is termed Ch'i Kung and involves three general stages, all aimed at allowing the practitioner to accept the reality of inner power on a par with the reality of a hand or arm. The first stage entails the practice of drills by rote, seemingly with no end result. In performing these drills in a regular manner, a student becomes accustomed to giving time over to exercise the ch'i and spending other times to practice physical and mental development. The second stage develops the skills needed to learn to consciously harness ch'i and use it for goal-directed activities. This stage is often a great impediment to further study because many people become enamored by their "super powers" and are unable to move on to the third stage. This final training stage teaches the practitioner how to amplify the mental and spiritual faculties. The subtlety of developing the ch'i energy at this stage makes it likely that only a handful of practitioners who reach this level will successfully complete their training. Traditional *iron palm* techniques were developed largely because internal methods took so long. By contrast, one can develop the *iron palm* in two to three years of diligent practice.

Ch'i Kung is not to be entered into lightly. Though most early exercises are harmless, there are many opportunities for personal injury to occur. It is inadvisable for an unsupervised student to undertake such practices. Some injuries may occur along vital meridians, on points that may not manifest symptoms for weeks or months after performing an improper technique. If the guidance of a master is not available, then a student would do better to take up the inner power exercises of T'ai Chi Ch'uan or Pa Kua. (Try to avoid the instructors/schools who have given the style a "New Age" face-lift by dropping the "Ch'uan" from "T'ai Chi Ch'uan." The art possesses tremendous efficacy as both a fighting art and as a method for training ch'i, but many "teachers" of the art transmit a watered-down version.)

Ch'i can be conceptualized a little like electricity. It is neither "good" nor "bad" but depends on the user to define its purpose. In practicing basic ch'i exercises, it must be remembered that you are much more likely to hurt a training partner than yourself. Think of the electric eel: it can discharge enough current to kill a horse, but the eel remains uninjured. Ch'i is not really any different. However, in doing many of the training drills, especially those for hand conditioning, it is easy to hit acupuncture points that may result in later self-injury.

Several concepts are fundamental to Shaolin Ch'i Kung training, including knowledge of vibrations, their special manifestations, and exercises. These exercises will focus on centering energy in the body's ch'i center known as the **tan t'ien**. The tan t'ien is known as the source of inner energies, but is actually more like an antenna to receive energy and distribute it throughout your body. The tan t'ien lies about two inches below the navel (about three finger-widths below the navel, and about three finger-widths back from the surface), and beneath this is the cauldron, which contains uncirculating, or stored, ch'i. Initial Shaolin training requires abstention from sexual acts, which causes accumulated ch'i to heat the cauldron, thus resulting in ch'i boiling over into the acupuncture meridians. The excess ch'i from suppressed sex acts as a crucial catalyst. After six weeks of training, the body is strong enough to resume sexual intercourse.

The first week of ch'i training aims to strengthen the heart, lungs, and spleen. Practitioners will generally be free of later cardiac arrest. Other weeks will train the brain (to eliminate dead cells and increase memory capacity), the nervous system, the circulatory system, the skeleton, and muscle structures.

There is a ch'i maneuver (*dragon's talon*) wherein you direct ch'i and use it as an invisible hand at a distance from you. Projections, the throwing techniques of many styles, are done *inhaling* to draw in the foe's ch'i so the defender can redirect it. When you want to fling someone away without inflicting damage, *exhale* and expel ch'i, like water from a fire hose.

Vibrations

The emotional state of a person can be measured as a vibratory rate. Changes in this vibration output are measured in part by lie detectors. Our human minds are well tuned to Klaviermusik (Bach, et al.), basic percussion drumming, and deep resonant sounds. These vibrations can help bring us into meditative states. Such deep contemplative states intensify our ability to study, cure illness, relax, and concentrate. As the vibration rate increases, mental planes of operation increase also. Active music, for example, often inspires us to progress from thought to deed. Consider the effect of military march music on a crowd! However, your vibratory rate only increases if you are enjoying what you are doing. Otherwise, even though pulse and respiration rates may go up, the psychic vibratory rate goes down. This explains the detrimental effect of boredom or depression on a soul, slowing it down even in the presence of activity and "stress."

The most common method to increase the rate of vibration is to use incense to achieve a body quiet/mind active mode. Choose incense you like, though, because individual tastes vary. The use of "mood music" should be saved for much later in your training, lest your mind follow the music instead of the meditation exercises. Sweet smelling incenses such as fruit flavored will increase meditative awareness.

Various substances can help or hinder one's ability to sense, and harmonize with, vibrations. Natural (herbal) tea has an equalizing effect on vibrations. One should *not* drink alcohol because it upsets the physiology by increasing vibrations of the heart and lungs without increasing astral vibrations. This effectively puts the body in a state of severe disharmony. A small amount of beer, on rare occasions, will not have much of a detrimental effect. Chocolate is the most potent psychic stimulating food available. Caffeine at certain concentrations will stimulate psychic centers, but amounts in excess of this (and it varies among individuals) will shut down psychic centers.

Colors, representing wavelengths of visible light, are also vibrations. Color therapy will enhance or impede some aspects of mental training. Colors that promote studying are subtle blue and gray shades. Bright colors are distracting (e.g. red, orange). Off colors, such as olive green and muddy brown will drain your energy and tire you prematurely. White is generally seen as a neutral color. You can change the colors around you to alter your mood and, often, success. Complementary wardrobe color may enhance your success and self-image. Yellow, blue, and sometimes medium gray are colors of shirts worn by "upwardly mobile" people. The point here is that we can blend our vibrations into closer harmony with other vibrations through sounds, scents, and colors.

To people trained in seeing beyond the standard visible spectrum—into the ultraviolet or infrared—the energy field of a living thing may be perceived as a cloud around the body. The gross, easier to observe field is termed the "etheric field," or simply "etheric," while the more subtle and colored emanations are called the "aura." The width of the radius of these fields indicates the level of available ch'i energy present in the body. A dead body lacks both etheric and aura; indeed, it is believed by Buddhists (along with Hindus and proponents of other Asian philosophies) that death simply is the state of a body without ch'i.

Mundane physical objects also have vibrations, a connection long recognized among eastern philosophies. According to quantum physicists, all matter and energy are made up of vibrating fields rather than solid elemental particles. According to Albert Einstein, matter simply is energy - manifesting in a slightly different manner. Shaolin achieves Ch'i Kung mastery by attuning the practitioner's mind to these vibrations. Empathy and clairvoyance are skills that utilize fine-tuning of vibrations at various levels. In the last century, our physics has come to what may be an understanding of matter that is compatible with rather ancient, eastern concepts of ch'i.

Ch'i Kung Exercises

No student should move beyond the most basic Ch'i Kung exercises without regular supervision by a master instructor. Though there is potential for self-inflicted damage, there is also a greater likelihood that incorrect practice will simply block further development. Though many schools allow anyone to start ch'i training, we believe that this is not safe without a foundation in physical training. For one thing, though inner energy moves through subtle channels instead of through arteries or nerves, it nevertheless affects all organ systems in the body. A weak body cannot safely conduct intense energy any better than a thin wire can move a large current. Body and wire tend to melt down. That said, here is some information on the safer exercises that a beginner may perform.

Basic Ch'i Meditation: Prepare for increasing ch'i flow by sitting with your hands on your knees, palms down. Close your eyes while pushing the tongue upwards. Keep your neck and back straight, and begin by taking a few long, slow breaths. As you start relaxing, inhale through your nose for the count of four, exhale the breath for the count of four, then keep your lungs empty for the count of four. Use your heartbeat as a metronome. As you become more relaxed you will move to deeper meditative levels, and both your heart rate and breathing rate will slow accordingly.

Red Sand Training: (Note: This exercise is *not* what some practitioners call *"Red Sand Hand"* [or sometimes *"Iron Palm"*] training, which is designed to turn the hand into a formidable weapon by striking into heated sand.[178]) This is a sensitivity exercise accomplished by taking fine sand and grinding it between your palms. This drill requires concentration as you attempt to feel each individual particle of sand with your palms (not a very touch-sensitive part of the anatomy). Allow yourself to project ch'i into the sand. Over time, it is said that the practitioner will be able to move an object by opening the trained palms towards it. More fundamental, though, is the increased sensitivity so useful in sticky hands practice, and touching to help heal a sick or injured person. Perform this exercise for 3-5 minutes per day for the first two weeks, increasing by 5 minutes every week thereafter until you are doing a 30-minute session. Take a one-day break after every five weeks. Initially you use very fine (red) sand; beach sand often makes a good substitute. At roughly six-month intervals, increase the particle size of the sand until, eventually, you are using chickpea sized gravel.

Small Bell Exercise: Place your hands on your hips, relax, and assume a *horse stance*. Slowly raise your hands, palms up, to a point in front of your chest. Inhale through your nose as your hands rise. Pause and then slowly exhale through your mouth as you extend your arms, palm down, and straight out from the shoulders. At full extension, bend your wrists so your palms face front, fingers outstretched and fingers pointing upwards. Inhale again while moving your arms out to the sides, palm up. Slowly bend elbows and raise hands while exhaling. Return hands to your hips. Repeat this exercise ten times daily, preferably in the evening.

Nei-Kung: This practice eventually allows a practitioner to change the temperature of a body part by controlling blood flow in an area. Ch'i feels warm if it is "yang" type, and cool if "yin." The meditative practice that leads to this skill is highly influenced by Taoism. Increasing yin energy can relieve pain and aches caused by yang energy. Minimal nei-kung proficiency requires an hour of daily yoga or Ch'i Kung plus some gung fu practice.

Regarding the manifestation of ch'i during training: a practitioner should begin to feel ch'i entering the body at the fingertips during the palm-up phase of an exercise. It must be allowed to course down the spine to the tan t'ien, the spot just below the navel where ch'i is centered. Your breath, when exhaled, should be released slowly, so slowly that a single feather in front of your mouth will not be disturbed.

Any student who follows this training method will enhance their abilities to perform physical and mental feats. The ability to increase balance, recall facts, and maintain health will increase gradually with continuing practice. However, **no student should attempt to progress**

beyond the basic stage without proper supervision by an experienced sifu. Improperly practiced, ch'i development may permanently injure or kill the practitioner.

Those familiar with Asian philosophies and yogas may note the similarity between advanced ch'i manifestation and the practice of Kundalini. Both practices can be done safely, but rarely quickly. In ch'i training the student is guided through methods that both open energy conduits and develop control of that energy; in Kundalini practice, the student focuses on mixing opposite energies in a "cauldron" region and having that energy quickly gush forth up the spine. Ch'i training is best practiced alone, with frequent guidance from a teacher; Kundalini yoga is best practiced with a partner and under close guidance of a teacher. Finally, in both practices the goal is to achieve enlightenment, using inner energy to bind closer with the universe.

...valleys, because of their lowness, become the source of rivers...

Lao Tzu

Hidden Valley:
High-level Meditation and Ch'i Kung

Perhaps the greatest mysteries still extant in the martial arts of this century are those generated by the so-called internal mystical systems of Chinese gung fu. Few disciples ever followed a master into those realms, and thus there are few legitimate new practitioners today. One of the ancestral styles, leading to a purely spiritual concept called Seven Valleys, is the *Hidden Valley* style. The mystique around this art has managed to give rise to the popularization of some of its mythical aspects via the book and film *Lost Horizon*. Accordingly, western thought has neglected the study of this approach because of the depth of legend around it, yet virtually all refined meditation techniques used in Asia stem in part from it.

According to legend, the name "Hidden Valley" supposedly refers to the style's place of origin, the westernized "Shangri-La" of Tibetans. The legend states that there is a valley beyond the first peaks of the Himalayas where a tropical environment persists. The Tibetan monks who developed the type of Lamaism that paralleled Shaolin would make a pilgrimage to this valley upon completion of tests for becoming lamas. Here, in a strange and less inhospitable climate, secluded from the known world, they exercised a new form of ch'i, a self-exploration inspired by transportation into a truly new world.

The goal of the Hidden Valley exercise was to achieve Ch'i Kung, or a completely energy-based method of gung fu. Success was gauged by how little physical effort would be needed to avoid conflict. Several great grandmasters were reputed to be able to keep even the meanest antagonist from rising out of a chair merely by willing him not to rise. Elements of hypnosis, the power of suggestion, and the self-assurance of the practitioner make this art work. Shaolin have been ritually taught the exercises for this sort of control, and the art perseveres in small areas to this day.

Hidden Valley entails three training levels: Yin Ch'i, Yang Ch'i and Tao Ch'i. The first level concerns adapting all of one's martial arts training into moving meditation. In so doing, the artist places himself into a hypnotic state by learning to move ever slower. This allows the subconscious to surface more readily at the command of the disciple; it further teaches the autonomous reflex arches to come under conscious control. Completion comes when even the simplest set takes so long that many meals pass without the need for consumption, and when the priest can will his blood flow to slow noticeably.

For the Yang Ch'i phase, the practitioner must move his thoughts from his body, to allow the forms, and eventually all of his movements, to flow from themselves in accord with Tao. Before he completes this training, he will have mastered a great deal more than his monastery training alone provided. Some legends state that only one in a thousand masters ever attain this level. In fact, though, Yang Ch'i accomplishes the very Ch'an-based ideal of being completely submerged in the actions and being of *now*. It is from this total immersion in the moment and its action that new perceptions about old knowledge come to light.

Once body, mind, and spirit are under control and yet still able to express themselves, the final level awaits, wherein the adept need no longer utilize the physical body to affect his surroundings. He is said to be able to influence the needle of a compass, or move small things in a room without touching them. (Before dismissing this particular claim, recall that some people actually drain small batteries and cannot, therefore, depend on a wristwatch to tell time.) He has also attained the power to heal, or to cause disruption of bodily functions. This level has sometimes been called "dim mak" in Western literature, and certainly includes dim mak skills, but Tao Ch'i involves far more knowledge, control and expertise. Assuming that a monk would actually attain this type of enlightenment, he would leave the Hidden Valley to explore the world of his contemporaries, and ultimately become the head of a temple. An added benefit, legend claims, is that he would be unique from all other monks in containing in his or her brain all the knowledge of the arts, without ever having been formally taught. Of the temples that were in existence where these methods were practiced, only two or three might have such a monk at any given time.

Hidden Valley practice is really a codified curriculum of combining martial arts and meditation in a surrounding of mystique and ritual. Practitioners tended to be loners, and their achievements probably did not generally exceed those of more mainstream Ch'an devotees. The allure of a secret style is the elitism that comes from its secrecy—the membership of a special order within a special order. While such an attempt to become the "elite of the elite" sounds like a major transgression into ego stroking, the rigors and deprivations that accompanied Hidden Valley training insured that only monks most driven by right attention would undertake or complete the practices. In other words, the path one takes in Hidden Valley training was not amicable to those feeding their egos.

Yet while the Hidden Valley style seems an end in itself, it is merely an entrance to the ultimate knowledge, the pure enlightenment of the Seventh Valley. Throughout history, no more than one disciple per generation would be taught the intricacies of this method. Once the monk had reached the level of Seventh Valley meditation, the focus was on development of the skills and wisdom—far and above the attainment of "mere" knowledge—needed for the forthcoming role as a bodhisattva. Bodhisattvas, as incarnate buddhas ("awakened ones"), are responsible for helping other sentient beings achieve meditative awareness and eventual escape from the cycle of rebirth. As sages, their role would absolutely require them to have compassion and wisdom in equal doses. In a very real sense, these "arrived and awakened" masters could be seen as empathic and therefore be of immense help to others, because upon attaining enlightenment and the realization that all things are part of the one, they could truly empathize and understand the suffering of others.

Chapter Thirteen

Coming Full Circle: Integrating Principles and Gung Fu

May you live in interesting times.

ancient Chinese curse

When the senior priests of the Shaolin Order brought their wealth of knowledge to America, they did so hoping that the school would find a place in the "free" world where natives could interpret its core meanings to western students. Since the time when they began transmitting the Shaolin corpus of knowledge, the West has become a land of spiritual plenty. Old religions are revived and hive into new branches, while others mix and match into New Age and crystal worship. Teaching circles now offer integrated lessons combining Hopi spiritualism with Confucian humanism, African ancestor worship with gospel singing and Japanese koans. This is no mere renaissance of spirituality, but an all you can eat buffet of generally "feel good" philosophy mixed with precious little spiritual growth.

In assessing the value of an Asian school's philosophical worth, please bear in mind that all the great Asian philosophies and religions are first and foremost exercises in transformation. In each practice the goal remains to elevate the spirit to the highest levels attainable for the human condition, and the universal requisites to these practices are compassion, detachment, recognition of our interrelatedness, and recognition that all things are transitory. To the detriment of these teachings and, we dare say, the shame of their earlier masters, most of the esoteric and spiritual courses offered today direct their efforts to emptying your wallet by offering to make you wealthier, sexier, or more competitive in society and business. Anyone who seriously reads the texts of Buddhism, Taoism, Hinduism, and such, will find great difficulty reconciling the true teachings with these "short course" objectives.

Consider the example of the desecration of the Tibetan Buddhist art of Tantra. Tantric practice includes meditation, breathing exercises, artwork, and the use of odors to enhance the emergence of ch'i energy in the body. Each level of practice aims to liberate the spirit from the mundane so it may dwell more regularly in its "natural habitat" plane of being. In America and Europe, though, the focus has been on the formerly most secret and powerful concepts, which use sexual union to promote, strengthen, and control the spiritual self. Instead of teaching these practices after a foundation of the other basics has been laid, the new courses jump right into ways to "prolong sex" and "become a better lover." In turning sacred Tantra into narrowly and physically-focused encounters between two loving (or merely amorous) tantrikas (practitioners), the spiritual smorgasbord of modern society has turned this art into little more than prurient debauchery. We do not mean to denigrate sexual union or its value in a healthy human relationship. Rather we ask that couples having sex call it such and be glad of it, and understand that true Tantra is not for sale nor is it anything like the community center offerings and self-help seminars seen all too often.

In addition to the advice we provide in an earlier chapter about finding a good instructor, let us add that a spiritual teacher will never advertise that spiritual training will make you more affluent, popular, or satisfied with life. In many cases the spiritual path will make us poor, unpopular, and (at least for a time) unsatisfied. Once we begin to make progress towards seeing through the veil of illusion, we see reality in all its forms, and many are ugly and hard to accept. It is especially difficult for a Shaolin to accept the sheer amount of misery in the world, and to recognize that almost all of it is self-generated. The spiritual teacher makes no promises of happiness and joy, but warns that the path of training wisdom and compassion is difficult! But take heart. The Buddha promises that his teaching leads ultimately to the cessation of suffering, an so far as we can tell, he makes good on his promise.

True spiritual practice leads to a state often known as the "little death," representing a pointed time when the person emerges on the other side of a portal of understanding. The event is nothing less than an enlightenment experience, and once through that portal nothing in the world will ever seem quite the same as it was before. This new way of seeing is a path from which there is no going back. Once you have heard a symphony orchestra in person, you might forget the tune, but never the complexity, clarity, and magic of the sound. This is the way of enlightenment, of the expansion of consciousness. You may not see the world the same way ten years later than you did the first day, the fact is that you *can't* ever see the world as you once did. Buddhists think of this experience as moving past the veil of illusion, because in the pre-enlightenment stages we see only dim images of reality, as if we are viewing the world through a thin curtain.

Once the spiritual path is seen and followed to its intended conclusion, the person has become transformed. The practitioner is still human, but in the moment of enlightenment recognizes that he or she is also everything else, too. We are made of atoms that formed in the core of an exploding sun, the same elements that make up the closest parasite and the farthest quasar. Enlightenment, which comes when we move from *knowing* about this reality to *understanding* it, transforms us. We no longer care about such transitory and, ultimately unimportant things (in themselves) such as money, status, politics, or time. This is not a divine or supernatural position, but a simple recognition that we are neither terribly special nor completely worthless, either. We simply are, and that state of being is without time or place. Only our temporary form and way of perceiving our nature differ from existence to existence.

Martial Arts, Combat, and the Spiritual Wanderer

What makes…a great warrior is that he has no opinions; he is simply aware.

Chögyam Trungpa

No Shaolin practitioner will be comfortable being termed a "warrior," "warrior monk," or any similar military title. Our supreme goal is to practice compassion and evolve our spirit to the level of the bodhisattva. Yet many people will wonder how an essentially religious order such as Shaolin, embracing the most peace-based of major teachings, can also warmly embrace combat.

It has been observed of humans that we are often at our best when things are at their worst. The selfless and compassionate acts people perform for each other during wars, natural disaster, or accidents are often beyond belief because they take caring to levels we rarely hear about in normal circumstances. What is it about the human spirit that allows a soldier to draw lethal enemy fire so a companion known for perhaps only a few months (or hours) may live? What makes a woman jump into a frozen river to help rescue people from a crashed airliner? Where does the motivation come from for a fireman to brave, often certain, death in an effort to save a stranger, one who may otherwise have been viewed as unworthy of notice? To answer the question of how such courage and compassion may be cultivated, we might examine Shaolin in light of two very different sides of its Ch'an coin: compassion for sentient beings and the one-point of life and death situations.

Compassion is Buddhism's most important component, for it guides our attitude towards all life, past and present. Compassion allows us to try walking in another person's shoes and, if that's not possible, to at least accept that another person might be seeing the world in a quite different way than anything we can imagine. No matter how much we may disagree with another person, accepting that they can have another viewpoint is our first step in trying to reach an understanding. True, some positions are so diametrically opposed that peaceful resolution is not possible. Awareness of such situations gives us a better position from which to defend our own beliefs should conflict result.

Combat puts us into potentially life or death situations, even in practice. Our opponent might fail to properly pull a technique, or we might inadvertently walk into one. Weapons slip and techniques sometimes fail, and all these possibilities are magnified when combat is real. But in combat there is an elegant simplicity: there is only the combat. All other realities vanish, at least briefly, leaving the mind more focused and intense than perhaps at any other time. When we are in combat we do not worry over a late bill payment, nor whether we have to pick up milk tonight on the way home. There is no thought of mowing the lawn or getting children to soccer practice. Once the mind drifts to any of these topics we have lost the combat.

Much of life puts us into positions that may not be "life or death" but nevertheless have broad ramifications on our lives and the lives of others. One kind of spiritual combat that Shaolin prepares for through physical combat drills is the combat that involves morality and ethics. Can the monk see evil without "defending" goodness? Can the monk make a sacrifice when necessary? It *is* possible to train strength of character in advance, although we all too often hear that moral (or indeed, any) courage comes from actions forced on us by circumstances. Consider an example that might be invoked by someone promoting the notion that courage is born of circumstances. The soldier who falls on a grenade to save his comrades from death or severe injury did not plan to do the brave act, and may actually have long talked disparagingly about those who performed such feats before him. But when the moment of crisis arrived, he ballooned with courage and saved his fellows. But the simple fact that these sorts of things occur is no evidence that the courage to do the right thing is somehow parasitic upon circumstances. In Shaolin, we believe that in accepting the impermanence of all things (including life) we take an important and large step towards accepting that doing the right thing may be costly to us—but we must act when faced with such a situation. We believe, like former president Harry Truman, that "the buck stops here," meaning we are ultimately responsible for our actions and choices. In concert with living a Buddhist lifestyle, we use gung fu to develop spiritual strength.

For Shaolin, gung fu *is* a spiritual practice. Separating gung fu from Shaolin would be like taking communion from Christians, the Koran from Muslims, or celebrating Passover from Jews. This is a literal and *essential* comparison, for without the mental and physical dynamics of gung fu practice, Shaolin loses its heart. A brain (Buddhism) and body (education) cannot live without a heart.

Shaolin in the 21st Century: Contributor or Anachronism?

Weak mind, weak fist; strong mind, no need for fist.

Shaolin saying

As with the generations that came before us, we too will face many challenges. Some of these challenges are truly unique in human history, such as global warming and other difficulties enabled by technological advance. Other obstacles to a peaceful and wholesome planet are as ancient as humanity. Wars and diseases readily come to mind. Historical events of old seem to recur in cycles, even if they fail to do so with astronomical precision. The latter half of the twentieth century has been a period of seemingly unbounded prosperity. As a result, many people today harbor a sense of limitless growth for humanity.

Our unbounded growth, however, leads to excessive consumption of natural resources. There is irony here: the same science we use to increase the complexity of our tools and our mastery over the physical universe also informs us that a belief in unbounded growth is disconnected from reality. Science tells us that balance will one day come. We can ignore the message, bury our heads in the sand, and eventually collide head on with a harsh and unpleasant future. We can also listen, learn, and exercise our abilities to ensure that our planet is a vibrant and healthy one for ourselves and future generations of plants and animals. Just as we create new problems for ourselves by only listening to the scientific deliverances we wish to hear, inattention to our past mistakes and our "it's not my problem" attitude towards exercising compassion sabotages attempts to develop lasting peace. The Buddha's teaching on mindfulness can be of service here. In Shaolin, we are mindful so that we may make appropriate decisions on behalf of ourselves and our communities, yet we also recognize that things get better and worse in a neverending cycle.

Shaolin is, as we have discussed, a pragmatic school in which hope and serendipity are not acceptable currencies upon which to base decisions.

Neither is it a font of unfounded optimism that seeks to make people feel good regardless of circumstances. In its insistence on examining reality and taking the measure of multiple variables, Shaolin forces its adherents to look long and hard at the world and to accept the basic reality that all we can change in this lifetime is ourselves. Mahatma Gandhi perhaps said it most eloquently: "We must become the change we want to see in the world." From this vantage, we may only act as lighthouse-like beacons to others who would walk the path with us. Enough committed souls could effectively modify the future to make it more palatable. The challenge is enormous, for even if changes are made now, today, the number of people and problems we must steer through to ensure adequate food, health care, education, hygiene, and basic human comforts will be staggering.

What has Shaolin to offer? Perhaps the nature of its practices, focusing so much on mortal combat, can be translated into working with life to avert needless and premature death. When we face our mortality, it makes us stronger or we succumb. A future in which people become less disciplined will be a future with more fear, leading in turn to hatred and warfare. Making hard choices becomes easier and, we believe, more just *and* merciful, when we have the skills that allow us to chose among subduing, hurting, or killing an adversary. Perhaps people have become technological giants but have remained morally and spiritually infantile as they continue to let priests and ministers do the "work" of spirituality for them. Shaolin teaches us to be independent, and though we use priests and priestesses in ceremonial roles, we do not expect them to bear the weight of spirituality alone. Most religions began with leaders who urged each follower to become "as a priest," but that message got lost in the wake of political struggle and the demands of making livings. Following Shaolin advice, we should each take responsibility for our own spiritual growth and, in fact, all our actions. This self-reliance will distribute strength to each person, rather than centralizing it in the hands of "leaders."

But we must also place compassion in a foremost position, for discipline without compassion is cold and inhumane. Discipline without compassion is the stuff of dictators and easily becomes twisted into true evil. No hard decision should be made without compassion, and few compassionate decisions will seem easy. Buddhism has a general attitude of reverence for all sentient life, and avoids any unnecessary taking of life, no matter how small or "insignificant." In learning to avoid unnecessary killing, by doing things such as helping trapped wasps get out of our homes and not stepping on insects, we reinforce the image of life as valuable and irreplaceable. Killing for food is considerably different from killing for fun or without thought. When we become aware of each killing act for what it is, we have moved another large step towards spiritual awareness and towards building the ethical muscles we need to become truly strong.

Many Buddhist sects eschew the eating of meat, for the adherents believe that all animals represent sentient life. In Shaolin there is less of a distinction between "sentient" and "non-sentient" life forms, and acceptance that *all* animal life—including humans—exists by eating other living things. Long after Tamo was gone, and the Order was developing its trademark animal styles, it became apparent to our monks that plants have a life cycle, just as animals do. The true difference between plants and animals may be seen as one of degree. Some Japanese Buddhist thinkers believed that plants possess buddha-nature as well.[179] Shaolin accept that all living things fulfill their nature by surviving, and while we do not kill animals for sustenance, eating meat was, and is, not prohibited. It may interest readers to know that Shaolin did keep chickens for the purpose of harvesting and consuming eggs.

The Buddha specifically forbade the eating of tigers, bears, elephants, humans, and some other animals. He also said that a Buddhist monk should not cause animals to be killed for food. Within these parameters the Shaolin monk is indeed allowed to consume meat as a normal part of the human diet. Historically, the Shaolin diet was often largely or completely vegetarian by necessity, but never by religious regulation. (More orthodox Mahayana sects may be critical of the Shaolin path as regards vegetarianism, for a variety of reasons. Without delving into the morass of issues, let us simply point out that the Buddha urged compassion and respect for all life without requiring vegetarianism of the Sangha. Like many Buddhist sects in Japan and Sri Lanka, Shaolin both embraces the message of the Buddha and allows the consumption of meat.) When it comes to food, all food, we believe it is important to know where that sustenance has come from, and to respect and value that source. As each of us moves through this life, we cannot help but cause the deaths of living creatures. Awareness of this fact, and taking responsibility for our own actions, is a hallmark of Shaolin Ch'an.

As an aside, there is a popular legend about how, when the young Shaolin Order helped T'ang Emperor T'ai-tsung ascend to the throne, the grateful emperor decreed that Shaolin would thenceforth be allowed to drink wine and eat meat. From a Shaolin perspective, this is merely a popular tale. Our Buddhist practices have never been dictated by a secular power, emperor or no. Imagine the Italian parliament passing a law stating that the pope can marry. That just wouldn't make any sense. Why would the Italian government care? The pope would disregard any such law anyway. And so it is with the Shaolin. Our practices come from our own internal philosophy and tradition.

Shaolin's strong attention to a complete education—for all people—is paramount to empowering humanity with the essential mental tools and discipline it will need to overcome the staggering problems it faces. Several independent studies, including a major paper prepared for the United Nations, have spelled out two near-absolute requirements for improving conditions in developing countries: universal education and equal rights for women. Nations lacking either of these components face serious hurdles to long-term survival. While Shaolin ethics will not allow forcing anyone to do anything, Shaolin proponents may certainly assist with improving both education and human rights wherever an invitation to do so exists.

Strength will become a key commodity if we are to create a favorable future for the coming generations. This strength must be founded on compassion and our willingness to take full responsibility for ourselves, and our actions. Part of this strength must come from spiritual, philosophical, or even religious teachings. This strength must be founded on the core and, too often, most difficult teachings from our different cultures. That means embracing and practicing the golden rule, and truly "loving thy neighbor." These dictates *absolutely must* take precedence over the petty and shortsighted use of religion to justify murder, mayhem, discrimination, war, and intolerance. Humanity has too many peoples, cultures, and belief systems to tolerate any creed that at any time says, in essence, "Love *my* god or die!" As oxymoronic as it may sound, we have come to a point in time where we cannot tolerate intolerance.

Those who assist their rulers with the Way,
Don't use weapons to commit violence in the world.
Such deeds easily rebound.

Lao Tzu

The Shaolin priest and priestess have learned to defeat the weaknesses in their hearts, to overcome fear and intolerance through ritual combat aimed ultimately at conquering the self. We augment meditation with combat to kill our egos, and in the end hope that we emerge, like a butterfly from its cocoon, as a new creature. In our dedication to compassion and the eightfold path, we find a way to live in harmony with others who would, at best, welcome us into a diverse community or, at worst, simply leave us alone. Such inner strength can be used by people from any culture or background to stand up to political and "spiritual" ideologues and tell them that they have abdicated their authority, and neither rightness nor godliness have, or ever will, come from the barrel of a gun.

Shaolin are Buddhists who incorporate Taoist ideas into our beliefs. We are not necessarily vegetarians or celibate. We promote peace, yet train hard to learn fighting skills. We welcome men and women into the highest levels of the Order. We are iconoclastic and independent, and though always a small group, we have also cast a large shadow. Shaolin walks a crooked and complex path, never a highway, and this strange heritage is part of our core identity.

In the final analysis, the role of Shaolin Ch'an is to serve as a path for people who seek spiritual improvement, with eyes focused on becoming qualified to help others in their quest to escape suffering in this world. You, as a practitioner of whatever level, will need to adhere to your own personal code of ethics and learn to escape the initial pitfalls of ego building *and* hypocrisy. The path of a Shaolin initiate is not a well-paved path, but is more like the yellow brick road that led to Oz. Along the way are adventures and learning opportunities, dangers and traps, new friends and cryptic teachers, loneliness and noisy crowds. From these scenarios we experience a wide variety of life's offerings, experience which in turn provides us with the knowledge that we need in order to form wisdom. The way is not easy, but then few valuable things in life are easily attained. Looking back over an entire century of Shaolin in the New World, we can only relate that it has all been worthwhile. Should you also choose to walk the path, may it be illuminating and wonderful.

As the raft is of no further use after the water is crossed,
it should be discarded. So these arbitrary conceptions of things
and about things should be wholly given up
as one attains enlightenment.

Shakyamuni Buddha

Glossary

Arhat— The Hinayana ideal, the arhat ("lohan" in China) is an enlightened individual who has achieved that state through strict practices, and who will not be reborn again. The arhat is passionless and removed from the world of common people.

Asceticism— A philosophy mandating rigorous self-denial as a vehicle for spiritual development.

Bardo— Tibetan for "in-between state," there are different kinds of bardo, some characterizing aspects of life, and some characterizing the time between death and rebirth.

Block— A defensive technique which pits force against force, and can often double as a strike.

Bodhidharma— The founder of Shaolin, Bodhidharma was born in Kanchi (in the southern Indian kingdom of Pallava) as one of the brahmin— the third son of King Simhavarman. He was taught the Dharma and told to go to China by his teacher, Prajnatara. Called "Tamo" by the Chinese, Bodhidharma set Shaolin on its unique course and introduced Ch'an (which would evolve into Zen) to China. He is credited with introducing a physical regimen at the Honan Shaolin Temple. Referred to in Tibetan writings as "Bodhidharmatara."

Bodhisattva— 1. In Sanskrit, it means "spiritual being," or "spiritual warrior." A bodhisattva is an enlightened person, or buddha, who postpones entering a state of nirvana to instead return for another life with the intent of helping other sentient beings become enlightened. Compassion is the most important characteristic for a bodhisattva. This is the fourth and highest level of Buddhist mastery. 2. The *Maha Prajnaparamita Sutra* defines a bodhisattva as one who "ceaselessly seeks unexcelled, perfect enlightenment as well as the happiness and welfare of all beings." In a sense similar to this one, the word "bodhisattva" is often used in sutras and other Buddhist writings to refer to Shakyamuni Buddha prior to his enlightenment (although this is not the standard use of the term). Also note that some scriptures will use the term "bodhisattva" to refer to those who are not yet enlightened, but who have made considerable progress on the path.

Bon— The dominant religion of Tibet prior to the introduction of Buddhism. Bon has many deities, spirits, heavens, and hells. Bon's two creator deities are the principles of good and evil, and the religion is similar to shamanism. Bon blended with Buddhism to create Lamaism.

Boxer— Very broadly, any exponent of gung fu may be considered a Chinese boxer. But the term most often refers to members of secret societies such as the Triad Society, the White Lotus Society, and many more who worked to restore the power of the Ming (in name, at least), and who later fought to expel foreigners. The term "boxer" is most often used in connection with the Boxer Rebellion, when many Chinese used their gung fu to fight western powers in an attempt to expel them from the country. Most of these boxers were members of secret societies.

Buddha— 1. The historic Indian Prince Siddhartha Gautama who attained enlightenment in the northern village of Benares in the 4th century B.C.E., and went on to teach his path for the rest of his life. After leaving his teachers to find enlightenment on his own, he was called "Shakyamuni," for "sage of the Shakya clan." He is often referred to as Shakyamuni Buddha to differentiate him from other buddhas. 2. (not capitalized) Any person who achieves the full state of enlightenment.

Buddha Hand— A Shaolin style of gung fu which employs many knife edges and spear hands.

Buddha-nature— The original mind, or what remains of the self once ego is extinguished.

Buddhism— The Asian philosophy, originating with Shakyamuni Buddha (who was born as Siddhartha Gautama), that teaches the elimination of suffering by following a path of detachment and compassion. Buddhists use the term "Dharma" to describe the Buddha's teachings. Buddhists are those who accept the truth of the four noble truths and commit to living their lives in accordance with the eightfold path.

Caste— What westerners call the "Caste System" arose in India out of Hinduism. There were four traditional castes and one "anti-caste." The brahmin were priests and holy leaders, the kshatriya were warriors and nobles, the vaishya were artisans and merchants, and the shudra were laborers. Then there were the "untouchables," basically shudra who were conquered peoples, non-Hindus, or otherwise unsavory to the rest of the populace. Up until some point, between 500 B.C.E. and 500 C.E., a person in India could actually change caste (scholars disagree at which point things began to change), but after that point people were stuck in whatever caste they were born into. Each caste had very different dietary restrictions and education, and typically did not inter-marry (although there are broad exceptions). Generally, the brahmin were of northern, Aryan descent and had lighter skin. Separate but integrated into the castes is the class system. Classes are more like professional divisions, although other factors are relevant as well. The number of classes in India today is quite large. One thing to keep in mind regarding castes and classes is that Indian social structure is rather complex; oversimplification should be avoided. From the Shaolin, and indeed the overall Buddhist, perspective, the key thing to keep in mind is that the Buddha's message did not neatly fit into the prevailing Indian social structure. Since the castes were religiously derived, this amounted to a rejection of Hinduism, much as the Buddha's philosophy of anatman was the polar opposite of Hindu atman.

Centerline— An imaginary rod that extends from the center of your skull, out the base of your spine and to the ground, and around which your balance shifts. Centerline styles are so-called, as they are especially known for strong attention to defending their own centerlines, and attacking the centerlines of their opponents.

Ch'an— The practices of meditation that form the core of the Mahayana path towards enlightenment. Known in Japan by its more familiar name, "Zen." Ch'an is known as "Thien" in Vietnam, and as "Son" in Korea.

Ch'i— The subtle inner power that distinguishes living from non-living things. Also known as "ki" (in Japan) and "prana" (in India), the early promotion of the concept of ch'i is sometimes attributed to the Chinese philosopher Mencius. Ch'i is often seen as the universal life force.

Ch'i Kung— Practically a style in its own right today, Ch'i Kung focuses on the development of the practitioner's ch'i. Prior to the mid-19th century, Ch'i Kung was not really seen as a discipline separate from typical martial study (think of how yin and yang join in an inseparable union). But since then, Chinese martial styles have increasingly come under the academic scrutiny of occidental culture, which has (perhaps inappropriately) drawn very sharp distinctions between internal training and external training. Ch'i Kung is sometimes called "Nei Kung," and seeks to improve the practitioner's health, longevity, and martial prowess by increasing the flow of ch'i, and then harnessing the ch'i for specific purposes.

Chih— The philosophical practice of "uprightness," or knowing the difference between right and wrong. By itself, it could be interpreted as the moral "high ground," for which reason its potential for pretentiousness is counterbalanced by the practice of jen.

Ch'in na— Grappling and locking. Every style has some ch'in na, if only a little. Within Shaolin, Black Crane probably has the largest quantity of ch'in na techniques. Certain pais outside the Temple tradition have taken ch'in na to tremendous heights and developed many techniques. Within the Shaolin, we focus primarily on the different ch'in na techniques that accompany each animal style. Outside of Shaolin, Northern Eagle Claw and non-Temple White Crane employ wide ranges of ch'in na manuevers.

Ch'uan fa— Literally, it means "fist art" or "way of the fist," and is another synonym for "gung fu." The Japanese translate "ch'uan fa" as "kempo."

Cobra— Cobra is an ancient, northern style of Shaolin gung fu. The style is now nearly/mostly extinct, but its remnants are often studied by Tiger and Snake stylists.

Compassion— A crucial trait for a bodhisattva, and indeed for any Mahayana Buddhist. Compassion is very important within the Shaolin Order. Wisdom and compassion together constitute "skillful means" for attaining enlightenment.

Confucian(ism)—The philosophical, almost religious practice of the guidelines for "proper living" as propounded by Confucius, or K'ung Fu-tzu. Paramount in Confucian practice is the recognition and deference to a hierarchy among people, with the imperial family and nobles at the top, and elders at the head of each community and household. Confucianism is a philosophy of humanism.

Crane— The Crane styles of gung fu mimic the movements of the crane. Black Crane is alternately referred to as a "system" and a "style." Before White Crane came into Shaolin, what is now called "Black Crane" was Shaolin's only Crane style. But today, there are three distinct systems, Tibetan, White, and Black, all under the umbrella of the Crane style. So don't get wrapped up in whether we are using "style" or "system" to refer to any of them. They're just names. Traditionally, Crane practitioners also focus on some aspect of the healing arts.

Dharma— 1. The teachings, way, or law of practice of the eightfold path. The Dharma also includes core Mahayana doctrines such as anatman, pratitya-samutpada, and shunyata. 2. (not captialized) "dharma" also translates as "basic element of existence," or simply thing," and is used this way frequently in the sutras.

Dhyana— It means "meditation," and is the source for "ch'an na" which became Ch'an and "zen na" which became Zen.

Diamond Sutra— In addition to the teachings of Tamo, the *Diamond Sutra* (literally the *"Sutra of the Diamond-Cutter of Supreme Wisdom"*) is a critical part of Shaolin philosophy. The *Diamond Sutra* is the most important of the traditional Mahayana sutras to Shaolin. In general, Shaolin is not focused on analyticity and intellectualizing. We are a very pragmatic school. But the message of the *Diamond Sutra*, that the phenomenal world is not ultimate reality, is a key Shaolin teaching. Understanding Shunyata, or Emptiness (which is rather distinct from nihilism), helps us overcome our egos and awaken to our own buddha-natures. The sutra also outlines important ethical principles, in the way of the paramitas: charity, selfless kindness, humility and patience, perseverance, tranquility, and wisdom. The *Diamond Sutra* is the oldest printed book in the world, dating to 868.[180] A copy may be seen at the British Museum.

Dim mak— The *delayed death touch*, a variant of acupuncture technique that allows a practitioner to strike an opponent with a subtle touch, causing the opponent to die at a later time, possibly weeks later. *Dim mak* techniques are prominent in Snake and Southern Praying Mantis, but *dim mak* is common to the study of many styles.

Disciple— 1. A member of the Shaolin Order of intermediate rank, above students and below masters. 2. A skilled entrant upon the path towards enlightenment, representing the first and most basic level of Buddhist mastery. Disciples could be of two degrees, a) Stream-entered, learning of the path and following Buddhism in this lifetime, and b) Returned, coming back after having lived previously as a Buddhist.

Dragon— A style of gung fu from which many systems have developed. It is based on a variety of real and imaginary creatures, and was strongly influenced by Taoist beliefs.

Ego— The aspect of the human psyche that draws an essential distinction between the self and everything else, the ego is an obstacle on the path that must be overcome to reach enlightenment. The ego is transitory, mutable, and constructed of the five aggregates—hence the ego is susceptible to suffering. In Shaolin Ch'an, we seek nothing less than the extinction of the ego, and work to achieve this through meditative practices, which in turn help eliminate craving, hate, and delusion.

Eightfold path— The guidelines for living included in the fourth noble truth, the eightfold path is an organic entity. Each aspect of the path intertwines with the others, and following the path prepares the mind and spirit for the transcendence of enlightenment. The eightfold path is the Buddha's cure for the suffering in the world—applied at the level of the individual, which is the only level at which the cure can successfully be applied.

Enlightenment— The state of bliss and fulfillment achieved by following the eightfold path as set forth by the Buddha. Enlightened souls are free from the rounds of birth, death, and rebirth. The experience of enlightenment entails awakening to one's buddha-nature, which is identical to the nature of the universe. The twin aspects of enlightenment are compassion and wisdom.

Expedient device— A method which is used to prod the ignorant towards enlightenment/liberation/awakening. Expedient devices have historically included Kung-an ("koan" in Japanese), parables, theories, maxims, physical pain, silence, and more. These devices are the means Buddhist masters employ to help their students along the path. They are tools, called "expedient" as a caution not to take them literally, thereby "mistaking the finger for the moon" (mistaking the tool for what it can accomplish). Shakyamuni Buddha and Bodhidharma were both extremely skilled in employing the appropriate expedient device for each particular disciple. Because Buddhist, and especially Ch'an Buddhist, means of teaching focus on expediency, it is very common for the same master to say logically contradictory things to different students.[181]

Fang chang— This is the Chinese-language term for "chief monk," or "first abbot."

Five Elements— The five traditional Chinese elements are water, wood, fire, earth, and metal. The elements are very roughly analogous to the elements of European alchemy, and play an important role in both Taoist alchemy and traditional Chinese medicine (where the goal is to keep the elements in balance). Here are the basic relationships: water has a tendency to create or transform into wood, wood creates fire, fire creates earth, earth creates metal, and metal creates water; water controls or moderates fire, wood controls earth, fire controls metal, earth controls water, metal controls wood.

Five-Formed Fist— The first "style" of Shaolin, incorporating different animal movements, but also a generic name for Shaolin gung fu. Today, there is also a Five Animals style, which could appropriately be called the "Five-Formed Fist." This style is sometimes called "Ngo Cho Kune" (which means "Five Ancestor Fist," literally), and is of Shaolin descent, although it is distinct from the Shaolin Five Animals style which is practiced within the Order. "Five-Formed Fist" can mean many different things.

Four noble truths— His deep realization of these truths is often seen as constituting the Buddha's enlightenment. Simplified, they are: there is suffering, suffering is caused by craving, suffering can be eliminated by eliminating craving, and the way to eliminate craving is by following the eightfold path. If suffering is the ailment, then the eightfold path is the cure—but this cure cannot be administered by a doctor. Buddhist worthies and the Sangha can help, but you have to effect the cure yourself. And it's the toughest quest you will ever undertake, if you choose to undertake it.

Fu Jow— Fu Jow (or Fu Jow Pai), meaning "Tiger Claw," is a reasonably common non-Temple variation of Southern Tiger. Of course, it is only common compared to Shaolin's Southern Tiger style; compared to Tae Kwon Do, Fu Jow Pai is extraordinarily rare.

Fut doo— This term refers to the monks who returned to, and then remained at, the temples. They were the "lifers" who had chosen to dedicate much of their lives to the Order and the Shaolin path.

Grandmaster— A Shaolin master who has elevated a disciple to the rank of master. "Grandmaster," in Shaolin, is not a rank, but a title. At various points, the Order has had many grandmasters.

Guardian— The term "guardian," although sometimes used within the Order to refer to the guardian successor, properly refers to any abbot/style master within the Order. Style masters are those who are responsible for a complete style (or multiple styles).

Guardian successor— The one person in the Order who is responsible for knowing everything taught within the Temple (meaning, the entire Shaolin Order). It is no wonder that guardian successors typically begin immersion in Shaolin education while still very young. Normally, there is no more than a single guardian successor in a generation. Being the guardian successor isn't like being the president, king, or pope. Shaolin's hierarchy is as relaxed as possible. From the perspective of internal politics, the guardian successor is kind of like a chief advisor and facilitator. Additionally, the guardian successor has some special responsibilities.

Gung fu— "Gung fu" means something like "excellence," "skilled activity," or maybe even "time/energy." It is not unlike the Greek term "arete," and may be applied to people in a general, or specific, way. For instance, you might say of a friend, "He is a gung fu painter!" Or after watching a person do something amazing which requires a lot of focus and talent, you might say, "Great gung fu!" Historically, it was more common for Cantonese to refer to martial arts as "gung fu". Northerners more often used the term "wu shu" which literally means martial art. Today, "gung fu" most often applies to Chinese martial arts. But why are there the different spellings, "gung fu" and "kung fu?" This is yet another result of western linguists confusing both eastern and western speakers. In the once near-universal Wade-Giles spelling, a Chinese "g" sound was written in English as "k", while what the Chinese pronounced as "k" was transcribed as a "k" followed by an apostrophe. Thus if "kung fu" were to be pronounced with a "k" sound, it would have been written as "k'ung fu." When Bruce Lee introduced American audiences to his martial art, he both spoke and wrote the American "g," hence "gung fu." More recently, the Chinese Pinyin system has revised the transliteration of most words so that you will now frequently see the spellings "gonfu" and "gongfu." Confused? Don't worry about it, so is everyone else... (See the entry below for Wade-Giles.)

Hidden Valley— A high level Ch'i Kung style, Hidden Valley is heavily influenced by Tibetan Buddhism and Taoism.

High style— A martial art that places considerable emphasis on ch'i development from its most basic exercises. In contrast are low styles that emphasize physical power until late in training. In essence, a "high" style is both "soft" and "internal."

Hinayana— It literally means "Small Vehicle," and is often perceived as a mildly derogatory term for this strict interpretation of Buddhism. Since Theravada is the only extant school of Hinayana Buddhism, see the entry for Theravada.

Hsing-I— Sometimes called "Hsing-I Ch'uan," or "Mind Form Boxing," Hsing-I was developed in and around the Wutang Temple. The style revolves around the five elements and the twelve animals; and a single stance, called the "three essentials" stance provides a foundation for combat.

Hui-k'o— Tamo's student and the second patriarch of Ch'an Buddhism.

Hung Gar— This style of gung fu is sometimes known as "Southern Tiger-Crane," and "seeped" out of the Fukien Temple. Consequently, Hung Gar is sometimes called "Fu Hok Pai." The situation with Hung Gar is analogous to that of Northern Praying Mantis. Both were Shaolin-originated styles, and both were often taught to rebels trying to restore the Ming dynasty (or at least hamstring the Ch'ing).

Jeet Kune Do— "The Way of the Intercepting Fist," a philosophy (not a style) of combat devised by Bruce Lee in 1967-1973. It is predicated on eliminating flowery techniques, dispensing with low-efficiency techniques, and striking first and fast.[182] As a philosophy, it is intended to be particularly useful to the experienced martial artist—not to the neophyte. Many commercial martial arts school have "cashed in" on Bruce Lee's popularity by emphasizing that they teach Jeet Kune Do, or "Jeet Kune Do concepts." Even in 1970, Lee remarked that "there have already been rumors of people claiming to teach Jeet Kune Do…in fact, I have heard that one guy has already learned all eight of Bruce Lee's forms! Funny, though…" To the prospective student of such a school: do your research! What style does the school teach? What will you really be learning? Bruce Lee's Jeet Kune Do philosophy is spelled out in his book, *Tao of Jeet Kune Do*, which you can buy for only $16.95.

Jen—The philosophical practice of benevolence, treating all people and sentient creatures with respect and kindness. Coupled with chih it helps a person to follow a spiritual path of "goodness." Jen is the Confucian concept of humanity.

Karma/karmic cycle/karmic debt— "Karma" is the Sanskrit word for "deed," and is the universal law of cause and effect. This law manifests as follows. Karma is essentially a measure of debt or accumulation that impedes the advancement of the spirit to a higher level. Karmic debt is seen as incremental moves away from enlightenment. Sometimes, karma gets divided into "good" karma and "bad" karma. There is no such thing as "good" karma; one either acquires karma (not good) or eliminates it (the goal of meditation). Although different Buddhist sects use the term in a variety of ways, all agree that it isn't primarily the action that causes a karmic effect to arise, but rather the intention behind an action. Certain intentions, whether actions result from them or not, cause accumulation of karmic debt. Once hate, craving, and delusion are eliminated from intention (for the Shaolin, gung fu and Ch'an meditation aid in achieving this—which, you will note, sounds a lot like eliminating the "ego"), one cannot accumulate karma. Liberation ensues. The term "karmic cycle" refers to the fact that the effects of karmic accumulation are not often manifested in the same lifetime as the individual whose intention gave rise to the karma. Talk of the "karmic cycle" can also be another way of referring to the universal law of cause and effect.

Kuen— The Chinese term for "form" (known as "kata" in Japanese, and sometimes called "pattern"), a kuen is a pattern of movement. Most styles have three or more such kuen, which serve as training tools (for both meditative and more practical purposes) and encyclopedias of martial knowledge. "Kuen" is also written as "ch'uan" and literally means "fist," although it is frequently, colloquially used to mean "form."

Kuoshu— It means "national art," and is often used instead of "gung fu." The term is especially popular among the descendents of the nationalists, the Taiwanese.

Kwoon— This is the place where martial arts are learned and practiced ("dojo" in Japanese, "dojang" in Korean).

Lama— "Lama" literally means "none above," and although the term can be used to refer to any Tibetan Buddhist monk, it especially applies to lamas who have received a very specialized training. "Lamaism" is a word often used for Tibetan Buddhism because the religion prominently features lamas. Tibetan Buddhism has also been called "Mantrayana" (vehicle of holy words), "Tantrayana" (vehicle of manuals), and is now most often called "Vajrayana" (vehicle of the thunderbolt; "vajra" also means "diamond," so one possible translation is "diamond vehicle"). There are many parallels between Chinese Ch'an and Tibetan Buddhism. For instance the yang and yin correspond to the Tantric male and female elements of Shiva and Shakti.

Lao Tzu— A librarian-philosopher who recorded his teachings (for a gate guard, as legend has it) in the book, the *Tao Te Ching*. "Lao Tzu" means "Old Master," roughly, and so was not his given name.

Leopard— Leopard is a style of gung fu that has been absorbed as a system under the Tiger style. It is a very fast style employing often extremely low stance work. Leopard systems and many pieces of Leopard systems have survived outside of the Temple as pai styles.

Lohan— 1. Lohan is a style of Shaolin gung fu that originated in the North, and presently enjoys some degree of popularity in Malaysia. 2. (not capitalized) An enlightened person, or buddha, who enters a state of nirvana after death, instead of returning for another life with the intent of helping other sentient beings to become enlightened. Known as an "arhat" in India, this is the third level of Buddhist mastery.

Low style— A martial art that places emphasis on physical techniques and strength, timing, or both. In essence, a style is "low" if it is primarily both "hard" and "external."

Mahayana— Translated as "Great Vehicle," Mahayana is the middle way of most Buddhists living in Tibet, China, Japan, Europe, and the Americas. A key aspect of Mahayana is the bodhisattva ideal, as opposed to the arhat ideal of Theravada. Mahayana also stresses the buddha-nature of all sentient beings over the importance of the historical Buddha, places less value on monasticism, and seeks to provide liberation for all.

Mandala— Very important in Tibetan Buddhism, mandalas (the word "mandala" literally means circle) are graphic representations of cosmic forces that serve as meditative aids. By meditating on the mandala, a lama works to grasp the simple natural order hidden in the complexity of the design. Throughout Shaolin history, our Tibetan comrades have made many gifts of mandalas to the Order. Most all of these pieces of art have been lost or destroyed.

Mantra— A mystical invocation, a mantra is a syllable or phrase chanted as an adjunct to meditation.

Master— 1. The highest level of practitioner in the Shaolin Order. 2. In Buddhism generally, the second level of Buddhist mastery, in which practitioners follow the path of Dharma, but do not quite attain the severing of ties needed to reach nirvana.

Meridian— These are the channels through which ch'i flows. Pressure points, often identical with acupuncture points, are located along these energy channels.

Metaphysics— The field of philosophy engaged in the study of the really real, or ultimate reality. "Metaphysics" is sometimes used to refer to all sorts of "New Age" and psychic notions, but we do not employ the term in this way. By "Metaphysics," we mean what Aristotle meant: that which comes "after" (meta), or beyond, the physics. Metaphysicians are interested in questions like: "Is there a god or intelligent creator?", "Do we have free will, or are our lives predetermined?", "What is reality?", and so on. In a very real sense, Taoists and Ch'an Buddhists are metaphysicians; but metaphysicians who have, like Wittgenstein, not bought in to the notion of self-created, logical entities which have little or nothing to do with reality.

Monk— The generic term for any participating member of a Buddhist sect, including students, disciples, masters, priests, priestesses, and nuns.

Naga— Supernatural and often beneficent snake beings; "naga" means "serpent" or "dragon." The naga Mucilinda was said to have sheltered the Buddha from inclement weather, and some branches of Tibetan Buddhism maintain that nagas protect Buddhist scriptures.

Ng Mui— 1. The creator of Southern Dragon, circa 1570. 2. The creator of Wing Chun, circa 1776.

Nirvana— Nirvana is like the Tao in that an accurate description is insufficient to capture the idea. Nirvana is experiential. For Shaolin, nirvana is the state of freedom from attachment, and of grasping at an intuitive level that the practitioner is one with the universe.

Novice— A student at the time he or she is formally introduced to Shaolin teachings, usually after being a student for six months to a year. Traditionally, students beginning Temple life were evaluated for six months to a year before being deemed worthy of learning the uniquely Shaolin curriculum. Today, there isn't much distinction between a novice and a student, as students are introduced to Shaolin teachings as soon as they commence study.

Ordator— The creator of the original Tibetan White Crane style.

Pai— Roughly, "pai" means "family," yet the connotation is often somewhat richer than that, including the sense of an association, school, or style. Most styles of gung fu are pai styles, meaning that although they may have roots in one of the temples, they are practiced foremost as martial arts, and not as a Buddhist practice. In most pai systems, there is a designated "grandmaster" who is the head of the style. This can lead to confusion, as "grandmaster" does not have this meaning within the Shaolin Order. Pais are the most widespread transmitters of Chinese martial arts, and there are many excellent sifus spread out among the various pai schools. Tjoa,

Draeger, and Chambers offer an excellent, concise description of what traditional pai training was like.[183]

Pa Kua— A style developed around and at the Wutang Monastery. The kuen are performed walking in a circle. The style specializes in non-linear lines of attack, and also works to develop the practitioner's ch'i. "Pa Kua" means "Eight Directions," or "Eight Trigrams," as the style is based on the eight trigrams of *I-Ching* philosophy. Each trigram has an associated martial movement. Initial training is soft, latter training is hard. Like T'ai Chi Ch'uan, many students who never advanced to the external, hard phase of training set themselves up as teachers of the style. So, like T'ai Chi Ch'uan, the style suffers from a plethora of half-trained instructors teaching the public only a part of the style.

Pak Mei— The Chinese-language translation of "White Eyebrow." Pak Mei was a dark figure in the Order's history, and not to be valorized in any way. His style was preserved because of its usefulness. We remind ourselves of his actions not to inflate him or his role in Shaolin, but as a way of cautioning ourselves so that we do not repeat his mistakes.

Parry— A defensive technique which requires minimal force and which does not pit force against force.

Path— By necessity an ambiguous term, "path" can refer to the eightfold path, the way of Taoism (the Tao), and more. In this text, when the term "path" is invoked by itself, it usually refers to the totality of the Shaolin way of life (we sometimes just use the word "way"), which includes the eightfold path, the teachings of Lao Tzu and Tamo, and Shaolin customs.

Patriarch— A term used especially in Chinese Buddhism, "patriarch" refers to the founder of a school and his direct lineage. Generally, Ch'an Buddhism traces its history through a series of patriarchs to the Buddha himself. Each successive patriarch is "qualified" to spread the Dharma by his predecessor. Some prominent patriarchs are Kashyapa, Nagarjuna, and Bodhidharma.

Prana— Meaning "breath," prana can roughly be translated as "ch'i."

Praying Mantis— Styles of gung fu modeled at least in part on the defensive and hunting techniques of the insects known as praying mantids.

Priest(ess)— A fully ordained master of the Shaolin Order.

Quando— A pole-arm weapon with a short, curved blade affixed to the end.

Rank— The level of responsibility and education of a member of the Shaolin Order. Ranks are student, disciple, and master, and indicated by colored sashes. "Rank" is also used specifically to denote the level of a disciple or master, such as 3rd rank, or 7th rank. This use of numbered ranks is a recent innovation. Prior to the 1970s, we only used dragon titles to indicate specific level of attainment in the arts and Buddhism of our order.

Reincarnation— In traditional Hinduism, every person had an atman, or soul. After death (and a suitable waiting period), the atman would swoop in and "inhabit" a suitable sperm/egg combination, and be reborn into the world. This cycle of death and rebirth would continue until the atman was liberated. The Buddha rejected the theory of atman with his anatman (no-self), but anatman with respect to the individual soul flows from a larger idea: that no thing is permanent and no thing exists by itself. The personality (or soul), like all things, is a temporary and constantly changing collection of elements. So then, what gets reincarnated? One perspective: realize that the psychic aggregates that make up a "soul" can be re-instantiated in living creatures until the ego is subsumed and enlightenment occurs. Whatever nature our animating force is (ch'i, for instance), the notion is that this force is undifferentiated. Ch'i is ch'i, whether it is yours, mine, or a cat's, it makes no difference. Once this is deeply understood, and we let go of the differentiations clung to by the ego, we become liberated and suffering is ended. One thing to keep in mind with respect to Shaolin and reincarnation is that Shaolin is pragmatic and reincarnation is supernatural. Shaolin permits a wide latitude in the belief of its adherents. So ponder reincarnation. If it makes sense to you, and makes your life better, believe it. If not, do not.

Samsara— A Sanskrit word that literally means "journeying," samsara is the cycle of rebirths which continues until nirvana is achieved. Sentient beings are trapped in samsara by hatred, craving, and delusion. Samsara is often employed to mean the phenomenal world. But in that sense, "samsara" and "nirvana" just become empty names, since what we call the "world" is simply a collection of mental representations. Escaping samsara is heavily dependent upon extinguishing the ego, which wipes out hatred, delusion, and most craving at a single stroke.

Sangha— 1. The body of followers of Buddhism, the Buddhist community at large. 2. A specific Buddhist community, such as the Shaolin Order. In Sanskrit, "sangha" means "group" or "congregation." Interestingly, some Ch'an traditions use the term "ts'ung-lin," or "woods" instead of "sangha" to denote a monastic community. The idea is that the "harmonious life of a monastic community is analogous to a thicket where trees and grasses grow together".[184] Perhaps this is at least a partial explanation of why "lin" shows up in the name of so many Ch'an monasteries.

Sanskrit— Sanskrit is the ancient scholarly language of India, and many terms from both Hinduism and Buddhism are Sanskrit words. Buddhism migrated early into southern India and Sri Lanka, where a dialect of Sanskrit called "Pali" predominated. In pronouncing Sanskrit words, it is important for English speakers to realize that the next-to-last syllable usually carries the emphasis, and that a consonant followed by an "h" has an aspirated pronunciation. So, Tathagata is pronounced "tat-ha-GA-ta," where the "…t-h…" junction is not pronounced like "th" in English. The "tat" and "ha" sounds are mostly separated.

Sect— A Ch'an sect is simply a school, or way, of Ch'an. Practitioners should avoid getting caught up in the notion of a "sect," however, as this leads away from the path. Master Dogen was renowned for disliking the term "Zen sect," feeling that the Zen way is simply the right way of Buddhism.[185] There are many sects of Ch'an and although they may prefer to employ different expedient devices, the core teaching remains the same. None of these schools is better or worse than any other—they merely offer vehicles suited to different kinds of people. For this reason, Shaolin have just as much reverence for other Ch'an traditions as they do for their own.

Sentience— More orthodox Buddhists apply the term "sentient" to all animals (and not plants), but the term is used in a more limited fashion in Shaolin to refer to creatures that are significantly self-aware. Sentient beings, then, are capable of being liberated. In the Shaolin sect, we strive not to get hung up on the precise definition of terms like "sentience," however. We believe in compassion and respect for all life, and that humans are a part of the same natural world as other animals, and plants. This philosophy is not merely "lip-service" coming from the recognition that humans are *mammals*; our survival as physical and spiritual beings is inherently linked to other terrestrial life, and our Buddhist practice reflects this belief. However, Shaolin does not require vegetarianism as an unavoidable consequence of this philosophy.

Shakyamuni— See entry for "Buddha."

Shaolin/Sil Lum— The Buddhist order founded by Bodhidharma at Shao Lin Temple. Although the Temple had existed for a few years prior to Tamo's arrival in 520, it bore no relationship beyond a geographical one to what we now call "Shaolin." "Sil Lum" is an equally acceptable translation, as that is how "Shaolin" is spelled/pronounced in southern China. The Order of Shaolin Ch'an is committed to sharing (but not proselytizing) the Shaolin teachings with those ready to learn them. The Order is similar to many Japanese and Korean Buddhist orders (such as the Won Buddhists in Korea) in that we are a Ch'an/Zen organization that does not follow the more orthodox path of some Theravadins and Mahayanins. That is, we allow members to marry. We allow members to consume meat. We are not especially ritualistic. And our notion of meditation is not confined to an activity that is performed only at set times. We seek to achieve a continual meditative state, being where we are, doing what we are doing, with complete focus.

Shiva— In Hindu theology Shiva is a major god, known as "Shiva the Destroyer." He destroys ignorance through his dark consort, the goddess Kali, but creates order and new life through his gentle light consort Shakti (also known as Tara). The concepts behind Shiva are an important part of Shaolin mythology. Shiva is also known in western mythology as Dionysus, Adonis, and Apollo.

Shorin— This is the Japanese pronunciation of "Shaolin," and represents a derived school of Zen based somewhat on Shaolin. Shorin (usually known as "Shorinji Kempo," the non-Temple derivative is Shorin-ryu) has both meditation and martial teachings, though the Japanese martial forms are radically different from traditional Shaolin gung fu. Shorinji Kempo is fairly popular in Japan, with somewhere between one and two million practitioners.

Shunyata— The Buddhist notion of emptiness, shunyata (often spelled "sunyata") plays an absolutely essential role in Ch'an philosophy.

Sifu— Pronounced "see-foo," a sifu is a teacher. In the Shaolin Order, "sifu" is a title for mid-level disciples. Depending upon how it is translated it means something like "honored father," "father teacher," or "honored monk." Shaolin prefers the latter translation, especially given that female teachers are also sifus! In Mandarin, the corresponding word is "shifu," pronounced something like "shr-fu."

Snake— Style of gung fu modeled on striking techniques of snakes, emphasizing finger strikes to vital pressure points.

Stance— The footwork of a style, particularly in reference to foot position and relationship of the person to the ground.

Student— Traditionally, Shaolin students were responsible for the household duties around the temples, but also received a liberal arts education which included gung fu training. Today, students still occasionally mow lawns for lessons (but not necessarily) and they also still learn the basics of Shaolin gung fu and Ch'an.

Style— The most encompassing level of referring to a martial arts group. Tiger, Crane, Wing Chun, and Aikido all represent styles. A style may, in turn, be composed of several different systems.

Sutra— "Sutra" is a Sanskrit word ("sutta" in Pali) for "thread." From this meaning, sutras came to be strings of words of holy lessons. Like strings of pearls, sutras are seen as strings of precious jewels—the wisdom of the Dharma. The sutras are collected in the second part of the Buddhist canon, and two basic types are found: sutras based on faith, which stress devotion and cite many miracles, and philosophical sutras that form the core of Mahayana thought. This second group of sutras focuses on the notion of Emptiness. The most important sutra to Shaolin is the *Diamond Sutra*, which falls into the group of philosophical sutras.

Swastika— Derived from the Sanskrit word "svasti," or "happiness," the swastika is a famous symbol of the teachings of the Buddha. In China, it often symbolizes the limitless nature of the Buddha's teachings, and in Japan it often symbolizes the seal of the buddha-mind that was transmitted by Zen patriarchs. The swastika, in a reversed form, was perverted by the Nazis into a symbol of evil.

System— A system is a branch of a much larger martial arts style. For example, Fu Jow Pai and Leopard are descended from the more encompassing Tiger schools, or style, of martial techniques. Karate is a style in this hierarchical classification, while Shotokan, Shito-ryu, and Goju-ryu are all systems. (Some authors choose to employ "style" and "system" a bit differently: "system" referring to a more complete entity and "style" referring to a less complete entity.) In any case, in most places where we use "system," it would be perfectly acceptable to also use "style."

T'ai Chi Ch'uan— A style of gung fu developed by Chang San-feng (although there are many versions of its origins[186]) which is both a potent martial art and a therapeutic practice. T'ai Chi Ch'uan is often promoted as "Tai Chi" by a New Age crowd who by and large don't understand the art. There are authentic teachers out there, however, and studied as a martial art, T'ai Chi Ch'uan has much to recommend itself. To the prospective T'ai Chi Ch'uan student: search for an instructor who actually possesses combat effectiveness within the style (this would be at least one indication that the teacher is transmitting the whole style and not just the initial soft aspects).

Tamo— The name given to Bodhidharma by the Chinese, it is short for P'u-t'i-ta-mo. In southern China, Tamo was known as "Dot Mor."

T'an-lin— "Armless Lin," as he was sometimes called, was the Sanskritist who recorded a short biography of Bodhidharma and the *Two Entrances*. T'an-lin was likely a student of Hui-k'o, the second patriarch of Ch'an Buddhism.

Tan t'ien— A point some two inches below your navel that serves as the origin of your ch'i energies. Meditation upon this point ("contemplating your navel") gradually gives the meditator greater control over his or her inner power.

Tao— The philosophical concept that reality is made up of merging, constantly moving polar opposites (yin and yang). Examples of these opposites are positive-negative, male-female, light-dark, and good-evil. The totality of opposites make a true whole, termed the "Tao." "Tao" is also sometimes translated as "meaning" or "way," but keep in mind: the Tao that can be named is not the true Tao. In this text, we often use the words "path" and "way" in place of "Tao." Even the meaning of "Dharma" is sometimes interchangeable with "Tao," depending of course upon the context. "Sil Lum Tao," or "Shaolin Tao," refers to the Shaolin way of life, and includes Ch'an Buddhism, Taoism, gung fu discipline, and other Shaolin philosophies.

Taoism/Taoist— First a philosophy, then an alchemy, and finally a religion, Taoism sprung from the work of Lao Tzu, and was further developed and popularized by Chuang Tzu. Taoists are those who adhere to Lao Tzu's philosophy, which prominently features the ideas of yin and yang, and various principles such as wu wei.

Tao Te Ching— *"The Book of the Way and its Power,"* or *"The Book of the Path and its Virtue,"* the *Tao Te Ching* may be the most widely read, widely printed book in all of history. This book is the primary source for Taoist philosophy, and was written in opposition to the ideals of Confucius. Written by Lao Tzu, the *Tao Te Ching* and the philosophy it engendered played a strong role in the development of Shaolin Ch'an.

Temple— When capitalized, "Temple" can refer to a specific Shaolin temple or to the Order as a whole. So, for instance, when we write, "The teachings of Lao Tzu were highly regarded in the Temple," what we mean is that the Order values Lao Tzu's teachings. When not capitalized, "temple" is being employed as a generic term. The different temples were much like small, liberal arts universities. They were also occasionally refuges for those in trouble with the government. As a Buddhist Order, a Chinese citizen could renounce his family ties and join a Shaolin temple. In an important way, monks were outside of the political class system in China and not subject to a variety of laws. And the Shaolin often took such people in if they "professed" a true desire to follow the path. Refugees such as these rarely became priests in the Order, and typically did not remain in the temples for very long. Because the Order has had such a tumultuous history, the word "temple" might now refer to any gathering of Shaolin, approved by the abbot, for the purpose of Shaolin Ch'an training. The term is also used to differentiate non-Shaolin from Shaolin arts, as in "non-Temple style" and "Temple style."

Theravada— It literally means "Doctrine of the Elders." Theravada is the only surviving school of Hinayana Buddhism and stresses the liberation of the individual. It takes the arhat as the ideal state, and strongly emphasizes monasticism and ritual. Theravada is a very analytical school. It is the most common form of Buddhism in southeastern Asia, including Sri Lanka, Thailand, Laos, and other nations in that region.

Tibetan Buddhism— "Tibetan Buddhism" is a very broad term. Sometimes called "Lamaism," it encompasses traditions known as "Vajrayana," "Tantrayana," and more. There are four major monastic traditions in Tibetan Buddhism, and their differences might be likened to the differences between Ch'an sects in China. All of Tibetan Buddhism stretches deep roots into both Buddhism and the Bon religion. Tibetan Buddhism emphasizes mandala meditation and ritual. In Tibet, religion is more tightly interwoven with lay culture than in most other places in the world. For perhaps 1000 years, there have been links between certain Tibetan Buddhist orders and the Shaolin Order; these ties were strongest during the Ch'ing dynasty. Also, see the entry for "Lama."

Tiger— Tiger is a vicious, powerful, and popular style of gung fu. Southern Tiger is the classic Shaolin style of Tiger, although many sub-systems are practiced within the Temple tradition. Elements of Tiger have found their way into many family styles of gung fu and many martial art styles outside of China.

Tong— Tongs were Chinese community associations, primarily designed to help people out. At various points in the early 1900s, many tongs were overtaken by organized crime. But traditionally, a tong (from the word for association: "t'ang") was just an organization, and tongs in early Chinese-American communities were founded to help recent arrivals to America.

Training master— 5th and 6th rank Shaolin masters. These masters were often responsible for the majority of teaching within the temples.

Wade-Giles— The transliteration system used before Pinyin was instituted by the PRC. Most martial sources with respect to the gung fu and Shaolin tradition use the Wade-Giles system, as do most Buddhist sources. Pinyin probably makes learning how to pronounce Chinese words a little bit easier, but we use the Wade-Giles system for the stated reasons. Here is a brief summary to help understand how some major Wade-Giles-transliterated sounds should be pronounced:

Written	Pronounced
ch	j
ch'	ch
e	short "u" as in "pun"
j	"r" as in "red"
k	g
k'	k
p	b
p'	p
t	d
t'	t
ts	dz
ts'	ts
hs	sh
Vowels	As in German

Wang Lang— Living sometime in the early to mid-17th century, Wang Lang is credited with creating Northern Praying Mantis by blending simian footwork with mantis hand technique. His base style gave rise to many variations, including the Northern Praying Mantis of the Shaolin Order, which is T'ai Mantis.

Wing Chun— Southern gung fu style developed in 1776 by Shaolin priestess Ng Mui, founded on techniques of White Crane and Snake. The style was named for her first student, Wing Chun ("Blessed Springtime"). As with so many Chinese to English translations, this term is spelled in a variety of ways including "Ving Tsun," "Wing Choon," and "Weng Tson."

Wushu— Literally, "martial art," but the term is most often used in reference to Modern, or Contemporary, Wushu, which is a sport activity. Modern Wushu was created by combining elements of western ballet and gymnastics, and traditional gung fu (mostly Long Fist style). Wushu is a fun and healthful activity (though not really suitable for anyone but the young), but not a martial art in the sense of emphasizing self-defense applications and combat effectiveness.

Yang— The Taoist hard/light principle. The yin/yang symbol that has become so popular in the West has its roots in very ancient Chinese astronomical charts. The symbol, sometimes called the "T'ai Chi" symbol, represents celestial activity such as the cycle of the sun, the four seasons, the foundation of the *I-Ching* (*Book of Changes*), and more. Thus, the yin/yang symbol truly is all encompassing.

Yin— The Taoist soft/dark principle. On the yin/yang symbol, see the entry for "Yang."

Yoga— A yoga, literally meaning "yoke," is simply a path towards the Truth (note the capital "T"!), where Truth is something you experience by an experiential union with the divine (or universe). This is sometimes called a "mystical experience," and is a very specific psychological and spiritual experience. There are many yogas in the world, and those who follow these paths in search of the mystical experience that entails this sense of unity are properly referred to as "yogis." Of course, "yoga" is frequently used to refer to the early stages of such mystical disciplines, which are primarily oriented towards control, and healthful development, of the physical body.

Zazen— A sitting meditation where the mind clings to no object yet is alert. Undertaken diligently, and coupled with the appropriate training, zazen may result in enlightenment.

Zen—The Japanese equivalent of Ch'an, the practice of quiet meditation as the way to achieve enlightenment.

The chief monk of the Shaolin Order, circa 1974

Additional Resources

There has been so much written about Shaolin that a comprehensive review of the literature is impossible and a meaningful review worthy of a volume in its own right. Part of the difficulty in finding high quality sources of information is that almost all portrayals of the Order are mostly fictitious—including many novels, motion pictures, and the *Kung Fu* television series—while others are second or third hand accounts by people who are not Shaolin. Further compounding the problem has been Shaolin's fame, since many martial arts schools claim to teach "Shaolin" (or "kung fu") because the name is familiar, even though the materials taught have nothing to do with Shaolin. We are aware of several competent, sincere, honest individuals who teach "Shaolin" arts because they were told that is what they had been taught. These people were misled, and should not necessarily be seen as frauds or confidence men.

The Order of Shaolin Ch'an approved the compilation and publishing of this book, in large part, as an educational project. Further volumes are planned, especially a series of style-specific books. The Order was reestablished in America, in New York City, in 1927 and has operated in a low-key manner ever since. All founding members were expatriate senior monks (grandmasters) who fled China in order to insure the survival of Shaolin practices and philosophy. If you are interested in studying Shaolin Ch'an, or for any other inquiries, you can find the Order of Shaolin Ch'an, a non-profit organization, online at www.shaolintemple.org. Tax deductible donations in support of the OSC's mission of preserving and perpetuating Shaolin teachings can be mailed to:

Order of Shaolin Ch'an
P.O. Box 566
Beaverton, OR 97075

Finally, we encourage readers to explore the selected bibliography. *All* of the listed works have something to offer, providing valuable information on both philosophy and martial styles.

Selected Bibliography

Austin, James H. *Zen and the Brain*. Boston: MIT Press, 1999.

Blundell, Arthur. "The Power of the Past." Middle Way. 45, (4), 1971.

Broughton, Jeffrey. *The Bodhidharma Anthology: the Earliest Records of Zen*. Berkeley: University of California Press, 1999.

Chao, H.C., ed. *The Striking Snake Maneuvers*. Taipei: Meadea Enterprises, 1985.

———. *Chinese Praying Mantis Boxing: Book II*. Taiwan: Unitrade, 1986.

Cheng, Hsueh-li. "The Roots of Zen Buddhism". Journal of Chinese Philosophy. 8, 1981.

Cheng, Man-jan. *Lao-Tzu: "My Words are Very Easy to Understand"*. Translated by Tam C. Gibbs. Berkeley: North Atlantic Books, 1981.

Cheong Cheng-leong, and Mark V. Wiley. *The Secrets of Phoenix-Eye Fist Kung-Fu: The Art of Chuka Shaolin*. Boston: Tuttle, 2000.

Cheung, William. *Kung Fu Dragon Pole*. Burbank: Ohara Publications, 1986.

———. *Advanced Wing Chun*. Burbank: Ohara Publications, 1988.

Chin, David, and Michael Staples. *Hop Gar Kung Fu*. Hollywood: Unique Publications, 1980.

Chow, David, and Robert Spangler. *Kung Fu: History, Philosophy, and Technique*. Burbank: Unique Publications, 1977.

Cleary, Thomas, ed. *Classics of Buddhism and Zen*. Volume One. Boston: Shambala, 1989.

Conze, Edward. *Buddhism: Its Essence and Development*. New York: Harper and Row, 1959.

———. "The Buddha's Bodies in the Prajnaparamita." Buddhist Studies 1934-1972. Oxford: Bruno Cassirer, 1967.

———. *The Large Sutra on Perfect Wisdom*. Berkeley: University of California Press, 1975.

de Bary, William Theodore. *The Buddhist Tradition in India, China, and Japan*. New York: Vintage Books, 1972.

Draeger, Donn F. *Modern Bujutsu and Budo: The Martial Arts and Ways of Japan (Vol. 3)*. New York: Weatherhill, 1974.

Draeger, Donn F., and Robert W. Smith. *Comprehensive Asian Fighting Arts*. Tokyo: Kodansha, 1981.

Dumoulin, Heinrich. *Zen Buddhism: a History: Vol. 1*. New York: Macmillan, 1989.

Echard-Musgrave, Stephen. "Eight Steps to Freedom: Following the Buddha's Eightfold Path in Modern Life". Unpublished essay: 2003. [available from www.buddhanet.net]

Eisen, Martin. "Classical Versus Modern Gong-Fu: Gin-foon Mark Interview". Journal of Asian Martial Arts. 2, (1), 1993.

Eng, Paul. *Praying Mantis Kung-Fu: Spear Hand*. Sunnyvale: Carroll Street Press, 1984.

———. *Praying Mantis Kung-Fu: Bong Po*. Sunnyvale: Carroll Street Press, 1986.

———. *Praying Mantis Kung-Fu: Steals the Peach*. Sharon Center, Ohio: Alpha Publications, 1993(a).

———. *Praying Mantis Kung-Fu:Plum Blossom Hand*. Sharon Center, Ohio: Alpha Publications, 1993(b).

Eng, Tak Wah. *Entering the Fu-Jow Pai*. New York: Tak Wah, Inc., 1988.

Ferguson, Andy. *Zen's Chinese Heritage: The Masters and their Teachings*. Boston: Wisdom Publications, 2000.

Funk, Jon. "Northern Praying Mantis—The Complete System". Inside Kung Fu. 23, (6), 1996(a).

———. "The Shaolin Temple Hoax". Black Belt. March, (21), 1996(b).

Furuya, Kensho. *KODO Ancient Ways*. Santa Clarita: Ohara Publications, 1996.

Giles, Herbert A. *Chinese Sketches*. Originally published in 1876. Indypublish.com, 2002.

———. *The Civilization of China*. Originally published 1911. Indypublish.com, 2003.

Goddard, Dwight. *A Buddhist Bible*. Boston: Beacon Press, 1966.

Hallander, Jane. "Leopard Kung Fu: Fast, Fierce, and Aggressive Techniques Characterize this Shaolin Animal System". Black Belt. 35, (9), 1997.

Henning, Stanley E. "Chinese Boxing's Ironic Odyssey". Journal of Asian Martial Arts. 8, (3), 1999.

———. "What's in a Name? The Etymology of Chinese Boxing". Journal of Asian Martial Arts. 10, (4), 2001.

Hiroyama, A. *A History of Chinese Secret Societies*. Shanghai: Commercial Press, 1935.

Hong, Wai. *The Secret Iron Hands of Fu-Jow Pai*. New York: Fu-Jow Pai Federation, 1978.

Hongjun Wang, ed. *Tales of the Shaolin Monastery*. Translated by C. Lonsdale. Hong Kong: JPC, 1988.

Hu Shih. "P'u-t'i-ta-mo k'ao." Hu Shih wen-ts'un. Taipei: Yüan-t'ung t'u-shu kung-szu, 1953.

Hyams, Joe. *Zen in the Martial Arts*. Boston: Tarcher/Houghton Mifflin, 1979.

Inada, Kenneth. "Zen and Taoism: Common and Uncommon Grounds of Discourse". Journal of Chinese Philosophy. 15, 1988.

Iyengar, B.K.S. *Light on Pranayama*. New York: Crossroad, 1981.

———. *Yoga: the Path to Holistic Health*. London: Dorling Kindersley, 2001.

Jacobsen, Knut A. "Humankind and Nature in Buddhism". In *A Companion to World Philosophies*. Edited by Eliot Deutsch and Ron Bontekoe. Oxford: Blackwell, 1997.

Jenner, W.F.J. *Memories of Lo-yang: Yang Hsüan-chih and the Lost Capital (493-534)*. Oxford: Clarendon Press, 1981.

Kamata, Shigeo, trans. *Zengen shosenshu tojo. Zen no goroku 9*. Tokyo: Chikuma shobo, 1971.

Kasulis, Thomas P. "The Buddhist Concept of Self". In *A Companion to World Philosophies*. Edited by Eliot Deutsch and Ron Bontekoe. Oxford: Blackwell, 1997.

Kohn, Michael H., trans. *The Shambala Dictionary of Buddhism and Zen*, by Ingrid Fischer Schreiber, Franz-Karl Ehrhard, and Michael S. Diener. Boston: Shambala, 1991.

Kong, Buck-sam. *The Tiger/Crane Form of Hung Gar Kung-Fu*. Santa Clarita: Ohara Publications, 1983.

Kong, Buck-sam, and Eugene H. Ho. *Hung Gar Kung Fu*. Burbank: Ohara Publications, 1972.

Lamotte, E. *L'Enseignement de Vimalakirti*. Louvain: Institut Orientaliste, 1962.

Lao Tzu. *Tao Te Ching*. Translated by G. Feng and J. English. New York: Vintage, 1972.

Lao Tzu. *Te-Tao Ching: A New Translation Based on the Recently Discovered Ma-wang-tui Texts*. Translation and commentary by Robert G. Henricks. New York: Ballantine Books, 1989.

Lee, Benson, and Lawrence Tan. "Kung Fu: Survival or Extinction? The Legacy of Northern Eagle Claw Kung Fu". Inside Kung Fu. 12, (7), 1985.

Lee, Bruce. *Chinese Gung Fu, the Philosophical Art of Self-Defense*. Oakland: Oriental Book Sales, 1963.

———. *Tao of Jeet Kune Do*. Burbank: Ohara Publications, 1975.

———. "Toward Personal Liberation (Jeet Kune Do: IV)." *Bruce Lee: Artist of Life*. Edited by John Little. Boston: Tuttle, 1999(a).

———. "Wu-Hsin (No-Mindedness)." *Bruce Lee: Artist of Life*. Edited by John Little. Boston: Tuttle, 1999(b).

Lee, James Y. *Wing Chun Kung Fu*. Burbank: Ohara Publications, 1972.

Leung Ting. *Seven Star Praying Mantis Kung Fu*. Hong Kong: International Wing Tsun Leung Ting Martial Arts Association, 1980.

———. *Skills of the Vagabonds*. Hong Kong: Leung's Publications, 1983.

———. *Skills of the Vagabonds II: Behind the Incredibles…*. Hong Kong: Leung's Publications, 1991.

Lingpa, Dudjom. *Buddhahood without Meditation*. Junction City: Padma Publishing, 1994.

Luk, Charles. *Ch'an and Zen Teachings*. London: Rider, 1960.

Maliszewski, Michael. *Spiritual Dimensions of the Martial Arts*. Tokyo: Tuttle, 1996.

Meng, Benny, and Alfredo Delbrocco. "The Secret History of Wing Chun: The Truth Revealed." Dayton, Ohio: Ving Tsun Museum, 2003. [available from home.vtmuseum.org]

Meng, Benny, and Richard Loewenhagen. "The Holy Land of Martial Arts: Southern Shaolin Temple." Dayton, Ohio: Ving Tsun Museum, 2003. [available from home.vtmuseum.org]

Merton, Thomas. *The Way of Chuang Tzu*. New York: New Directions, 1965.

Ming Zhen Shakya. *Seventh World of Chan Buddhism*. Nan Hua Chan Buddhist Society, 1996. [available from www.hsuyun.org]

Miyagi Chojun. *Karate-do Gaisetsu*. Written in 1934. Compiled and translated by Patrick and Yuriko McCarthy in *Ancient Okinawan Martial Arts Volume Two: Koryu Uchinadi*. Boston: Tuttle, 1999.

Nagaboshi, Tomio [Terrence Dukes]. *The Bodhisattva Warriors*. York Beach: Weiser Publishing, 1994.

Nakamura, Hajime. "The Non-logical Character of Zen". Journal of Chinese Philosophy. 12, 1985.

Nakamura, Hajime. *Indian Buddhism: A Survey with Bibliographical Notes (Buddhist Tradition Series Vol. 1)*. Edited by Alex Wayman. Blue Dove Press, 1999.

Nan, Huai-chin. *The Story of Chinese Zen*. Boston: Tuttle, 1995.

Nisker, Wes. *Buddha's Nature: Evolution as a Practical Guide to Enlightenment*. New York: Bantam Books, 1998.

Ogata, Sohaku. *The Transmission of the Lamp: Early Masters*. Durango: Longwood Academic, 1990.

Oyama, Masutatsu. *The Kyokushin Way*. Tokyo: Japan Publications, 1979.

Parker, Edmund. *Secrets of Chinese Karate*. Englewood Cliffs, New Jersey: Prentice-Hall, 1963.

———. *Infinite Insights into Kenpo. Volume 1: Mental Stimulation*. Los Angeles: Delsby Publications, 1982.

P'ng Chye Khim, and Donn F. Draeger. *Shaolin Lohan Kung-Fu*. Tokyo: Tuttle, 1979.

Profatilov, Ilya. "The Traditional History of Plum Blossom Praying Mantis Boxing". Journal of Asian Martial Arts. 10, (4), 2001.

Rahula, Walpola. *What the Buddha Taught*. 2nd edition. New York: Grove Press, 1974.

Ralston, Peter. *Cheng Hsin: The Principles of Effortless Power*. Berkeley: North Atlantic Books, 1989.

Red Pine [Bill Porter], trans. *The Zen Teaching of Bodhidharma*. Compiled from texts believed to have been written by Bodhidharma or his students. New York: North Point Press, 1987.

———, trans. *The Diamond Sutra: The Perfection of Wisdom*. Contains text and commentaries translated from Sanskrit and Chinese sources by Red Pine. Washington: Counterpoint, 2001.

Reps, Paul, and Nyogen Senzaki, trans. *Zen Flesh, Zen Bones*. Tokyo: Tuttle, 1957.

Ross, John F. "Kung Fu U.". Smithsonian Magazine. May, 2002.

Senzaki, Nyogen, trans. *The Iron Flute*. Kyoto: Tuttle, 1961.

Shaolin Gung Fu Institute. www.shaolin.com. [The Order of Shaolin Ch'an gave permission to the Shaolin Gung Fu Institute to publish some of the OSC's materials on the World Wide Web *prior* to the publication of this text.]

Sheng-yen. *Faith in Mind: A Guide to Ch'an Practice.* Elmhurst, New York: Dharma Drum Publications, 1987.

Shiozaki, Cory. "Kung-Fu Grandmaster Ark Y. Wong." Inside Kung Fu. 1, (1), 1973.

Shum, Leung. *The Secrets of Eagle Claw Kung Fu: Ying Jow Pai.* Boston: Tuttle, 2001.

Sprackland, Robert. *Instructor: Teaching the Martial Arts.* Belmont, California: Young Forest Company, 1998.

Staples, Michael. *White Crane Gung Fu.* Burbank: Ohara Publications, 1973.

Strong, John S. 2001. *The Buddha: A Short Biography.* Oxford: Oneworld Publications, 2001.

Suzuki, Daisetz T. *The Lankavatara Sutra.* London: George Routledge and Sons, 1932.

Taisho shinsu daizokyo (Great store of scriptures). This work contains not only sutras, but also Tao-hsüan's *Hsü kao-seng chuan (Continued Biographies of Eminent Monks)* and many other writings. 85 vols. Tokyo: Taisho issaikyo kankokai, 1924-33.

Tao Yuan. *Transmission of the Lamp.* Translated by Sohaku Ogata. Wolfeboro, New Hampshire: Longwood Academic, 1989.

Thich Nhat Hanh. *The Heart of the Buddha's Teaching.* Berkeley: Parallax Press, 1998.

Thich Thien-An. *Zen Philosophy, Zen Practice.* Berkeley: Dharma Publishing, 1975.

Tjoa Khek Kiong, Donn F. Draeger, and Quintin T.G. Chambers. *Shantung Black Tiger: A Shaolin Fighting Art of North China.* Weatherhill: New York, 1976.

Trungpa, Chögyam. *Meditation in Action.* Boulder, Colorado: Shambala, 1969.

Ts'un-wo-chai chu-jen, ed. *Shao-lin Ch'uan-shu mi-chueh.* Shanghai: Chung Hua Publishing, 1915.

Un H.B. *Pak Mei Kung Fu (White Eyebrow).* London: Paul H. Crompton, 1974.

Vermeer, E.B., ed. "Development and Decline of Fukien Province in the 17th and 18th Centuries". Sinica Leidensia Volume XXII. Leiden: New York, 1990.

Wang Yi-t'ung. *A Record of Buddhist Monasteries in Lo-yang: By Yang Hsüan-chih.* Princeton: Princeton University Press, 1984.

Watson, Burton, trans. *The Vimalakirti Sutra.* New York: Columbia University Press, 1997.

Wesbrook, Adele, and Oscar Ratti, contributor. *Aikido and the Dynamic Sphere.* Rutland: Tuttle, 1970.

Wong, James I., ed. *The Praying Mantis System, Volume One: History and Introductory Forms*. Stockton, California: Koinonia, 1979.

Wong, James I., ed. *A Source Book in the Chinese Martial Arts, Volume I: History, Philosophy, Systems, and Styles*. Stockton, California: Koinonia, 1978.

Wong Kiew Kit. *The Art of Shaolin Kung Fu: The Secrets of Kung Fu for Self-Defence, Health and Enlightenment*. Rockport, Massachusetts: Element Books, 1996.

Yampolsky, Philip B. *The Platform Sutra of the Sixth Patriarch*. New York: Columbia University Press, 1967.

Yanagida, Seizan, ed. *Zen no goroku: Daruma no goroku* (*Discourse on Zen: Discourse on Bodhidharma*). Tokyo: Chikuma Shoten, 1969.

Yang Jwing-ming. *The Essence of Shaolin White Crane: Martial Power and Qigong*. Jamaica Plain, Massachusetts: YMAA, 1996.

Yang Jwing-ming, and Jeffrey A. Bolt. *Shaolin Long Fist Kung Fu*. Burbank: Unique Publications, 1982.

Yee, J. "Brendan Lai: The Seven Stars Praying Mantis". Inside Kung Fu. 1 (1), 1973.

———. "Inside Techniques: Yow Kueng Moon". Inside Kung Fu. 1 (12), 1974.

Yeow, L. *Chinese Praying Mantis Boxing*. Singapore: Tiger Press, 1973.

Ying Zi, and Weng Yi. *Shaolin Kung Fu*. Kowloon: Kingsway International, 1981.

Young, Robert W. "Shaolin Temple: A Quest for the Truth About Bodhidharma and the World's Most Famous Martial Arts Monastery." Black Belt. September & October, 2001.

Zeuschner, Robert. "The Understanding of Karma in Early Ch'an Buddhism". Journal of Chinese Philosophy. 8, 1981.

Index

K

L

M

X

Y

Z

Endnotes

[1] Nakamura, 1985.

[2] Inada, 1988.

[3] Nagaboshi, 1994.

[4] Ross, 2002.

[5] Henning, 1999.

[6] P'ng and Draeger, 1979.

[7] Kohn, 1991.

[8] Broughton, 1999; de Bary, 1972; Maliszewski, 1996; Red Pine, 1989.

[9] Broughton, 1999.

[10] Hu, 1953; Jenner, 1981; Taisho shinsu daizokyo, 1924-33; Wang, 1984.

[11] Broughton, 1999; Nagaboshi, 1994.

[12] Red Pine, 1989.

[13] Broughton, 1999.

[14] Broughton, 1999; Kohn, 1991; Nagaboshi, 1994; Red Pine, 1989.

[15] Nagaboshi, 1994.

[16] Nagaboshi, 1994.

[17] Taisho shinsu daizokyo, 1924-33.

[18] Ying and Weng, 1981.

[19] Broughton, 1999.

[20] Hiroyama, 1935.

[21] Draeger and Smith, 1981.

[22] Meng and Loewenhagen, 2003.

[23] Leung, 1983.

[24] Leung, 1983.

[25] Wong, 1978.

[26] Chow and Spangler, 1977.

[27] Yang, 1996.

[28] Wong, 1978.

[29] Ts'un-wo-chai chu-jen, 1915.

[30] Hallander, 1997.

[31] Yang, 1996.

[32] Henning, 2001.

[33] Ts'un-wo-chai chu-jen, 1915.

[34] Yang, 1996.

[35] Yang, 1996.

[36] Draeger and Smith, 1981; Henning, 2001.

[37] Chow and Spangler, 1977.

[38] Vermeer, 1990.

[39] Chao, 1986; Funk, 1996(a).

[40] Chao, 1986.

[41] Draeger and Smith, 1981.

[42] Henning, 2001.

[43] Draeger and Smith, 1981.
[44] Kong, 1983.
[45] Young, 2001.
[46] Giles, 1876.
[47] Strong, 2001.
[48] Kohn, 1991.
[49] Ming Zhen Shakya, 1996.
[50] Ming Zhen Shakya, 1996.
[51] Strong, 2001.
[52] Cleary, 1989.
[53] Red Pine, 2001.
[54] Nakamura, 1999.
[55] Conze, 1967.
[56] Red Pine, 2001.
[57] Broughton, 1999.
[58] Strong, 2001.
[59] Rahula, 1974.
[60] Goddard, 1966; Rahula, 1974; Kohn, 1991; Ming Zhen Shakya, 1996; Echard-Musgrave, 2003.
[61] Nan, 1995.
[62] Rahula, 1974
[63] Lee, 1999(a).
[64] Cheng, 1981.
[65] Lamotte, 1962.
[66] Blundell, 1971; Luk, 1960; Senzaki, 1961; Zeuschner, 1981.
[67] Kohn, 1991.
[68] Inada, 1988.
[69] Parker, 1963.
[70] Cheng, 1981.
[71] Chin and Staples, 1980; Ming Zhen Shakya 1996.
[72] Parker, 1963.
[73] Chow and Spangler, 1977.
[74] Reps and Senzaki, 1957.
[75] Lee, 1999(a).
[76] Kohn, 1991.
[77] Rahula, 1974.
[78] Red Pine, 1989.
[79] Broughton, 1999.
[80] Taisho shinsu daizokyo, 1924-33.
[81] Broughton, 1999.
[82] Yanagida, 1969.
[83] Zeuschner, 1981.
[84] Lee, 1999(b).
[85] Inada, 1988.
[86] Lee, 1963.
[87] Kasulis, 1997.
[88] Goddard, 1966.
[89] Trungpa, 1969.
[90] Broughton, 1999.
[91] Cheng, 1981; Rahula, 1974.
[92] Taisho shinsu daizokyo, 1924-33.

[93] Kamata, 1971.
[94] Broughton, 1999.
[95] Broughton, 1999.
[96] Nan, 1995.
[97] Shiozaki, 1973.
[98] Red Pine, 1989.
[99] Furuya, 1996.
[100] Chow and Spangler, 1977.
[101] Draeger, 1974; Lee, 1963.
[102] Iyengar, 2001.
[103] Lee, 1999(a).
[104] Chow and Spangler, 1977.
[105] Yang, 1996.
[106] Chow and Spangler, 1977.
[107] Ross, 2002.
[108] Ross, 2002.
[109] Nagaboshi, 1994.
[110] Meng and Loewenhagen, 2003.
[111] Funk, 1996(b).
[112] Young, 2001.
[113] Eisen, 1993.
[114] Yang, 1996.
[115] Leung, 1991.
[116] Leung, 1991.
[117] Chow and Spangler, 1977.
[118] Wesbrook and Ratti, 1970.
[119] Draeger and Smith, 1981.
[120] Miyagi, 1934.
[121] Chow and Spangler, 1977; Yang, 1996.
[122] Lee and Tan, 1985.
[123] Draeger and Smith, 1981.
[124] Yang, 1996.
[125] Parker, 1963.
[126] Lee, 1975.
[127] Draeger and Smith, 1981.
[128] Cheong and Wiley, 2000.
[129] Cheung, 1986.
[130] Cheong and Wiley, 2000.
[131] Parker, 1963.
[132] Yang, 1996.
[133] Yang, 1996.
[134] Giles, 1911.
[135] Parker, 1963.
[136] Eng, Tak Wah, 1988.
[137] Tjoa, et al., 1976.
[138] Kong and Ho, 1972.
[139] Parker, 1963.
[140] Chao, 1985.
[141] Profatilov, 2001.
[142] Chao, 1986; Funk, 1996(a).
[143] Wong, 1979.

[144] Chao, 1986; Wong, 1979.
[145] Chow and Spangler, 1977.
[146] Yee, 1973.
[147] Eng, 1986.
[148] Wong, 1979.
[149] Profatilov, 2001.
[150] Profatilov, 2001.
[151] Funk, 1996(a).
[152] Chao, 1986.
[153] Shum, 2001.
[154] Wong, 1979.
[155] Chow and Spangler, 1977.
[156] Lee, 1975.
[157] Yee, 1974.
[158] Parker, 1963.
[159] Kong and Ho, 1972.
[160] Un, 1974.
[161] Lee, 1975.
[162] Meng and Delbrocco, 2003.
[163] Meng and Delbrocco, 2003.
[164] Cheung, 1986.
[165] Wong, 1979.
[166] Wong, 1979.
[167] Cheong and Wiley, 2000.
[168] Maliszewski, 1996.
[169] Eng, 1993(a).
[170] Maliszewski, 1996.
[171] Furuya, 1996.
[172] Trungpa, 1969.
[173] Broughton, 1999.
[174] Trungpa, 1969.
[175] Yang, 1996.
[176] Chin and Staples, 1980; P'ng and Draeger, 1979; Yang and Bolt, 1982.
[177] Yang, 1996.
[178] P'ng and Draeger, 1979; Yang and Bolt, 1982.
[179] Jacobsen, 1997.
[180] Nagaboshi, 1994.
[181] Nakamura, 1985.
[182] Lee, 1975.
[183] Tjoa, et al., 1976.
[184] Nakamura, 1985.
[185] Nakamura, 1985.
[186] Draeger and Smith, 1981.